The Poverty of Affluence

The Poverty of Affluence

A Psychological Portrait of the
American Way of Life

Paul L. Wachtel

THE FREE PRESS
A Division of Macmillan, Inc.
NEW YORK

Collier Macmillan Publishers
LONDON

The Free Press
A Division of Macmillan, Inc.
866 Third Avenue, New York, N. Y. 10022

Collier Macmillan Canada, Inc.

Printed in the United States of America

printing number

2   3   4   5   6   7   8   9   10

Library of Congress Cataloging in Publication Data

Wachtel, Paul L.

   The poverty of affluence.

   Includes bibliographical references and index.
   1. Economics—Psychological aspects. 2. Economic development—Psychological aspects. 3. Wealth—United States—Psychological aspects. 4. Consumption (Economics)
HB74.P8W3 1983   339.4'7'0973   83-47655
ISBN 0-02-933540-X

For Ellen, Kenny, and Karen

Contents

Part III   AGAINST THE TIDE

Preface

IN SOME RESPECTS a preface is a conceit. It is the author's re-ward to himself for the hard work invested in the pages that follow, an opportunity to reflect on the experience of having spent several years in an activity that is at once self-indulgent and self-denying. It is written in that special state of conscious-ness that derives from completing any large and intense proj-ect — an odd altered state, half elation and half depression, when defenses are exhausted on both counts. It thus gives the reader something of a special opportunity. My argument really begins with the Introduction, but those with a taste for eaves-dropping may find this self-reflective interlude useful.

This book is both a highly personal statement and an ex-tension of my scholarly work. Its style reflects its dual roots. Where I have quoted others or cited facts or trends, I have doc-umented and provided references. But in many places its tone is informal, and throughout I hope the prose is considerably livelier than is usually expected from the pen of a professor.

The discerning reader will readily detect the influence of a number of venerable figures who are scarcely discussed in the text. Veblen, Tawney, Fromm, Weber, Marx, and others have been suggested to me by various readers of earlier drafts as can-didates for more explicit attention. In the interest of reaching a wider readership, however, I have chosen not to provide the kind of detailed review of the literature that might be appropriate in a more strictly scholarly work. My intent is a serious one, not a "popularization," but I do wish to limit the scholarly apparatus to what is strictly necessary to bolster or substantiate my contentions. I hope to contribute to the literature in a way that will prove useful to psychologists, economists, sociologists, and other professional scholars, but most of all I want to make my arguments accessible to the general reader. I believe the topic to be too urgent for scholarly discourse alone. I have no quick and easy remedy for the disillusionment and confusion that have gripped so much of our citizenry, but I do think I can offer the first step toward such a remedy — a diagnosis of some of the basic assumptions that have led us astray.

I must confess, however, that concern with liveliness of presentation is not the only reason I have not reviewed in detail the prior scholarly work from which the present arguments derive. I am also simply less clear about the sources of the ideas in this book than I usually am about what I write. Given the breadth of the topic, practically everything I have read since my freshman course in Contemporary Civilization at Columbia 25 years ago might have contributed to the shape my thoughts have taken. In addition, at least some of the decisive influences have no doubt filtered down to me through conversations and secondary sources in a way that makes it impossible fully to reconstruct the origins of the lines of thought presented here.

In attempting to familiarize myself with the broad range of literature relevant to the present study, I have been heartened to find that the conclusions I had reached from a psychological starting point converge in important ways with those of a number of other writers who have approached the problems we face from the perspective of other disciplines. Among those who should be mentioned in this regard are, in particular, Robert Heilbroner, William Leiss, E. J. Mishan, Tibor Scitovsky, E. F. Schumacher, Jeremy Seabrook, and Philip Slater. It will be particularly apparent that the present work derived great nourishment from the continuing efforts of John Kenneth Galbraith to challenge our national fantasies about how our economy really works. Without his bold and authoritative analyses to lean upon I might well have shrunk back from the conclusions to which my own explorations led.

I am sharply critical in the book about the way most of us in America lead our lives. This does not mean that I offer myself as an exemplary exception. Indeed, a key point in the book's argument is that the concrete realities of our society as it is today make it difficult for all but the most extraordinary individual to extricate himself from the temptations and exigencies of the consumer life on his own. From street crime to a shortage of public recreational facilities to peer influences on oneself and one's children there are a range of forces that make individualistic and consumerist choices hard to eschew. Understanding how our present choices are self-defeating is a crucial step in the process of change, but so too is understanding how the social and political context makes such self-defeating choices seem almost inevitable.

One of the reasons that for a short time in the Sixties young people could so radically alter their lives is that they did so jointly, with mutual support and within informal social structures that made it easy (and one of the reasons that the change was so short-lived was that this crucial influence of context and mutuality was insufficiently recognized). If the ideas in this book make sense to readers, they will not be put into practice by individuals one at a time. It will require efforts to provide mutual support and persistent input counter to entrenched ideas and pressures, and it will require as well work on a still broader front aimed at social and political reforms that can reinforce changes in values and grounding ideas.

In presenting my arguments, I have stressed the American context and provided examples mostly from American life and culture. That is not because I believe the situation I describe is uniquely American, but only because it is easiest and safest to focus on the familiar. I believe that the present analysis and the recommendations that flow from it are relevant as well to such societies as those of Western Europe, Japan, Canada, and Australia, and hope that the book eventually finds a readership in those places. Recognizing the commonality of our situation will certainly increase the likelihood that benign changes can be achieved.

I wish now to comment on a matter of style. There has been increasing concern in recent years that deeply ingrained linguistic habits may contribute to maintaining harmful stereotypes about men and women. The use of the male pronouns *he*, *him*, or *his*, for example, when one is referring to an abstract individual who could really be male *or* female (e.g., "when a surgeon faces his patient . . .") may contribute to locking us into assumptions we need to transcend. I have struggled unsuccessfully to adapt my writing style to this concern. It will be readily apparent to the reader that my forte is not the simple declarative sentence. Something deep in my cortex has a fondness, or perhaps a need, for sentences with a fairly complex structure. When I try to change "he" and "his" to "he and she" and "his and her" what comes out sounds like German sentences with English words.

Other commonly offered solutions also have seemed to me to have an impact on how precisely and pleasingly the tool of language is employed. Use of "they" and "them" instead of "he" and "him" sometimes works, but often it lacks the immediacy that is required. Substituting "her" for "his" as the general form some of the time seemed to me at first the ideal way to reconcile aesthetic and moral concerns, but I found that when I encountered this form in reading others' writing it was distracting. Locutions such as he/she or (s)he jumped off the page even more.

I am presenting my struggles with this issue in some detail because I do not want the linguistic choices I have made to be taken in any way as an endorsement of those who dismiss the seriousness of feminist concerns. Where the structure of particular sentences or the precise communicative intent permitted, I did use forms like "his or her" or shifted to the plural. In many places that did not seem possible without doing damage to what I wanted to get across. That is simply evidence of how deeply rooted in our aesthetic and linguistic sense are the very habits now being questioned. Let me ask the reader to be aware that there are numerous places in the text where words like "he" or "mankind" appear as the unfortunate legacy of centuries of bias and should be read as including that half of the human race that our language can seem to render invisible.

My work on this book was aided by a great many people (as well as a canine named Rascal, who seemed to know precisely when a visit from a creature of indomitable playfulness was precisely what was needed). At its inception, a grant from the National Endowment for the Humanities permitted me to spend a year at the Institute of Society, Ethics, and the Life Sciences in Hastings-on-Hudson, New York. Both time to reflect and stimulating people to argue with were provided aplenty in a heady interdisciplinary atmosphere. Will Gaylin and Dan Callahan, the President and Director of the Institute, were extremely gracious and supportive, and they, along with Ron Bayer, Ruth Macklin, and Marilyn Weltz, made very helpful comments on early drafts.

Because this book ventures into territory for which a clinical psychologist is not formally prepared, I found it necessary to conscript more than the usual number of friends and colleagues into the task of reading and commenting on the manuscript. The following all gave me valuable feedback on one or more chapters: Marsha Amstel, Arthur Arkin, Stephen Bendich, Marshall Berman, George Kaufer, Patricia Laurence, Stuart Laurence, Jane Lury, Ronald Murphy, Stanley Renshon, Oliver Rosengart, Lloyd Silverman, Robert Sollod, Deborah Tanzer, Michael Tanzer. My brother-in-law, Joel Finer, read every chapter with a commitment and energy that were especially appreciated.

Miles Orvell, in particular, helped shape this work during countless hours of conversation whose loops and byways no computer could track. To the degree that this book is "the real thing" it owes much to both the seriousness and the playfully bantering spirit of our dialogues.

I am grateful as well for the feedback offered by my students in seminars where portions of the manuscript were considered, as well as in more informal conversations. The Ph.D. program in clinical psychology at City College is a remarkably open and intellectually fertile place. There are few clinical programs in the country where I could have received such consistent support for a project so disregarding of disciplinary boundaries, and none, I believe, where the commitment to critical thought at the very highest level is so ably carried through by students and faculty.

It is a pleasure to offer a very special note of thanks to Robert Coles, John Kenneth Galbraith, and Robert Heilbroner. The interest they showed in the book at a crucial stage was of inestimable value, and their comments were as perceptive as I had hoped. I wrote to them each as a stranger whose ideas I thought they might find congenial. The generosity of spirit they showed, in the face of extraordinarily busy schedules, is something I will long remember.

Very special thanks are also due Seymour Sarason, an inspiring teacher of mine at Yale, a friend to be counted on, and a *mensch*. Not the least of the many things I owe him is introducing me to Kitty Moore, my editor on this book but also a shrewd psychologist who managed my behavior with consummate skill and wrung from me a manuscript far better than the one that first caught her interest.

One final note of thanks: Once again my family has helped me to maintain the balance so many authors seem so proud of losing; they saved my evenings and weekends rather than my ruining theirs. We are all happier for it. But I cannot extend to them the ritual disclaimer I offer — with considerable truth, by the way — regarding all the others mentioned above: that what is meritorious in the book owes much to them and what is baneful owes to my stubbornness. The fact is, the heart and soul of this book comes from my experience with my wife, Ellen, and my children, Kenny and Karen. My view that feelings, relatedness, and human experience count more than the nonsense we are told today is "the bottom line" comes most of all from knowing and being with them; if that central idea is wrong, it is they who have led me astray!

ONE

Introduction

WE ARE USED TO THINKING of economic concerns, of dollars and cents, as eminently practical and rational matters. In this book I will present a quite different picture. I will argue that our society's preoccupation with goods and with material productivity is in large measure irrational and serves needs similar to those which motivate neurotic defense mechanisms in individuals. Despite the many benefits we have derived from our capacity to produce ever more and newer products, there are important ways in which our quest for abundance has become self-defeating.

A mood of pessimism and a sense of imminent decline have become increasingly evident. Sober warnings that the era of affluence is drawing to an end resonate with the daily experience of millions. It is not really affluence, however, that is threatened, but growth; we have confused the two for reasons that go to the heart of our national psychology.

Economic growth has been a foundation stone of our way of life. Whether viewing their current station in life as one of comfort and fulfillment or one of deprivation and discontent, Americans have viewed the future as rightfully providing them with more. Even those who doubted that the future *would* so provide had little doubt that it *should*. It seems only natural to

1

us that we should all have more than our parents had. To be "standing still" seems to many in our society a sign not of stability but of stagnation and failure.

This way of thinking has led to our current impasse. If even to stand still we must move ahead, then an ever larger supply of energy and of natural resources must be made available. For many years we managed to satisfy the prodigious appetite of our economic system, but the enterprise has begun to collapse under its own weight. We are finding it increasingly difficult and expensive to meet what have become our needs. Moreover, we have learned that there are severe side effects to our productivity. Health-threatening pollution of air, water, and food has grown along with the economy; "Love Canal," "Three Mile Island," and "PCBs" have become unwanted additions to our vocabulary. As a consequence, an "atmosphere of limits" has descended upon us, and fear of the future and a sense of austerity have become widespread.

But our present problems stem not so much from physical and economic limits—real as those are—as from our miscalculations as to what really works to provide us with security and satisfaction. Our economic system and our relation with nature have gone haywire because we have lost track of what we really need. Increasing numbers of middle-class Americans are feeling pressed and deprived not because of their economic situation *per se*—we remain an extraordinarily affluent society—but because we have placed an impossible burden on the economic dimension of our lives. So long as we persist in defining well-being predominantly in economic terms and in relying on economic considerations to provide us with our primary frame of reference for personal and social policy decisions, we will remain unsatisfied. A central task of this book will be to show how our excessive concern with economic goals has disrupted the *psychological* foundations of well-being, which in a wealthy society like ours are often even more critical.

It is common today to claim that we are already too preoccupied with psychological matters, that we are a culture of narcissism, a "me" generation. I will argue that we are not psychological enough, that the psychological impact of our decisions about how to commit our resources and energies and how to organize our lives has been insufficiently addressed. The critics of psychology have raised important issues. Many of their arguments are useful and compelling. But in examining these critiques, I will try to show how they have been based on a rather narrow and limited conception of psychology—narrow both in terms of the kinds of psychological theories that are considered and with regard to what the possible role of psychology in our culture might be.

This is not to say that psychological considerations ought to become our exclusive concern. A narrow psychologism would hardly be an improvement over our present way of thinking about things. But it is important to recognize that paying greater attention to the psychological dimension can facilitate the attainment of other important values as well. A shift in emphasis from an economic to a psychological definition of wellbeing, for example, makes far more feasible the attainment of a harmonious ecological balance. To the degree that we measure our lives in terms of social ties, openness to experience, and personal growth instead of in terms of production and accumulation, we are likely to be able to avoid a collision course with our environment without experiencing a sense of deprivation.

The shift in values and guiding assumptions I am suggesting does not imply reneging on our commitment to social justice or to the poor and disadvantaged. Initially, I will be addressing myself to considerations that bear most clearly on the experience of the middle class. I will try to show that much of the dissatisfaction currently being expressed by middle-class Americans stems not really from material deprivations but from deprivations more psychological in nature, and I will argue that most of us are considerably more affluent than in our present mood (and with our present assumptions) we are able to recognize. But real poverty will not go away by magically redefining it as affluence. There are many millions in America who really are poor, and there are still more enormous numbers throughout the world for whom the considerations with which this book begins seem sadly irrelevant. Before I am finished, however, I hope to show how the changes in thinking I am hoping to foster can play a role in relieving the plight of those who go to bed hungry or who lack jobs, decent housing, or the luxury of being able to reflect on whether or not their deprivations are real.

Even with regard to the middle class, it is not very useful to argue that their complaints are based on needs that are not "real." The way we have set things up, people really do experience a need for the things they buy (or wish they could buy).

Any argument that does not take this very real experience as a starting point is unlikely to find many followers. But the experience of economic needs in our culture is an artifact of how we *have* set things up—with little regard for the psychological consequences of our single-minded striving for material productivity. For all of the books on self-actualization and personal growth, all of the therapy sessions, all of the claims that we are a "psychological society," we are really a society that is psychologically quite unsophisticated. We need a new set of values and guiding assumptions to live by—assumptions that will let us *enjoy* our affluence and will enable us to translate the achievements of our technology into a life that is experientially richer and more secure.

My concern in this book is not primarily with the technical matters that concern economists. Rather, it is to raise some questions about the human reality that lies behind their imposing charts and figures. I want to have us look afresh at what money, goods, and jobs mean to us as individuals trying to make some order—and get some pleasure—out of our lives.

In criticizing the misuse of economic thinking and its excessive dominance in the ordering of our lives, it is not my intention to criticize the profession of economics or the individuals who practice it. Indeed, it is often the economists who are most aware of the limits of applicability of an economic approach and who complain that economists are asked to provide—and then criticized for not providing—guidance of a sort that economics was never intended to provide (for example, indicators of general welfare instead of indices of material productivity).

The aspects of our lives for which economic analysis is useful are limited but extremely important. It makes no small difference whether our resources are deployed in ways that permit us to achieve our goals or are frittered away in needless and frustrating inefficiencies. But however sophisticated its analyses, however cleverly it tries to include (and impute a dollar value to) such "externalities" as clean air, leisure, and life span, economics remains the science of "bread alone." When it ceases to be employed as a tool in the service of larger ends, and becomes instead the guiding framework of our lives, economic thinking becomes destructive. This has, to a disturbing degree, become the case in contemporary America.

Our discussions of critical ethical and social issues and our decisions about the priorities by which we will live tend today to be couched in terms of what we can "afford." The "bottom line" has become our favorite metaphor for what really matters. Now, no one would deny that a clear understanding of the economic impact of any course of action is essential in order to make an informed and intelligent decision; a recognition that our resources are finite and that deploying them in one direction limits what is available for other things is a mark of wisdom. But often our use of economic justification for policies masks deeper and less readily acknowledged values, fears, and prejudices. We pretend to ourselves that we are simply dealing with matters of accounting and budgeting and we thereby can avoid—for the moment—facing the more difficult choices that are really at issue.

But these deeper questions will not go away. By attempting to solve them by proxy, by pretending that they are limited to the arithmetic of dollars and cents, we fail to gain the clarity necessary for effective and satisfying resolutions. We can defer the sometimes painful process of examining whether our grounding assumptions are still valid, we can delay confronting our real beliefs about what is right and wrong—and whether we live up to those beliefs—but the price for this temporary comfort is a compounding of our difficulties as we try to make sensible choices while squinting at reality. In far too many instances we have limited our vision to economic considerations alone, and in so doing we have permitted what should be a subordinate aspect of our lives to intrude and dominate.

I believe it is time for a fundamental reexamination of our assumptions about the relation between economic productivity and personal well-being. Much of what we produce we neither need nor really enjoy. In many instances, the adverse effects upon both the physical and the social environment have far outweighed the benefits of the goods produced. Indeed, it may not be too far-fetched to suggest that as we now pay farmers not to grow certain crops, we might derive a certain societal benefit by paying workers—at least over a transition period—*not* to produce certain goods we have been paying them *to* produce.

Such a line of argument has the danger of being perceived by the reader as puritanical, masochistic, cranky, or downright foolish. The pleasures and advantages of our affluence seem so obvious that it appears to many that only a lunatic or a fanatic would question them. I hope I shall be able to make it clear that I am as capable — and desirous — of enjoying material pleasures as the next person and that I do appreciate what those pleasures are. All other things being equal, *of course* the more the better.

But all other things are *not* equal. The toll taken on our lives and health by pollution, for example, is staggering — and growing every day as we try to make our material product grow. Moreover, as I will particularly stress in this book, our frantic pursuit of growth ends up *working against* the attainment of secure and lasting satisfaction. The siren call of growth has us enthralled. But like the sirens of antiquity, it calls us to a disastrous course.

It is not the achievement of lives of pleasure and security I oppose; it is the illusion that the path to such a life must be lined with factories spewing smoke and billboards stirring envy and insatiable desire. A rich material life is in our grasp, and I hold no brief for poverty. But riches that do not yield satisfaction are worthless. By failing to understand our experience we make ourselves poorer than we need to be.

PART I

False Profits

TWO

The Illusions of Growth: Economic Abundance and Personal Dissatisfaction

IT IS VERY LIKELY that the reader of this book feels more pressed economically than he or she did a decade or more ago. The sense of economic decline is widespread nowadays. Both left and right, while disagreeing on methods and priorities, seem to agree that we must "get the economy moving again." Consequently, this book may seem at first to fly in the face of everyday experience when it argues that greater economic productivity is not what will relieve our distress and that the pursuit of economic growth may actually make things worse.

You will find, however, that the analysis that follows is very much rooted in everyday experience. It does not deny the *feeling* of deprivation and economic difficulty that today pervades our society. It questions the explanations for why we feel that way. The common answer is that declining productivity has pinched our pocketbooks, that inflation has eaten up our buying power, that we can't catch up, much less get ahead. This common perception, however, is at odds with a number of facts about the actual performance of our economy.

9

Let us look at some figures which must be taken into account if we are to understand what is happening to us. They suggest that our distress is not due as much to objective economic conditions as we have been led to think. For the entire decade of the 1970s, for example — a decade marked by a major OPEC oil shock, a serious recession, the onset of "stagflation," and discouragement of Americans about their economic situation — real per capita income rose 28%. This increase was about equally divided between the first and second half of the decade, and is almost identical to that of the 1960s, a decade looked back upon as one when the economy did work well.[1]

A similar picture emerges from a comparison of the boom years 1966-1972 and the inflation-ridden years 1972-1978. Real per capita income — again after correcting for both taxes and inflation — rose 17% in the first period and 16% in the second.[2] 1979 did bring a slight decline, and a somewhat larger one followed in 1980. But when the period 1976-1980 is looked at as a whole — a particularly significant span since it was the period referred to by Ronald Reagan when he asked, to great rhetorical effect, the key question of the 1980 Presidential campaign: "Are you better off than you were four years ago?" — it turns out that people *were* better off in 1980 than in 1976, at least as measured by objective economic indicators. *The Wall Street Journal* reported that even after correcting for inflation and taxes, per capita income increased 6% during the Carter years. Moreover, according to the *Journal*, that figure substantially underestimates the increase in total economic benefits; in the same period social security benefits, unreported income, and other sources of economic support not considered in the Commerce Department figures on which the article was based rose at an appreciably higher rate. The *Journal* concluded that the widespread conviction that most people were worse off economically was contradicted by the facts.[3]

A number of other considerations make these figures — so at odds with our national mood and with the subjective experience of so many of us — even more striking. First of all, they do not include the "underground economy," all that income and exchange that goes unreported and is not taxed. Estimates of the underground economy for 1980 range between $80 billion and $650 billion,[4] and most experts believe it is growing, thus further raising questions about whether Americans actually have less now than they did. Moreover, all this has occurred despite an unusual age distribution in the population at present. Because of the "baby boom" of the 1950s, we have a considerably higher percentage of young people in the work force, who typically have less skills and earn lower income than those with more experience. Also, because of advances in medical care, we have a higher percentage of older, retired people in the population than in the past. These individuals do not earn income, but their numbers reduce the per capita income figures for the entire population. Thus, the comparisons of the *rest* of the population with their counterparts of 1960 or 1970 underestimate how well they are doing.*

Other figures also suggest our problem is not as much a strictly economic one as we typically suppose. Many people are dismayed by the price of new cars, for example, yet if one considers, say, the cost of a full-size four-door American sedan, the average American family had to work about 25 weeks to earn enough to buy one in 1960, about 18½ weeks in 1970, and only 17 weeks in 1981.[5] Or, to approach our material situation from another angle, figures released by the Department of Commerce for up to 1979 reveal an increase from 1970 to 1979 of approximately 37% in the proportion of homes with air conditioners, a 62% increase in the proportion with dishwashers, a 38% increase for clothes dryers, a 43% increase for home freezers, a 24% increase for clothes washers, and an increase of 111% in the proportion of homes with color television sets (from 42.5% of homes in 1970 to 89.8% in 1979).[6]

The above figures, moreover, present the more conservative of two possible comparisons. One must also recognize that the number of households increased substantially during this period. Thus, to yield an increasing proportion of homes so equipped, the supposedly sluggish economy had to provide an even more dramatic increase in the total number of such items. Furthermore, with a trend toward smaller households, these items were shared by fewer people in each house. If one looks at the absolute number of homes containing these items, there was a 70% increase in the number of homes with air condition-

---

*The number of older people (and probably, therefore, the number of retired) is likely to continue to increase for a while. But when the "baby boom" generation enters its economic prime, the percentage of younger, less skilled workers in the work force should decrease substantially.

ers, a 101% increase in the number with dishwashers, a 71%
increase for clothes dryers, 78% for freezers, 54% for clothes
washers, and an increase of 162% in the number of houses with
color television sets.[7]

All these figures suggest that the widespread experience of
economic distress, the sense of having difficulty making ends
meet, is not due to our having a smaller stock of material goods
or less buying power than in the "good old days" when the economy was supposedly working as it should; indeed, they indicate
that we have more. As a psychologist, I certainly want to take
the *experience* of decline seriously. But I will argue that we
have largely misunderstood what that experience is due to.

The Exception: Unemployment

Before proceeding further, it is essential to acknowledge one
very important way in which the performance of the economy
really has been a source of distress in a fairly conventionally understood way. That is in the matter of unemployment. Unemployment rose in the early 1980s to its highest point in 40 years,
and its effects on millions of workers and their families have
been devastating. Especially is this true for members of minority groups and—to a degree whose implications for the future
of our cities are truly frightening—among minority youths.
Programs of unemployment insurance and public assistance
have placed some limit on the material deprivations that the
unemployed now undergo, but that deprivation is nonetheless
real and substantial for many, and demoralization and disruption of normal family life is experienced by still more. Further,
the effects of unemployment have an impact not just on the unemployed and their families but on those who are still working
but fear they will be the next to go. In this sense, there is no
question that our economy is a serious problem.

But the sense of economic distress that pervades our land
goes well beyond the confines of the unemployed or those soon
to be. It is widespread among the solidly middle-class and even
among many making quite substantial salaries, as numerous
articles and interviews have attested.[8] It is this more broadly experienced sense of decline and unease that elected Ronald
Reagan as president in 1980 and that constitutes the puzzle to

be addressed in what follows — the sense of deprivation amidst what once would have seemed like plenty.

Looking Back at "the Affluent Society"

It is possible to quibble about some of the figures I have cited. The choice of yardstick among, say, spendable income per capita, per household, or per wage earner will cause the picture to alter slightly. There are reasonable grounds for considering each as the appropriate criterion for judging our economic condition; depending on which one chooses, things look somewhat better or worse. For example, real income per family did not rise as much as real income per capita, but since families have grown smaller, an equivalent amount of money for a family now has to meet fewer people's needs and is therefore more ample. We may also note that Census Bureau reports on real family income do not include such implicit economic benefits as Medicare and Medicaid, which yield benefits to many families, and those benefits increased substantially from 1970 to 1980.

Some families have maintained their economic position by the woman's going to work for the first time. In some cases, this has led to an exaggerated estimate of economic well-being since there are often extra expenses associated with another family member's working and since valuable services previously performed by the wife (but not considered in official income statistics) are not as readily available. Yet this phenomenon too influences the set of figures available in contradictory ways: The increase in working women may lead to an effective overestimation of real family income but may lead to an *under*estimation of wage levels. This is because many women have entered the labor force in part-time positions, and their presence in the work force lowers the average weekly wage reported.[9]

These various complexities and ambiguities notwithstanding, the figures I have cited make it clear that there are a number of key respects in which — contrary to what our national mood would suggest — we have made real gains in the last decade or so. There can be little doubt, for example, that the average family's stock of major durable goods is substantially larger than it was a decade ago. And even the most pessimistic modes of analysis on real income do not reveal a precipitous decline.

But there is another comparison we can make that particularly demonstrates how misleading are interpretations of our apprehensive state simply in terms of economic decline. Whatever can be made of the ambiguities in examining the economic figures for the decade from 1970 to 1980, there can be no doubts whatever when comparing our present economic status to that prevailing in 1958.

The year 1958 is not chosen arbitrarily; I pick that year for comparison because it is the year that John Kenneth Galbraith's highly influential book *The Affluent Society* was published. Though some of Galbraith's policy recommendations were rather controversial, few questioned his characterization of the personal affluence of the American middle class; most agreed we were an extraordinarily rich society. Yet now we are feeling pinched at levels enormously above those of the "affluent society" period. The increase in possession of major consumer items is even more dramatic than in the comparison to 1970 cited earlier. The proportion of homes with air conditioners, for example, rose 484% (from 9.5% at the beginning of 1958 to 55.5% at the end of 1979). For some other representative items the figures were: freezers, 134%; clothes dryers, 356%; and dishwashers, a whopping 743%. If one looks at the absolute numbers of homes possessing these items, the figures are even more extraordinary: air conditioners, 838%; freezers, 278%; clothes dryers, 628%; and dishwashers 1268% (from 2.5 million homes to 34.2 million).[10] Even correcting for the increase in population over that period, the increase is unambiguous.

Why, then, do so many Americans seem to feel less pleased with their economic situation than did their counterparts in 1958? Part of the answer, to be sure, is a fear that present levels cannot be maintained. Many feel that we are on the edge of a precipice, facing imminent decline unless something is done to turn things around. But that does not really provide an adequate explanation; upon sober reflection, few would conclude that there is any reasonable likelihood of our "decline" really taking us back to the levels of 1958—that is, to the level when we were characterized as "the affluent society."*

---

*I am not considering here the possibility of a nuclear war, which would of course plunge us far indeed below 1958 levels of comfort, and which is made more likely by the very habits of mind I am criticizing in this book.

Inflation too contributes to the illusory sense of decline. Our real buying power has gone up, but not nearly as fast as our income in dollars. A salary of, say, $30,000 doesn't buy what one grew up thinking $30,000 would buy, yet psychologically at such an income one expects to live at "a thirty thousand dollar level." One forgets that the job one holds paid only $15,000 when one's image of what $30,000 would be was being shaped, and that one's buying power is greater than was the buying power of one's equivalent back then. Instead, mesmerized by the numbers, we are struck by how little "thirty thousand" is.

The economist Lester Thurow makes a similar point in a somewhat different way. Referring to the period from 1972 to 1978, when the sense of economic decline began to be widely felt, he notes that

> [w]hile real incomes were rising 16 percent, money incomes were rising 74 percent. Suppose a money man were to deliver $74 to your doorstep in the morning. You put on your bathrobe to go down to pick up the money along with the morning paper but find that when you get to your doorstep only $16 is there. Are you happy or mad? You are $16 better off than you were, but you have seen the $74 and can imagine what life would be like with it. You may even be able to convince yourself that your real standard of living has gone down."[11]

He adds that in some *psychological* sense people really may be worse off, a theme I will elaborate, though in a very different way.

Our decreasing sense of economic well-being is also due in part to changes in our living conditions that change the meaning of certain goods. For example, in 1958 to have two cars in a family was more likely to be a luxury than it is today. Now for many families two cars are close to a necessity and bring little sense of amplitude of living. More women work; more families live in suburbs, and particularly in the more sprawling suburbs of the South and West; the quality of mass transit has declined as we have placed our resources more and more at the disposal of the private automobile; suburban shopping centers have largely taken the place of urban commercial centers; and factories too have tended to move away from cities and into areas accessible only by car. All these factors now make two cars necessary for many in order to accomplish the tasks of shopping and getting to and from work with any degree of convenience. The reader will doubtless be able to think of similar arguments as to why many of the other things we now have in greater numbers do not mean to us what they once used to.

To some, this might seem to contradict the thrust of my argument, to offer an "objective" basis for the widespread feeling of not being able to make ends meet, of barely being able to address basic needs despite salaries whose numbers once would have seemed impressive. According to this line of thinking, we really do need more and our salvation does lie in expanding the economy and increasing productivity. I would contend, however, that the fact that we seem "really" to need more today is but one more reason why our emphasis on economic growth doesn't work for us; the way the growth economy has been constructed, it creates more needs than it satisfies and leaves us feeling more deprived than when we had "less."

The Growth Mentality

The creation of needs in a society organized for economic growth is not just a function of material conditions such as suburban sprawl and deteriorating mass transit. These are important, to be sure, but from another perspective they can be seen as the physical manifestations of a psychological state—an almost inevitable consequence of a set of values, assumptions, and habits of mind that characterize citizens of a growth-oriented society. Neither the material conditions nor the psychological state really are more basic; they continually co-determine each other, and both must be understood and addressed if we are to master our present state of crisis. I shall concentrate more on the psychological aspects, as befits my own professional background, but it is important to keep in mind that the psychology I shall rely on here is one that does not falsely and sharply dichotomize between the inner world of experience and the outer world of social and economic reality.

In another influential book that reflects the sense of affluence experienced in the late 1950s, David Potter's *People of Plenty*, American national character is depicted as shaped particularly by economic abundance. That book discusses a conclusion of Margaret Mead's to the effect that Americans judge their worth not by where they are but by how far they have come from where they started.[12] This propensity may perhaps characterize Americans in particular because of the specific historical circumstances in which American society evolved, but it is also largely accurate for all people living in societies organized around economic growth.

It is ironic that the very kind of thinking which produces all our riches also renders them unable to satisfy us. Our restless desire for more and more has been a major dynamic for economic growth, but it has made the achievement of that growth largely a hollow victory. Our sense of contentment and satisfaction is not a simple result of any absolute level of what we acquire or achieve. It depends upon our frame of reference, on how what we attain compares to what we expected. If we get farther than we expected we tend to feel good. If we expected to go farther than we have then even a rather high level of success can be experienced as disappointing. In America, we keep upping the ante. Our expectations keep accommodating to what we have attained. "Enough" is always just over the horizon, and like the horizon it recedes as we approach it.

We do not tend to think in terms of a particular set of conditions and amenities that we regard as sufficient and appropriate for a good life. Our calculations tend to be relative. It is not what we have that determines whether we think we are doing well; it is whether we have *more* — more than our parents, more than we had ten years ago, perhaps more than our neighbors. This latter source of relativity, keeping up with (or ahead of) the Joneses, is the most frequently commented upon. But it is probably less important, and less destructive, than our comparisons with our own previous levels and with the new expectations they generate. Wanting more remains a constant, regardless of what we have.

Our entire economic system is based on human desire's being inexhaustible, on there being a potential market for almost anything we can produce. Without always recognizing what we are doing or how we do it, we have established a pattern in which we continually create discontent, and we attribute the restless yearning to the spontaneous expression of human nature. This is not just something perpetrated by people in the advertising industry, though they are hardly innocent in it. And it is not the simple result of a deliberate conspiracy by the corporations, though they do indeed attempt to manipulate us to their advantage. Rather, it reflects a mentality we all share, something we all participate in. We are all afraid of stopping the merry-go-round, whether we view things from the perspective of businessman, worker, union leader, bureaucrat, parent, or consumer. I do think that advertising stirs desires that might otherwise not be there, and often to our detriment. But it does not write its message on a blank slate. We are all primed to receive its messages, and our priming, our state of mind, plays a critical role.

Growth, progress, the idea of "more" is so much a part of our consciousness that it takes very little to persuade us that any particular item is something we want or need. Ads influence what *particular* things we will desire (and in their very ubiquitousness they contribute to the growth state of mind as well), but it is our state of mind, linked as both cause and effect to so many interlocking features of our way of life, that it is particularly crucial to understand.

Let us consider a revealing article that recently appeared in the Columbia alumni magazine.[13] The writer describes a dinner party attended by a number of recent graduates in which the conversation (as it always seems to these days) "turned to the state of the economy and our personal finances." It was not the sort of group one would expect to feel hardpressed: "Graduates of the nation's top business and law schools and alumni of Ivy League universities, many of us are earning starting salaries our parents regard with amazement or envy," the author tells us. Yet the outlook of this elite group was "unrelievedly bleak."

The problem, it seems clear from the article, is that they are victims of the growth mentality. They are already, she acknowledges, enjoying a standard of living in their twenties and thirties that their parents did not attain until their forties or fifties. But they are dissatisfied because "our present material worth is irrelevant if we can't expect our future gains to surpass it." That is as eloquently stated a formula for personal and environmental disaster as one is likely to find. And unfortunately, the author is probably right when she says that is the cornerstone of what her generation was taught by teachers and parents.

Not all who are complaining about their economic circumstances are as privileged as these dissatisfied Ivy League graduates. Their situations highlight with unusual clarity how little the sense of economic distress and disappointment currently sweeping America has to do with real deprivation and how much with assumptions and expectations. In other cases the ambiguity is greater, and it is easier to lend credence to the illusion that the problem is primarily an economic one.

Many other members of their generation, for example — not as elite as those just described but part of that great majority of Americans who define themselves as middle class — are experiencing difficulty in buying a house. Inflation, it seems, is making impossible the "great American dream" of a house in the suburbs for every couple.

The problem, to be sure, is not just a matter of expectations. A number of factors, all coming together at once, have combined to hit the housing market with special severity. Certainly inflation and interest rates must be considered, as well as other traditional economic categories and particular economic policies that have prevented adequate construction and maintenance of housing. We must recognize as well that housing costs in the past did not honestly reflect the environmental impact of the expansion of our population in numbers and into new territories. Costs of providing for proper sewage, for access to water, and other such necessities have contributed substantially to the increased cost of housing; present home buyers are paying the environmental debts of their predecessors.[14] Pressure on the housing market is also enormously increased by the huge influx of new home-seekers as the "baby boom" generation enters adulthood and by the simultaneous tendency toward smaller households. More young people are living alone, as are more of the elderly, thus increasing still further the number of units needed to satisfy the demand. In the long run, the decline in the American birthrate, if it is maintained, may go farther toward solving the housing crisis than any economic policies.

But for those caught in it in the present, it is essential to understand how, again, assumptions and expectations are as much a cause of distress as any "objective" considerations. Let us return for a moment to the words of our privileged Ivy League graduate, for here her experience is, even on its face, not very different from that of many of her generation. "When my parents were married," she says, "they did what their parents had done: watched expenses, did without conveniences, and saved for the down payment on a house." That indeed was the typical pattern until quite recently. People *didn't* expect to move into their own suburban dream house right away. And they didn't feel that things were going all to hell if they couldn't.

A recent article in *The New York Times Magazine* confirms that the change in expectations is not confined to the Ivy League.[15] Reporting on conversations with couples seeking housing and with real estate agents from Queens to Des Moines, the article describes how couples "find it difficult to save because their tastes and style of living were formed during their relatively affluent adolescences" and how they, like their Ivy League brethren, are unwilling to start out in the kind of neighborhood their parents did. By an odd and ultimately self-lacerating logic, this makes them feel poorer than their parents.

The Logic and Illogic of Growth

So immersed are we in the assumptions of growth, so inured to what we actually have and preoccupied only with whether it is more than we had before, that our ability to make certain basic logical distinctions has declined; for many of us not having more has become equivalent to having less. This is part of what accounts for the paradox noted earlier—that at an enormously higher material level than in the late 1950s, we no longer feel like an "affluent society" or a "people of plenty." We *have* much more, but our *rate of increase* has declined.

The sociologist Paul Blumberg, in an influential analysis of the social consequences of our present economic situation, notes that

> . . . for Americans, as well as for theorists of the American class structure, what has always been crucial is not merely the absolute level of living, but the progress from year to year, decade to decade, generation to generation. . . . [I]t is this expectation of continuous improvement that recent developments now threaten.[16]

There is much that is useful in Blumberg's analysis, yet like many who have tried to come to terms with what is happening he also contributes in certain ways to the very problem he is analyzing. His depiction of an "age of decline" when discussing a lack of *increase* in income is consonant with his references— hardly unique to him—to the "stagnation" of living standards or to workers whose living standards "barely are holding their own."[17] Were one not so mired in the language and perceptions of a growth ideology, one might as accurately portray living standards as "stabilized" or as "maintained at a level higher than those of the affluent 1950s and 1960s." The confusion so many of us seem to experience between our level of affluence and whether it is increasing still further is captured beautifully in his term "the falling rate of affluence," which again refers not to a decrease in living standards but to a decline in the rate at which they continue to increase still further.

Blumberg's fall into the habits of growth-think is only partly unwitting. In much of his book he seems quite aware of what he is doing, and it can be justified as an accurate phenomenological account of how workers *experience* the vicissitudes of the economy. Moreover, he is correct that these are real expectations whose social consequences can be ugly if they are not met. Other analysts seem to slide into describing a lack of increase as a decrease even when unambiguously speaking in their own voice; and when they are economists—and indeed economists more sensitive than most to what is happening to us—that is especially significant. Thus John O. Wilson, whose book *After Affluence* is subtitled *Economics to Meet Human Needs*, refers to an "end to affluence" by which he means, as indicated in the next sentence, "no *increase* in our consumption of nonessential goods and services" (italics added). Similarly, he says American workers' productivity had taken a "nosedive," yet later in the same paragraph it becomes clear that what he means by this and by a "drop in productivity" is that there was only a one-percent *growth* in productivity, whereas in other years growth rates were higher.[18]

I do not mean to suggest that Wilson did not understand the distinction, but rather to point out how pervasive and revealing are the almost tic-like language habits that creep into our speech undetected and constitute a kind of growthspeak or growth-think. If economists cannot keep these distinctions clear, even when carefully presenting arguments for publication, it is hardly surprising that the rest of us are unclear about these matters in our daily lives.

Affluence and Adaptation Level

One useful tool for understanding our confusions and the apparent lack of fit between our level of affluence and our experience of well-being is a psychological theory originally developed for studying processes of perception. The theory, called adaptation-level theory, was developed by Harry Helson.[19] It has found increasingly wider fields of application and is now used to address a broad range of problems in social psychology and the psychology of personality as well as in its original domains of application. Central to adaptation-level theory in all its applications is the recognition that our perception of events depends not just on their "objective" nature but on the expectations and assumptions that we bring to bear. In particular, our experience with previous events of a similar nature influences our perception. We tend to experience events in relation to what we are used to. Our perceptions are inherently comparative.

Thus, in a typical adaptation-level experiment, if a person is given a weight to pick up and asked to judge how heavy it is, he will judge it as heavier if he has previously picked up weights lighter than it. Similarly, in studies of the effectiveness of various rewards, it is found that the same reward may lead to greater or lesser effort depending on the reward that the person expects and on what he has been used to receiving in similar situations. Previous experiences and expectations produce an internal standard or norm, which psychologists call the adaptation level. New experiences are rewarding or disappointing not in terms of any absolute standard but in relation to this internal norm.

In judging how well off we are economically, similar processes seem to be involved. We assimilate new input to our "adaptation level." For many Americans, having one or several color television sets, two or more cars, a home in which there are more rooms than people—few Americans realize what an extraordinary luxury that is to most people in the world, even in the industrialized world—these and other features of their lives are experienced as the "neutral point." They do not excite us or arouse much feeling. Only a *departure* from that level is really noticed. Some pleasure may be afforded by our background level of material comfort, but unless we look elsewhere than the accumulation of goods for the main sources of pleasure and excitement in our lives, we are bound to be on a treadmill—one which, we are increasingly recognizing, can damage our health and shorten our lives.

The way off this treadmill, I will argue, lies in focusing more of our aspirations on experiences less subject to the adaptation-level effect. Attention to human relationships and cultivation of the senses and of aesthetic experience can point us toward domains where "more and less" thinking—while not completely absent—is not so dominant and where variety and novelty prevent the dulling of experience to a much greater extent. These dimensions of human aspiration have, of course, always been an important part of American experience, and there is evidence that they are in fact on the rise.[20] Nonetheless, when the director of the South Street Seaport Museum in New York was asked recently why he permitted the museum to become involved in a large-scale commercial development scheme he answered, with considerable accuracy I believe, "The fact is that shopping is the chief cultural activity in the United States."[21]

Social Limits to Growth

In addition to the psychological factors that limit the satisfaction which economic growth can bring, the late British economist Fred Hirsch discussed a number of more objective considerations as well.[22] Hirsch pointed out a major fallacy in the argument that economic growth can obviate the necessity of a redistribution of economic goods by providing a continually larger pie: In a society such as ours, in which for a substantial majority basic material needs are rather fully met,* the additional things that economic growth provides are inherently

---

*It is a shameful fact that for a minority of our population this is not the case—though even here the difference between American "poverty" and Third World "subsistence" is important to understand if one is to be helpful (see below).

scarce; that is, their enjoyment *depends* on others not having the same thing. This is more than just a matter of status-seeking or conspicuous consumption. Hirsch was at pains to demonstrate that there is as well an "objective, nonpsychological" basis for the limited capacity of economic growth to make us happy.

Hirsch's argument rests on a distinction between what he called the "material" and the "positional" economy. Goods of the first sort can increase with productivity and be of value to a wider and wider range of individuals. We needn't take telephones away from the rich; we can make them available to everyone. But with increasing affluence, more and more of what we strive for is of the second sort, either because of physical scarcity or because of the social nature of what is sought. The automobile is to some extent a positional good. Autos bring more pleasure to the few who drive them when they are a luxury than to the vast numbers who clog the roads when "growth" has made them accessible to all. Wider availability makes possession of an auto lose some of its value for everyone; even Rollses and Mercedes get stuck in traffic jams. Ownership of a beachfront home is even more clearly positional. The number of miles of ocean front set absolute limits to the number who can own such property. Building high-rises along the beach clearly changes the nature of what one can have. If a less urban, more serene or "natural" setting is desired, then redistribution—taking exclusive ownership away from those who now possess such houses—is the only alternative. Beyond a certain point, the pie can't get larger.

Increase in "productivity"—the standard answer to Malthusian and neo-Malthusian warnings about limits—is relevant, even if feasible, only for the material economy and for increasing production. But in the realm of consumption, Hirsch suggested, limits are "more" absolute than for production:

> An acre of land used for the satiation of hunger can, in principle, be expanded two-, ten-, or a thousand-fold by technological advances. . . . By contrast, an acre of land used as a pleasure garden for the enjoyment of a single family can never rise above its initial productivity in that use. The family may be induced or forced to take its pleasures in another way—substitution in consumption—but to get an acre of private seclusion, an acre will always be needed.[23]

"Growth" solutions to the desire of all for more are limited by other constraints that are more clearly social, rather than physical, in nature. Take, for example, the role of education in providing access to better jobs. When relatively few have high school educations, attainment of one provides many opportunities. When we have managed to provide a high school education to almost everyone, the "value" of such an education in this respect goes down *precisely because everyone now has one.* By making it available to all we have made it of value to none.

Now, of course the value of an education resides in more than just the leg up it provides in competing for a job, and in this (extremely important) sense, the economic growth that has enabled us to afford to provide everyone with more education has indeed provided greater benefits for all. Hirsch weakened his argument by seeming at times to ignore this aspect of such "goods" as education. (Clearly he recognized the value of education, and the apparent imbalance in his argument is partly a function of his trying to argue strictly as an economist and partly of his having his tongue at least lightly touching his cheek — and perhaps of his recognition that the two may not always be entirely different.) But — especially as the "standard" credentials for competing for a good job have increasingly become not just a high school but a college diploma as well — it must be acknowledged as a sad truth that for many people education is more of a cost than a benefit. And for this rather substantial group, the effect of making education more widely available by a process of growth has been to increase the effort required to get ahead, to place greater rather than less obstacles in the path of economic advancement.

Each individual's decision to get more education is still a rational one: He must do so to keep up with all the others who are doing so. But the total social costs (viewing education here as a cost rather than a benefit) have increased for all. Everyone must exert more effort to get to the same place. Because education (as preparation for a job, rather than as a valued end in its own right) is a "positional" good, the increased benefits of "growth" here are illusory.

Hirsch likened the effects of many of our seeming gains to those of standing on tiptoe to obtain a better view in a crowd. It works for any given individual considered separately (either giving him an advantage if he is the first, or at least helping him to equalize things if others have already done so). Clearly, his individual failure to act in this way would leave him with less benefits, and it would be irrational for him to choose not to stand on tiptoes. But, as Hirsch pointed out, if one calculates the aggregate benefit of all these individual acts, "the sum of benefits of all the actions taken together is nonetheless zero."[24] By assuming that what people are willing to spend to obtain something is a measure of its "value" to them, economists assign a value to the aggregate of all products and services by adding up these individual values. As Hirsch suggested, this sum produces quite flawed estimates of total value.*

Much of what we spend our money on doesn't really get us ahead; it merely keeps us from falling behind. We move to the suburbs to try to escape the problems we have created in the cities, and—by the time the presumed benefits of economic growth have enabled large numbers to partake of this solution—the suburbs become transformed and take on many of the same problems. It is then time for those who can afford it to move on to a "better" suburb—until growth enables many to afford that solution too—and again to nullify it.

We are, Hirsch suggested, subject to "the tyranny of small decisions." Given the particular choices open to us, each of us chooses in a way that we think will maximize our welfare. Yet the interacting effects of all our individual choices result in a situation that most people do not want. Our highly individualistic way of thinking about both personal and social choices does not let us pose our alternatives in a more communal way, to consider whether a *joint* response might result in greater welfare than the individualistic scrambling we now engage in.

Growth and the Poor

It is frequently argued—by an odd consortium of representatives of the poor and of corporate power—that calls by middle-class intellectuals to limit growth are selfish or short-sighted. Only with a growing pie, it is said, can those who have traditionally had smaller portions have their lot bettered. When ut-

---

*I will have more to say later about the limitations of such measures as gross national product and how they lead us astray.

tered by those who have worked so hard to assure that some people's slice was larger than the rest, this touching concern for the poor is somewhat suspect. When put forth by representatives of the poor themselves, this concern for growth is still, I think, misguided.

This view of growth is based on several questionable premises. The first concerns the matter of redistribution. Proponents of growth usually assume that redistribution of wealth is an unrealistic expectation. As a consequence, it appears to them that only if the total is larger can those at the bottom have more. It is interesting to note in this regard that social unrest does not seem to be quelled by growth. The 1960s were a time of high growth *and* great unrest — including calls not just for more but for a fairer share for those at the bottom. Simply dividing a larger pie did not yield contentment or social harmony.

It is certainly true that redistribution presents formidable political problems. But there are also grave problems in trying to improve the lot of the poor through the strategy of growth. "A rising tide lifts all vessels," said John F. Kennedy, and in certain ways this is true. On an *international* scale, for the poor of the Third World, many of whom are literally starving and others of whom have little more than a full belly to distinguish them from the first group, simply having "more" — in almost any sense — would indeed be a real gain. These people live at the margins of subsistence, and anything that can be done to better their material state is to be applauded. Since their numbers are so vast, it may well be that there is no way to achieve a measure of justice for them without — on a world scale — a good deal of economic growth.

This does not mean, however, that further growth in the developed countries will contribute much to the well-being of the world's poor. As things stand now, the developed nations use up or appropriate far more than their share of the earth's resources. Growth in the developed nations would exacerbate, not relieve, that problem. Moreover, the striving after more that is the essence of a growth economy does not breed generosity. The percentage of our gross national product that now goes to foreign aid is minuscule. If we continue to believe that we do not have enough ourselves, we are unlikely to increase our contribution very much. It is not difficult to imagine that with a more steady state economy — and a concomitant psychology of

contentment rather than increasing wants — the absolute
amount of our contribution might be greater even though our
gross national product, as typically measured, would be less.*

It must also be recognized that, for better or worse, we
tend to be the model toward which the less developed nations
strive. It is not easy to understand the problems and discontents
of a consumer society from the vantage point of genuine deprivation. If we set a material standard that is increasingly hard to
measure up to, we make the task of catching up that much
more difficult.

Realistically, affluence as we have tended to conceive of it
is beyond the reach of most of the world. To imagine a billion
Chinese using resources and polluting the air and water at the
rate we do, and in addition 700 million Indians, 400 million
Latin Americans, 500 million Africans, and numerous other
peoples as well, is to recognize that our present notions of what
constitutes the good life absolutely *require* that most of the
world be poor. *Only* by changing the way we use resources and
define our needs is there even a chance for all the world's bil-
lions to prosper.

If we shift our focus to domestic concerns, to the poor
within the affluent societies, the inappropriateness of a "rising
tide" solution is even greater. The misery of those at the bottom
of our society is not due simply to a lack of goods. It has elements of real material deprivation, to be sure, but it is also social and psychological. It is the *invidious* quality in their lives
that particularly constitutes their poverty; it is having *less than
everyone else* in a society that continually redefines and up-
grades what are regarded as necessities for a decent life, and
that through advertising and the media continually trumpets
that one *ought* to have this or that that one had hardly thought
of before. Increasing the size of the pie, without changing the
relative size of the slices, will do nothing to alter this invidious
sense of oneself. No matter how much "more" those at the bottom get in this way, they will still have "less" than the rest of us.
And being low man on the totem pole is painful no matter how
high the pole.

---

*Some argue that we help developing nations most effectively, and
least paternalistically, not by giving aid but simply by trading with them —
that it is the essence of trade that it benefits both parties to it. Chapter
Twelve will examine more closely the difficulties with such thinking.

The misery of those in our ghettos is not *all* a matter of invidious comparison, of course. There are certainly some absolute features of ghetto life that require correction and that might be improved by a "rising tide." Replacing crumbling, poorly heated homes infested with rats and roaches would be more possible in times of economic expansion and would contribute to well-being regardless of relative position. Certainly we should do all in our power to achieve this. Jobs too are more available in times of economic growth, and no one doubts that unemployment is one of the central causes of despair among the poor and minority population.

But even here, simply increasing the size of the pie may not have much beneficial effect. First of all, it is not at all clear that ghetto housing would be much of a priority even if "the economy" was "growing." We are far too prone to ask *how much* we are producing rather than *what*.

The same goes for jobs, in a slightly different way. It is not enough simply to provide jobs. Jobs without dignity, jobs that do not permit a sense of self-respect or a feeling that one can live well by working hard are not a great benefit. Elliot Liebow, in *Tally's Corner*, has provided a compelling account of the devastating social consequences of offering jobs at a level of pay that leaves people feeling they have no future even if they work full time.[25] In a society where many can work their way into a life of substantial comfort, giving work to a minority at marginal levels is a self-defeating exercise. Even if we lift the level of all, so that low-level jobs seem to pay more compared to current standards, if they remain substantially below what most people expect, and below a newly risen level of what seems standard, they will not make much of a dent in the despair.

Richard Easterlin, in a widely cited report on the relation between economic growth and happiness, draws the following conclusions from the evidence available from studies in the United States and throughout the world:

> *In all societies, more money for the individual typically means more individual happiness.* However, *raising the incomes of all does not increase the happiness of all.* The happiness–income relation provides a classic example of the logical fallacy of composition — *what is true for the individual is not true for society as a whole.*

The resolution of this paradox lies in the relative nature of welfare judgments. Individuals assess their material well-being, not in terms of the absolute amount of goods they have, but relative to a social norm of what goods they ought to have. [italics in original].[26]

There are more cars and television sets in the ghetto today than there once were in comfortable middle-class neighborhoods. Yet anger, misery, and despair are rampant. The pie has grown, but it hasn't really helped much. So long as those at the bottom are accorded markedly less than the rest of us — both in respect and in their share of the goods we are all taught to clamor for — they will feel poor. Growth is no substitute for greater equality. It may be tempting to think that growth can provide an easy way out of facing questions about the justice of present arrangements, but such questions will not go away. Growth proponents pose as hard-headed realists. But their vision of buying off the poor with the crumbs from their table is in fact a dangerously naive fantasy, no matter how sugar-coated the crumbs or grand the table.

THREE

The Unperceived Realities
of the Consumer Life

IN THE WORDS OF NOBEL ECONOMICS LAUREATE Herbert Simon, the basic model of economics posits that each person has "a complete and consistent system of preferences that allows him always to choose among the alternatives open to him; he is always completely aware of what his alternatives are; there are no limits on the complexity of the computations he can perform in order to determine which alternatives are best."[1] Most economists agree that such a description of human behavior is not realistic but regard it as a close enough approximation to be useful. Doubtless for certain purposes it is. But I will stress here another perspective that yields quite a different picture. I have already indicated some of the ways in which our thinking about the economic side of our lives is less realistic and less rational than we like to believe. In this chapter I shall consider some further ways in which we blur our experience or practice self-delusion about our lives as consumers.

Our economy absolutely requires that we nurture illusions if it is to persist in its present ways. Our image of what things mean to us and the homilies we share and repeat to each other have become increasingly at odds with the realities of our daily

31

lives. We magnify the satisfactions our material pursuits bring, while the sacrifices are either blotted out or reinterpreted in ways that make what we're doing seem to make sense.

To the psychotherapist, such a dedication by people to precisely the way of life that causes their distress is a familiar phenomenon. Irony and self-deception are abundant in the behavior patterns he studies. The psychotherapist's perspective is less superficially reassuring than the Panglossian circle of mainstream economics, which defines our real preferences as revealed—conveniently—by precisely what we buy. But there is something to be gained if one persists in the effort to examine experience a bit more closely than one's grocery list permits—perhaps not only self-knowledge but even the possibility of a kind of liberation considerably more satisfying than simply being "free to choose" what is on the shelves.

The Automobile as Dream Machine

Let us begin our examination of the self-deceptions of the consumer life by looking at the role of automobiles in our lives. Few products have had as powerful a role in shaping the way we live, for both good and ill, and few so strongly define and limit what options appear available to us. Moreover, few products have aroused such a complex of emotions in us or become so utterly indispensable to our way of life. The French semiologist Roland Barthes has even provocatively suggested that "cars today are almost the exact equivalent of the great Gothic cathedrals . . . the supreme creation of an era, conceived with passion by unknown artists, and consumed in image if not in usage by a whole population which appropriates them as a purely magical object."[2]

In Flannery O'Connor's *Wise Blood* we find one character saying "Nobody with a good car needs to be justified." Joyce Carol Oates says about the frame of mind of one of her characters, "As long as he had his own car he was an American and could not die." And lest one think such statements appear only in fiction, one finds in a *New York Times* article on the effects of energy shortages on people's lives the following statement by a social worker who had switched from solo driving to a car pool: "That first week of the car pool, when I knew my car was

not out in the parking lot, I felt like I had lost an arm or something."[3]

In America cars have been the lifeblood of the society of growth; it is not without reason that roads and highways are referred to as arteries.* Even those who live in cities, where automobiles may seem less of a necessity, depend for their very lives on the flow of automotive traffic. The seductive pull of the automobile — aided by huge government investments in a comprehensive highway system — has led to the atrophy of rail transportation, and since few of us grow our own food, we count on trucks and roads for the necessities of life.

Automobiles have reshaped our landscape, both geographically and culturally. At a time when few of us could see that the genie in the bottle looked very much like a smirking OPEC sheik, and when most of us probably thought that hydrocarbon emissions had something to do with putting bubbles in soft drinks, America took to the open road. Taking full advantage of our vast continent, we pushed ahead toward one last frontier — the relatively open spaces that surrounded our cities even after the Pacific had been reached and settled. The westward push that had dominated America's consciousness and expressed her vitality for so many years was replaced by an *outward* push. In every city, East and West, we expressed our expansiveness in this new way, forsaking the clustered way of life that had characterized city life for thousands of years. We created instead a *new kind* of city, freed from the old constraints imposed by time and distance. The automobile seemed to provide us with a way of keeping in touch, of sustaining the critical mass that is required for a lively culture, and yet enjoying as well the greenery and open space that we have always envisioned as Eden. Now, having tasted of the fruits of OPEC, we are threatened with expulsion from Eden — or perhaps, in the modern case, with house arrest instead of exile: Without the car, how could we get around? The structure of our living, shopping, and working arrangements seems to make the private automobile absolutely indispensable.

---

*One may whimsically note that these arteries — of concrete or asphalt — are *hardened* arteries, and that they are subject to clotting (especially at rush hour), a phenomenon which in turn raises the blood pressure in the more vulnerable arteries of drivers.

Automobiles are the core of our economy as well. Daniel J. Boorstin, historian and Librarian of Congress, asserts, "We cannot understand what we mean in America by competition or by monopoly, by advertising, by industrial leadership, or by know-how, unless we have understood the role of the automobile."[4] One in six jobs in America are directly or indirectly related to the automobile (not just in building them, but in selling, distributing, and servicing them; mining or producing the materials; drilling for, refining, and distributing the fuel for them; and so on).[5] Every 24 hours we add 10,000 new drivers and 10,000 new cars to our roads.[6] Estimates of how much of the average American's income goes to support his automobile—not just in paying for the car, but in interest payments, insurance, repairs, parking, tolls, fuel, taxes, and so forth—range from one out of ten to almost one out of every four dollars spent.[7] Indeed, our social fabric seems to be constructed out of automobile parts.

But automobiles are more than just a necessity to us. They are a way of life. Our involvement with them is more than just a matter of practicality; they serve us as a symbol of freedom, strength, speed, and adventure. Perhaps one of the reasons that solo driving to and from work has continued so persistently in the face of serious impracticalities is that it is so conducive to fantasy. Cars are our personal dream machines, and dreams are private experiences.

In many instances cars have been specifically designed to enhance this kind of fantasy. Interior and exterior design, model names, and the contents of ads all converge toward an image of driving that implies not only great speed but also far greater skill than is really involved. Everyday driving is in fact a rather passive, simple task that most of the time requires a bare minimum of skill. The effort to make cars "exciting," "sexy," and "supercharged" has helped to obscure the everyday experience of driving and to encourage us to make of cars a vehicle for our fantasies rather than merely a mode of transportation.

Looking into the not too distant past, even our sexual mores can be seen as intimately related to the automobile. Perhaps now that changes in sexual standards have become more pervasive and acknowledged, now that space and discretion are provided the young for their sexual experimentation, fewer initiate their sexual lives in automobiles. But for a transitional genera-

tion, the automobile was a boudoir as much as a mode of transportation. The possibility of young couples disappearing together for a few hours in an automobile did not *cause* a change
in sexual behavior in itself. There had to be a receptive culture
for this to be permitted in the first place. But the sense of freedom generated by the automobile did contribute to the background sense that young people were independent of and separate from their parents rather than part of a larger unit with a
well-defined and delimited place. And the mobility and privacy
provided by the automobile did make possible changes in sexual patterns which society at the time was willing to tolerate
(and perhaps even encourage) only if it did not have to see or
explicitly acknowledge them.

In return for the freedom, independence, spontaneity, and
excitement that cars are felt to give us, we have been willing to
pay an enormous price—though we have tended to deny the
price we pay. For one thing, riding in cars is one of the most
dangerous things we do in our daily lives. The highway accident rates we endure are astonishing—50,000 violent deaths,
4.5 million injuries each year,[8] as many casualties *each year* as
we sustained in the entire Vietnam War. Moreover, like war
deaths, highway fatalities take their toll disproportionately on
the young. More than half of the victims each year are in their
twenties or younger. Indeed, if present trends continue, 1 out of
60 children born in America today will die in an automobile accident before they are twenty-one.[9] But though few of us have
not known someone who was killed or seriously injured in an
auto accident, we relegate this unpleasant reality about the automobile to some nether portion of our consciousness.

The auto executives are probably telling the truth—
though a far more complicated and less honorable truth than
they would have us believe—when they say that most Americans "don't want" changes in cars that could make them safer
at the cost of higher prices or less "convenience." Indeed, even
the simple expedient of using seat belts and shoulder harnesses
is resisted. Though such devices enormously reduce the risk of
death or serious injury, it is estimated that they are used by only
15% of drivers.[10] This degree of disregard for the most basic
kind of protection against being maimed or killed speaks
poignantly to the fantasies of invulnerability associated with the
automobile and to our need to *feel* that we are unconstrained.

Cars are also, of course, a major source of air pollution. Here again, we use psychological mechanisms of denial and refuse to really take into account what we have wrought. Consider: In New York City the level of carbon monoxide in the blood of most taxi drivers is so high it cannot be used for transfusions to people with heart ailments.[11] When problems of pollution are brought to our attention, we deal with the issue in the language of "tradeoffs." We have become used to hearing a familiar litany: No one can live free of risks; life spent continually in fear of consequences is dull and not worth living; America wasn't built by frightened, cautious men; we need to try to reduce pollution, but we must be "reasonable"; pollution control, after all, is expensive, and someone is going to have to pay for it; a certain amount of pollution is a price we are willing to pay for the personal and economic benefits the automobile provides.

These arguments are not entirely without merit. In the abstract they make a fair amount of sense. But are the actual benefits really as great as we are accustomed to thinking they are? Are they enough to justify the very real risks to health, life, and limb for ourselves and our children?

To ride along a pristine country road on a beautiful spring day certainly *is* a pleasure, and one worth taking a certain risk to enjoy. A slightly longer life devoid of experiences of this kind may well seem not particularly attractive to many people. But is that what the bulk of our driving consists of? Or is it commuting to work along the Long Island Expressway, New Jersey Turnpike, or San Diego Freeway, stopping and starting and crawling along, breathing the fumes of the car in front; or driving along the "strips" that devour our landscape, stopping at traffic lights, assaulted by ugliness and, again, crawling along like thousands of other drivers, each wishing the others weren't there? Is *such* a commute so much more pleasurable than a comfortable train or bus? Is *that* worth endangering your children's lungs? And isn't *that* what most driving—especially most commuting—really is?

We nurture a *sense* or *illusion* of freedom that overrides the daily reality. Most days we do not "trade off" pollution and the risk of accident for a freer, experientially richer life; we trade these off for still another tradeoff, the daily grind on the expressway, another faulty compromise that mocks the supposed rationality of our decision-making. We eat gruel all week and tell ourselves it's dessert.

It can be argued, of course, that the transportation alternative I am implying doesn't exist in most places. Mass transit is often unreliable, uncomfortable, or not conveniently accessible. And even where it suits the needs of commuters, it is often not suitable for shopping. All this is true (though often exaggerated). Later I shall consider some of the social and psychological processes responsible for the poverty of choices we face, as well as some alternatives that might potentially be available. For now, though, I simply want to call attention to the difference between our *image* of the car in our lives (sometimes fulfilled on certain glorious days) and the reality of the daily commute that accounts for so many of our driving miles.*

Tons of Cotton Candy

Compared to the automobile, the mixed blessings of most of the other products of our industrial cornucopia are more subtle. Most other products do not so dramatically dominate our lives. They seem not to have the negative equivalent of traffic jams, and they don't pollute as obviously as the automobile does, where smoke comes out the exhaust as we use it.

Of course, our panoply of consumer items and the way of life associated with it are in fact responsible for a great deal of pollution—for emissions into the air from the factories that build the items and from the electric generating plants that later supply the energy to run many of them; for toxic chemicals spewed into the soil and water in the process of manufacturing; for environmental degradation associated with the disposal of plastics and the broader problem of waste disposal resulting from the hesitance to recycle which is part of our

---

*I cannot resist adding here an apocryphal tale reported in *The New York Times* in the context of a story about commuting on the Long Island Expressway. A local judge, it is claimed, once sentenced a chronic traffic offender to two weeks of driving on the expressway during the rush hour. The sentence was reversed on appeal—by a panel of judges all of whom themselves commuted on the expressway—on the grounds that it violated the Constitutional stricture on cruel and unusual punishment. Michael Norman, "Misery a Commute on L.I. Expressway," *The New York Times*, September 2, 1982, p. B1.

"consumer convenience" psychology. We are not really the "postindustrial" society we are sometimes made out to be. If we were, we wouldn't have the kind of pollution problems we do. To be sure, we put a greater portion of our effort and income into services than previously. But we are still a people preoccupied with products, and the state of our lungs and livers clearly reflects this.

If we probe further, we find that the pollution properly attributable to any particular consumer item is not limited to that which results from its own manufacture, use, and disposal; it includes as well an effect on how we manufacture *other* items: By seeking to maximize goods rather than other amenities such as leisure or clean air, we are required to manufacture each item in the cheapest way—that is, the way that leaves the maximum amount of money available for other purchases. If we imposed stricter environmental protection laws and backed them up with stricter enforcement, this would indeed "cost" us something; the price of the items involved would go up, and less would be available to buy other things. In choosing to aim for a large number of these "other" things, we are also *ipso facto* manufacturing many basic items in a less pollution-free way than we otherwise might. The new computer gadget may be relatively nonpolluting, but—implicitly but powerfully—we permit the manufacturers of other things to dump more into the air, water, and soil in order to have the money left over to buy it. The larger the array of consumer goods we aim for—and there is inevitably an implicit societal decision in this regard even if most of the manufacturing and buying is done privately—the more pollution we are almost certain to permit in the manufacture of each.

But again, these are the tradeoffs we claim to be making rationally and boldly in the pursuit of pleasure. Whereas for automobiles alternatives can readily be imagined that are potentially more pleasant for many purposes,* it is harder to make a similar case, based on clear experiential negatives, for stereo systems, video games, color TVs, boats, campers, air conditioners, and so on. There are no obvious equivalents of traffic jams here. These all seem to be rather pure plusses in experiential terms—leaving aside for the moment the effects of pollution, waste disposal, and the rest. To question them as real

*See Chapter Seven.

benefits, as something of genuine value to us, seems absurd at first.

But there is an odd phenomenon accompanying the accumulation of these goods. One might label it "the fallacy of the individual commodity." Somehow, as we examine the experiential impact of all our acquisitions, we discover that the whole is less than the sum of its parts. Each individual item seems to us to bring an increase in happiness or satisfaction. But the individual increments melt like cotton candy when you try to add them up. We are not any happier as a nation now than we were 25 years ago, despite having a good deal more of "the good things of life." This is attested to in a number of ways.

For one thing, surveys taken at various times of people's subjective sense of well-being do not show an increase over time corresponding to the increase in material possessions and comforts. Indeed, a higher proportion of Americans reported being "very happy" in 1957 than at any time in the next 20 years — despite a generally rising "standard of living" in the terms measured by economists.[12]

These findings for different time periods are paralleled by the results of a major cross-sectional study of happiness conducted a few years ago. Summarizing that portion of the study relevant to our present concerns, Jonathan Freedman notes that "once some minimal income is attained, the amount of money you have matters little in terms of bringing happiness. Above the poverty level, the relationship between income and happiness is remarkably small."[13]

The reason why economic growth no longer brings a sense of greater well-being, why the pleasures our new possessions bring melt into thin air, is that at the level of affluence of the American middle class what really matters is not one's material possessions but one's psychological economy, one's richness of human relations and freedom from the conflicts and constrictions that prevent us from enjoying what we have. Such a state of affairs is a consequence of affluence. In a Harlem tenement, or even more in a village in India, one might well expect improvements in the material basis of life to be strongly associated with improvements in feelings of well-being. But the middle class in the United States, Western Europe, and other industrialized nations constitutes what one might call an "asymptote culture," a culture in which the contribution of material goods to life satisfaction has reached a point of diminishing returns.

Economists take such matters into account to some degree in their concept of "diminishing marginal utility." Additional units of an item do not provide as much utility (pleasure, satisfaction, benefit) as do the initial units. Five thousands dollars extra a year does not mean as much to a millionaire as to a day laborer. A third or fourth or fifth helping of food is not the same as the bite we take when hungry.

But the economist's reckoning of what this implies about policies and values tends to be rather different from that presented here. To most economists evidence of satisfaction is in effect provided *ipso facto* by the act of purchasing. That consumers may behave irrationally, that their choices of what and whether to buy, or of whether to opt for goods or for leisure, may be far from optimal for them is not really considered. It is acknowledged that consumer autonomy and rationality are only approximations to reality, but the approximation is assumed to be sufficiently close to rely on. Moreover, it is held that to make judgments about whether consumers really make the right choices is morally and methodologically illegitimate.*

As a consequence, most economists do not fully appreciate the degree to which our pursuit of continuing economic growth is self-defeating. People's responses to the peculiar properties of a society characterized by massive advertising and a competitive economic system are taken to be simple expressions of "human nature." Lester Thurow, for example, argues that zero economic growth cannot make sense because "it does not jibe with human nature. Man is an acquisitive animal whose wants cannot be satiated." He further asserts that this characteristic of people in our society "is not a matter of advertising and conditioning, but a basic fact of human existence. To try to straight jacket human beings into 'small is beautiful' is to impose enormous costs."[14]

Consider in contrast the perspective provided by Kimon Valaskakis and his colleagues in the Canadian GAMMA group study of the "Conserver Society":

> If Americans were asked point blank whether they would agree to reduce their energy consumption by one-half, many would

*In Chapter Twelve I shall consider the problems associated with questioning the wisdom of consumer choices and suggest an alternative model to that which presently constrains economists.

probably recoil in apprehension and reject the idea. Yet energy consumption in 1960 was about half what it is now. Most of us remember 1960. Surely we had a civilized country then, with roads, electricity, entertainment, and so on. Yet we were consuming only half the energy we are using now. Have we, by doubling our energy consumption, doubled our happiness?[15]

Most of us would not have to think very long before answering in the negative. But we might have more difficulty in understanding quite why this is the case. How is it that we seem to enjoy each of the new things we buy and yet when all is said and done these pleasures don't add up to any greater sense of satisfaction?

The subjective sources of an answer to this puzzle are well captured in the following personal description by Jonathan Freedman, the author of the happiness study referred to above:

> As a student, I lived on what now seems no money at all, but I lived in a style which seemed perfectly fine. My apartment seemed then (and in retrospect still seems) like a lovely apartment, though it was not luxurious. I ate out as often as I thought I wanted to. I do not remember denying myself anything because of money, though I suppose I did. When I got a job, my income more than doubled. My rent also just about doubled. I ate out about as often as before, but the restaurants were a little more expensive. I do not remember denying myself anything because of money, though I suppose I did. As my income has grown since then, I have spent more on apartments and on restaurants and on other things, but it has always seemed to be just about the same amount of money and bought just about the same things. The major change is that I have spent more on everything, and I consider buying more expensive items. None of this has had an appreciable effect on my life or on my feelings of happiness or satisfaction. I imagine that if I earned five times as much, the same would be true—at least it would once I got used to the extra money. This is not to say that I would turn down a raise—quite the contrary. But after a while everything would settle down, the extra money would no longer be "extra," and my life would be the same as before.[16]

The point I wish to make is not that nothing makes a difference, that *any* change will leave our lives the same. It is that prevalent cultural assumptions and the nature of our economic system cause us to look in the wrong direction for a solution, to seek after changes that will not enhance our experience of richness in living rather than those that really can.

At the root of our present malaise, I would suggest, is our tendency to try to use economics to solve what are really psychological problems. This is not to minimize the importance of economics or to claim that the psychological dimension is more basic. Rather it is that the very success of our economic enterprise has made the economic side of our lives less important. Our economic productivity is now such that (at least in the West) we can readily provide enough for all to live well — provided we do not burden and distort the idea of living well by attempting to achieve via material accumulation what is more properly achieved through the cultivation of harmonious relations with other people and by a concern for those influences which expand or constrict the capacity for creative thought, aesthetic pleasure, and emotional sensitivity.

The general mood of pessimism and discontent described by so many social commentators, as well as the increasing tendency for Americans to consult psychotherapists or seek meaning or inner harmony with various cults, gurus, and quasi-therapeutic groups, attests to the failure of material goods to add up to a richer life. There are certainly positive features as well to these latter trends, as I will elaborate later in this book. In many ways they reflect a *healthy* discontent, a turning toward what really matters. But whatever correct intuitions may guide this seeking, it still indicates dissatisfaction with the kind of life our industrial civilization has produced. It reflects a sense that all our possessions have not made our cups run over. Somewhere there has been a hole in the bottom.

The Consumer's Forty Hours in Purgatory

Most consumers also work. The workers from whom we are always trying to exact greater productivity are none other than ourselves. Our society is geared to producing more and more so that we can enjoy the fruits. It is as consumers that we are to reap the benefits.* But we spend a great part of our day at the

---

*As I have suggested, those benefits are in fact rather ephemeral, but they are nonetheless the *raison d'être* for our way of doing things.

other end, as *producers* of our vaunted affluence. When we achieve productivity at the price of enormous stress and competitiveness, our productivity is not a free benefit. It has a cost which is largely disguised from us because we are robbing Peter to pay Paul—or, more precisely, robbing Peter to pay *Peter*. For it is out of our own flesh that the rewards of productivity are coming. It is we, as producers, who are straining and distorting our lives in order to satisfy ourselves in our other incarnation as consumers.

The stresses are more manifest and dramatic in the work lives of blue-collar workers than of those with "cleaner" or higher-status positions, though they are often kept out of view of the rest of us. Stuart Ewen has shown how advertisers consciously contribute to the disguising of the costs by systematically excluding the factory from the world the ads portray.[17] It may take a movie like *Norma Rae* or *The Deer Hunter* to remind us that factories can be unbearably noisy and ill-ventilated, or so run at the rhythm of machines that the human beings who attend the machines must be machine-like themselves in order to manage.

When work is organized in a way that makes it mindless and monotonous; when asbestos or cottonseed fibers or toxic chemicals threaten the health of the worker; when these and many other potentially correctable negative features of the work situation are left uncorrected, the justification usually given is, in effect, that these risks and unpleasantnesses are necessary in order to enjoy the benefits of the consumer society. When it is claimed that it would be "too expensive" to make the workplace safer, more pleasant, and more interesting, it must be understood what "too expensive" means. Certainly our technology is such that we could manage to improve working conditions substantially and still produce not only food, shelter, and clothing, but a good deal of other consumer goods too. What "too expensive" means is that we might not produce *as much* as under present conditions.* What would be produced would

*I say "might" not because there is in fact a good deal of evidence suggesting that present working conditions actually may *reduce* efficiency, and that absenteeism, poor motivation, and even intentional or only dimly disguised sabotage may result—and that performance may be improved by a change in working conditions that permits more varied and responsible participation in the production process.

still be quite considerable by world standards, or even compared to Western standards in earlier eras of prosperity, such as the 1920s. But it might be less than it is now, and on this basis rests the rationale for so much that we put up with from nine to five.

Now to be sure, those making the greatest sacrifices in terms of working conditions are not necessarily the ones who reap the greatest benefits of consumption. Part of what is involved is simply a matter of greater power for some people than for others; exploitation is certainly not absent in our economic arrangements. The executives who cite cost rationales for the levels of asbestos or other poisons that workers are exposed to do not choose to have similar levels piped into their own offices.

It must also be acknowledged that greater consumption is not usually the first or most obvious rationale provided in any particular instance for why the workplace is set up as it is. More likely, the explicit rationale is given in terms of *jobs*: If changes in the work setting make production more expensive, sales will go down and jobs will be lost.* The unions that represent workers are usually quite responsive to such considerations and play a substantial role in determining the level of compromise on work amenities deemed to be "reasonable." To be sure, unions have been active in efforts to eliminate the worst abuses, but a surprising amount of harm to workers is accepted by their representatives as in their interest in order to preserve their jobs.

But these considerations notwithstanding, I would suggest that behind all these influences—providing a level of assent that permits those at the bottom and in the middle to cooperate sufficiently to keep things running smoothly—is the idea that we are *all* better off being pushed (and pushing ourselves) as producers because we will reap the benefits as consumers. The afterlife in which Americans receive their just rewards for the virtue of hard work is found at the shopping center.

Much has been made in recent years of the transition in our culture from an emphasis on hard work, discipline, and self-denial to one centering on consumption, waste, and self-indulgence. No doubt such a shift has occurred in certain respects, and indeed much of this book is about the consequences of that shift, about the snares and delusions of the consumer society. But it must not be forgotten that behind all that con-

*See Chapter Eleven for a more detailed discussion of this issue.

sumption must be production, and that by emphasizing more and more goods to take out we are necessarily also emphasizing more and more—or more and more "efficient"—work to be put in. And though by and large we work fewer *hours* than we used to, not all of our greater "productivity" is achieved by machines alone. Some of it is a result of our treating *ourselves* as machines. The older ethic of delay and self-denial may be largely gone from the off-work hours; we spend (and borrow) now instead of saving, and we find the meaning of our activity in the luxuries we are able to buy rather than in hard work for its own sake. But in the workplace itself, where we spend much of our day, we continue to demand of ourselves—or to demand of others—the same performance imperatives our less "with-it" forebears did.

This stress on "productivity," on in effect turning oneself into a machine for a number of hours each day, is a general phenomenon of industrial societies, but it may be particularly pronounced in the United States. It is a very provocative finding that when asked whether they work alone or with another person, American workers tend to describe as being "alone" the same work arrangement described by their European counterparts as being "with others."[18] An American working, say, at a machine ten feet from another worker at a similar machine does not experience himself as in contact with that other person. Whether the Europeans actually talk to each other more or simply feel and value the other's presence more is hard to tell from the study that was done. But one might speculate that the American feels himself to be more of an extension of the machine, that he more exclusively experiences his purpose there as to work and not also to be with others. The recent concern over the smaller increase in productivity of American workers compared with those of other countries does not, it must be added, necessarily negate this picture of his single-mindedness. Indeed, this mistreatment of himself may well account for some of the problems with productivity.

The Work Life of the Middle Class

Lest it seem that I am discussing only what our mass consumption (and, again I must stress, also mass production) society does to those who are *directly* responsible for the production of goods, let us consider the effect on the life of the executive or professional. To be sure, there is something about such work that is less debilitating and more rewarding. Bertrand Russell's pithy observation still holds:

> Work is of two kinds: first, altering the position of matter at or near the earth's surface relatively to other matter; second, telling other people to do so. The first is unpleasant and ill paid; the second is pleasant and highly paid.[19]

Nonetheless, the lives of those at the "top" also bear the imprint of the particular way we organize and value things in our culture. They may have the satisfaction of playing a more active role in the priorities we set, but they are far from able to avoid the consequences of those priorities. Those of us in executive and professional roles enjoy comforts and power not available to others. But we too are cramped and damaged by the short-sighted choices that characterize our culture, choices which reflect little insight into the nature of personal satisfaction and self-esteem.

If the debilitating effects of our assumptions about work and the need for greater and greater productivity are more difficult to see in the lives of our upper middle classes, this is partly because the boundaries between work and the rest of life are less clear for those at the top. Indeed, the weaving of work values and attitudes so thoroughly into the fabric of living is itself one instance of how the middle class is affected by our orientation to productivity. Over the past 50 years, as the number of hours of work has consistently decreased for the labor force at large, the work week of managers and professionals has actually gone up. In many Western countries, professionals and managers now work close to 50% more hours a week than ordinary workers.[20]

To be sure, part of the reason for the longer hours of these individuals—who are more often in a position to set their own hours—is that they enjoy their work more. Much of the work of executives and professionals is challenging and stimulating, and leaves room for creativity and self-expression. But this is far from the whole story. I have seen—as patients, colleagues, and acquaintances—too many driven people claiming they love their work to accept such claims at face value very readily. There are, I would acknowledge, some rare individuals who truly enjoy their work so thoroughly and genuinely that even an apparently monomaniacal preoccupation with it represents a wise choice consistent with their true best interests and deepest satisfactions. But for a far larger number, loving their work is at best making a virtue of a necessity.

This is not to suggest that their work does not yield real satisfactions. Rather it is that the sheer number of hours spent working — or thinking and worrying about work during hours not explicitly viewed as work time — is often far greater than would yield optimum satisfaction for the person; that integrating more of leisure and cultural pursuits, family life, community life, or friendships into the structure of the person's life would, *together* with a strong commitment to one's work, yield fuller and deeper rewards in many cases. Further, it needs to be noted that even where the enjoyment in work is real, the pressured quality often remains and reveals itself in psychological and physical symptoms and in a generally high level of tension and irritability.

I am suggesting, then, that despite our being a consumption-oriented society — or, as will be apparent to those who are following the trend of my argument, precisely *because* the goals of consumption are so consuming — many members of our middle class are overly concerned with work productivity. Either by working harder than is optimal, or more generally by defining their lives and their self-worth in terms of what they achieve in the sphere of work, many people shorten their lives, decrease their overall pleasure in living, and enrich all those — from brewers to therapists to pharmaceutical firms — who make their living in dealing with tension and instability. Yet in present circumstances to work less hard, to relax more and reflect on what one really finds rewarding, is not very easy to do. It may seem to many an appealing goal but a naively utopian one.

For we live in a highly competitive and individualistic society, and the pressures on us to strive, to achieve, to "get ahead" are enormous. Moreover, when everyone else is racing to get ahead, not to do so is to fall behind. Although the advantages of being able to set one's own working hours, to determine when and how much one will work, are obvious, there is a compensating price to be paid as well — having continuously to face the question "Am I doing enough?" and, for many, *never* quite having the sense of one's work's being done and its being time to relax.

Like many other intellectuals, professionals, and managers, my life is rich but harried. I enjoy my work, but I wonder if I work more than I ought to. I am aware that although the kind of work I do is particularly self-directed, and presumably the amount and times of my work are in my control to a substantial degree, my assessment of what is an "appropriate" amount of time to put in is in fact not unrelated to what I know others are doing. It is not a simple expression of my personal desires, as I sometimes like to think. I pride myself on not working as hard as those individuals I cherish as bad examples and on devoting substantial and meaningful time to my family, to friendships, and to recreation; yet I often feel—as I suspect many readers of this book do as well—that if only everyone else would slow down a bit, I would like to also; that I have not really achieved the optimal balance, except for the factor of competition.

Pollution and the Vicissitudes of Denial

I turn now to the weightiest of all the denied realities of the consumer life—the problems of pollution and environmental limits. These problems have been addressed in passing thus far, embedded in the discussion of other issues, but it is time to address them more focally. I do so with some apprehension; these are topics about which many people feel "I've heard it all already," and I have wondered when some enterprising young product developer in a pharmaceutical firm will discover the extraordinary soporific effects of the word "environment" and market a nonabusable sleeping pill under that label. Indeed, it is our unwillingness really to pay attention to environmental dangers—as opposed to simply paying lip service or emitting occasional sighs of resignation—that I wish to address here, rather than a detailing of the disturbing facts themselves.

At an earlier stage in my conceptualization of this book I diligently collected numerous references detailing—in addition to more familiar facts about air and water pollution, dumping of toxic chemicals, acid rain, depletion of the ozone layer, and so forth—some extraordinary and lesser known evidence of the seriousness of what we had wrought: for example, that we had withdrawn so much water from the underground aquifers that constitute our largest potential source of fresh water that in Arizona the surface of the earth has fallen twelve feet since the 1920s;[21] that in the United States alone 12 square miles of farmland *a day* are converted into roads, shopping centers, housing developments, and factories (put differently, that is 3 million acres a year, or an area in the last decade equal to that of Vermont, New Hampshire, Massachusetts, Rhode Island, Connecticut, New Jersey, and Delaware combined);[22] that in addition 5 billion tons of topsoil on the land that remains cultivatable is lost to water and wind each year, a rate of soil erosion 25% greater than in the Dust Bowl years;[23] that our present antibiotics are being rendered ineffective—with the result already of many people's deaths—by the proliferation of dangerous resistant strains of bacteria, most likely greatly increased by the routine inclusion of antibiotics in the feed of cattle, pigs, and poultry in order to produce fatter animals more cheaply;[24] that cancer rates have been found to be higher around some nuclear power plants, decreasing in concentric circles with distance from the plant;[25] and that the rate of cancer of the testicles was 140% higher downwind from a nuclear weapons plant near Denver.[26]

I will not, however, be following through on these tantalizing allusions (the footnotes can direct the interested reader toward more detailed examination of these reports). In earlier drafts I had begun the book with extensive discussion and documentation of these matters; for my troubles I got yawns even from my best friends and warnings that this kind of thing was too familiar and that readers would tune out before getting to the "good stuff" in the rest of the book.

I learned my lesson. The perceptive reader may, in fact, conclude that what I have said in this section so far is based on the hope that forewarned is disarmed. To this I confess, and to it I will add that I intend to keep this section mercifully (and tactically) brief. The reader interested in learning in more detail about what the ecological price of our "standard of living" really has been can consult such excellent works as those of Barry Commoner[27] or Robert Heilbroner.[28] The facts that these and many others have documented were a crucial impetus for the point of view developed in this book. I shall confine myself here, however, to some questions of how and why we ignore them.

Nobel physics laureate Dennis Gabor captures well the frame of mind that until recently dominated our thinking. Few people, he said

> . . . dared to face the obvious fact that exponential growth cannot be continued indefinitely. *Growth had become synonymous with hope*, and man cannot live without hope. Under the day-to-day pressure of business even highly intelligent people refused to think of the long term, and if they thought about it at all, they unconsciously repeated St. Augustine's prayer "Lord make me good, but not yet!" Let exponential growth continue in my time! [Italics in original][29]

At root that attitude persists today. But after Three Mile Island, Love Canal, and almost daily reports of new problems with our air, food, and water as a consequence of our pursuit of growth, our denial has had to take a new form. On the surface, it appears that awareness of the environmental impact of unchecked growth has greatly increased. Even the most conservative businessman or legislator these days includes environmental effects in his calculations and regards it as reasonable that, at least to some extent, he should do so.

The new shibboleth, through which continue to pass tons of effluents a day, is "balance." We must strike a proper balance, we say, between the health of this and future generations and the needs of the economy, between our desire for clean air and water and our desire for material goods. We would like to have as many of the fruits of modern industry as possible without doing really serious damage to our health and as healthy an environment as we can without giving up the good things of life.

Such a framework tends to encourage a search for "moderation." Those who appropriate the middle ground in the debate seem like the voice of reason and those who place great stress on one or the other of the two poles tend to be labeled as extremists. Thus, strong environmentalists are cast in the role of fanatics or puritans or elitists or described as representing "special interests," as if only a certain class had lungs or kidneys.[30] The presence, on the other hand, of some businessmen who display rather wanton disregard for the environmental consequences of their activities enables those who acknowledge the need for more—but only a little—regulation to be viewed as responsible and realistic both with regard to the environment and about the needs of the economy.

Two things are misrepresented in this conception of "balance" or "moderation"—the real seriousness of the environmental situation we face and the real benefits of economic growth. The former is underestimated, the latter greatly exaggerated. Most of this book is concerned with our overestimation of the psychic benefits of increased material productivity. Here I would like briefly to address the other half of our misperception, our failure to appreciate the real extent and costs of environmental degradation.

It must be acknowledged that pollution has always been a byproduct of man's productive activities. As many critics of environmental "alarmists" point out, the air of nineteenth-century London was probably worse than that of twentieth-century Los Angeles, and the smell of horse manure on the streets of "Little Old New York" was no more charming than the smell of gasoline in "The Big Apple." But over the last few decades the extent of our pollution-producing activities has increased exponentially. Moreover, it has increased not just in scope but in kind. We have, for example, introduced into the environment chemicals that never before existed on this planet, and in relation to which organic life has no evolutionary history of adaptation.

Even the fact that, unlike horse manure or the black smoke that once choked industrial cities, much of modern environmental pollution cannot be seen or smelled presents new and unique problems. We are spared the unpleasantness but are also left without warning. Three Mile Island seemed a model of clean efficiency until the day before the accident, and Love Canal seemed just an ordinary working-class housing development until the toxic situation was discovered. Radiation, toxic wastes, invisible asbestos fibers, chemicals that can damage the ozone layer, changes in carbon dioxide levels that can create devastating changes in climate—all these and dozens of other threats are reported in the news daily, but they are not visible to the naked eye, so we shrug them off and go on about our business.

Moreover, not only are the offending substances invisible, but their effects are often considerably delayed. This too has serious consequences for our ability to make rational personal

calculation of costs and benefits. Very few people would choose
to have even the most fabled assortment of goods if it meant
getting cancer within the year. But the choice involves not the
certainty of cancer very soon but an increased *probability* of
cancer at some time in the future. The cancers are no less real;
millions will die painfully and prematurely because of what we
do to our environment. But the choice is not an easily visualiz-
able one, and our capacity for denial comes strongly into
play—as it tends to whenever we must weigh future costs
against immediate benefits.

Not everyone, of course, will develop cancer as a consequence of environmental pollution. In that particular lottery
some of us may come out winners. But all of us have to die of
something, and it is reasonable to conclude that for most of us,
as a result of the cumulative effects of all of the environmental
changes our industrial processes have created, that day will
come a couple of years earlier than it otherwise would have.

To this the man in the street says, in effect, "Well, we all
have to go sometime or other. And better 71 good years than 73
poor ones. Let me enjoy myself now and not be so preoccupied
with the future." Such an attitude—which I believe a little in-
trospection will reveal is in one form or another what most people hold—seems to be a reasonable choice framed in that way.

But consider this: offered even the prospect of another year
or two of life, most ill people choose to undergo surgery when it
is advised. If instead prospective surgery patients could magically be offered the alternative of saving their lives by paying
money instead of by the painful route of being cut open, does
anyone doubt that most people would be willing to pay a great
deal? Yet we do have a way to make it very likely that we will
live an extra year or two just by paying money. Investing more
of our capital in reducing harmful deterioration of the environment instead of in maximizing production as much as possible
would do just that: We would have somewhat fewer goods and
we would live longer. But the terms are too abstract and the
consequences too distant for most people to choose this way, so
the voices of growth dominate (even though they too would
probably choose the operation and the chance for a few more
years, and would choose to pay instead of having the operation
if that were magically possible).

There is a sense in which focusing on the most dramatic instances—the particular cancers that can be linked with fair

probability to a particular environmental source—can make the response of denial more likely. Most of us can say that it is likely that the victim in any particular instance won't be me. That is why I am focusing here instead not on particular cancer-pollutant links but on the overall effects on the lifespan of almost all of us—the subtle, cumulative, interacting effects of radiation, air pollution, toxic chemicals, and so forth that increase the wear and tear on our bodies and cause whatever it is we will die of to progress a bit more rapidly or happen a bit sooner. There are no data by which I can prove that the cumulative effect of all of this will take a year or two off your life or mine, but I suspect that most readers will regard this as a not unreasonable estimate. If we could keep the operation paradigm in mind to remind us of how precious a year or two of life really is to us, perhaps we might think twice about the priorities we now choose.

It is not only in overtly minimizing or distancing ourselves from environmental problems that we deny them. We do so at times via an almost opposite set of thought processes, which present environmental hazards as so thoroughly pervasive that they simply cannot be avoided. One sees such an attitude particularly in reports of carcinogenic substances in particular foods or additives. "Everything causes cancer, so why bother?" we say. "If you listened to all the reports, you wouldn't eat anything." There follows a slightly nervous laugh, a shrug, and mutual social reassurance that it makes sense to continue just as we have.

In fact, only a very small percentage of the substances added to food are identified by standard testing procedures as carcinogenic. Those tests, far from yielding the absurd—and necessarily ignorable—message that everything causes cancer, point very specifically to certain substances and not others.[31] We *can* greatly reduce the risk of cancer, and of other serious diseases as well, by altering our diet in particular ways. By saying the picture is bleaker than it is, we transform pessimism into cockeyed optimism; since nothing will make any difference, we don't have to do anything at all.

That has been our attitude toward many of the environmental challenges we face. We throw up our hands, then turn our backs. Because of the psychological meanings that growth has had for us, we find it difficult even to conceive of an alternative and hence see no way out. Deprivation or pollution seem our only choices. In fact, they are not, but to grasp the alternatives that are potentially available, we must recognize how our preoccupation with economic growth and possessions has caused us to deceive ourselves about the real sources of subjective well-being and about the realities of the way of life we have pursued.

The Hope of Technology

Environmentalists are often wrongly thought to be opposed to science and technology. In fact, it is only through the tools of modern science that the presence and the effects of most of the environmental hazards we currently face can even be detected. Solution of our problems requires not the abandonment of technology but its proper use.

The problem is that the impact of technology on our lives has been so extraordinary and, for the vast majority of us, its recent developments so beyond our comprehension in all but the most global outline that there is a tendency to retreat to a magical conception of it. Without quite knowing or seeing how, we count on technology to come through for us at the eleventh hour as a kind of *deus ex machina*. It is not unreasonable to consider the possibility that technological developments will enable us to solve environmental problems that today seem ominous or unyielding. But it is a dangerous fantasy to assume that we can simply continue as we have, secure in the expectation that at some point a technological breakthrough will bail us out. For "technology" is not a single entity, nor is it an autonomous force that impinges upon society by its own logic regardless of what we do. There are many different kinds of technologies with different consequences, and the kind that develops in any time and place depends upon the assumptions that people bring to bear and upon the concrete circumstances that make one kind of solution or another seem appropriate.

I will be arguing throughout this book that our assumptions are awry and, moreover, that the concrete circumstances we have created in accordance with those assumptions have caught us up in a poorly understood series of vicious circles, in which the apparent solution to each source of distress in fact only exacerbates the problem and sets the stage for still another problem-generating false solution. Unless we can confront directly the grounding assumptions that underlie our use of technology, the technology we choose is likely to be the wrong kind.

Technology is a two-edged sword. It is true that only technology can get us out of the environmental fix we are in; we have already done so much damage that we couldn't go back to "the simple life" even if we were psychologically capable. But technology is also the direct cause of the problems we are now hoping technology will solve. It is the prodigious capacities with which our technological expertise provide us that create such a threat to the environment. Those of us in the industrialized countries produce 50 times the amount of pollution per capita as those in the less developed nations.[32]

There is no such thing as "technology" *per se*. There are *particular* technologies, some of which are potential solutions to environmental problems and some of which are the problems for which a solution is sought. The great danger in the energy crisis is not that we will fail to supply ourselves with sufficient energy to run our industrial civilization but that we will succeed; succeed, that is, in a short-run, foolhardy way that will have serious, perhaps irrevocable, effects on our prospects for health and well-being. The assumptions about growth and satisfaction that this book is trying to challenge would make it likely that we will submit to the temptation to seek a quick fix, using not the kind of technology that can solve environmental problems but the kind that has created them.

FOUR

Vicious Circles

Economic growth, I have argued, does not work for us the way we think it does. Having more and more does not really leave us feeling fuller or more fulfilled. Though we have come close to the asymptote in the relation between material goods and a sense of satisfaction with life, we are nowhere near one with regard to desire. The less we get out of what we get, the more we seem to want. Now we are recognizing that the pursuit of this ironic cornucopia is literally poisoning us, that the air we breathe, the water we drink, and the food we eat are being contaminated. And still we persist, still we say we must have more. Why?

Some say it is simply a matter of human nature; it's natural to want more and foolishly idealistic to say it can be any other way. It would even be a betrayal of man's inherent dynamism and urge to transcend, according to some, if one were to "settle for less."

Others argue that our striving for growth is an expression of economic rationality. The laws of economics, they say, lead inexorably to the need for growth; they require that the economy expand if it is not to contract. George Katona, for example (ironically, one of the few writers on economic matters with a background in psychology as well), presents concisely a line of argument that is fairly typical of mainline economic thought. In discussing how to finance such public needs as construction of schools and hospitals, revitalization of deteriorated neighborhoods, or provision of funds for the old and sick and unemployed, he decries the idea that resources might be redeployed from consumer spending to public projects:

> Any attempt to cut down on consumer spending for the sake of increasing public expenditures might easily plunge the economy into stagnation or recession. Even maintaining current levels of consumer living standards would not suffice to do the job. It is precisely the wanting and striving for improvement in private living standards that forms the solid basis of American prosperity. Only if the so-called private opulence increases still further can we hope to overcome public poverty. The question is not one or the other; it is both or none.[1]

The idea of a steady-state economy — not to mention one in which we maintain a comfortable standard of living even while cutting back on production in order to conserve resources or reduce pollution — seems completely ruled out in such a view. We *can't* decide to spend on schools or social welfare efforts instead of video games and car stereos and a new wardrobe every season. Unless we make and buy the latter — and keep dreaming up new things to make and buy and want — we won't have any schools or hospitals at all. Growth, in this view, is the furthest thing from irrationality; it is the only way to have anything at all.

However accurate this may be as a description of our economic system as currently constituted, there is, I would like to suggest, another quite different source of our preoccupation with growth, both in economics and more generally in our culture. Our obsession with growth is the expression of neither inexorable laws of human nature nor inexorable laws of economics. It is a reflection of particular features of our culture, deriving from particular historical circumstances, which in turn derive from a distinct set of prior choices. It is a cultural and psychological phenomenon, reflecting our present way of organizing and giving meaning to our lives. Moreover, whatever value it once had in promoting a basis for a substantial degree of affluence and autonomy, it is now maladaptive. In fact, as I shall indicate shortly, as a social phenomenon it has many of the features that in an individual would merit the term neurosis.

This is by no means to suggest that all desire for more is neurotic. Aspirations to improve, to transcend one's condition, to explore new directions and expand one's knowledge and powers are certainly part of any reasonable definition of mental health. Indeed, their *absence* can be a sign of neurosis. But when this (or any) dimension of our psychological life becomes too dominant, when it leads to irrational and self-defeating choices and to the inability even to recognize that there are effective alternatives to those choices, then such a term as neurosis is merited.

It should also be clear that to suggest that certain behavior is neurotic is not to say that it has no basis in reality. On a social scale, as on the individual one, neurotic patterns of behavior create circumstances that then confront us as real and independent problems, which must be dealt with in their own right. Neuroses leave a residue, as it were, and that residue cannot be ignored. There is certainly much that is accurate in the economists' warning that our economy would be in trouble without growth, that we need growth to keep things going. However maladaptive and self-defeating our current economic arrangements are, we must be aware of them and take them seriously. We have gotten ourselves into a fix, and a clear understanding of the nature of that fix is essential in order to find the best way out (as is the recognition that it *is* a fix, and not just "the way things are and must be").

Social Neurosis and Vicious Circles

In applying a term like neurosis to a large-scale social phenomenon, it is necessary to be clear that one is engaging in a metaphorical extension of a term that has developed and been found useful in another context. Metaphorical extensions of this sort can be fruitful and stimulating, but they require a certain amount of caution and skepticism, especially when one is extending such a potentially value-laden term as neurosis. The language of mental health and mental illness is often used to spice a weak argument with gratuitous epithets that have a sub-

tle flavor of scientific respectability. Often, when a bit of behavior or a social trend is called neurotic, the term really means
little more than that the author doesn't like or approve of it.
Moreover, even in its original domain of applicability the term
neurosis is highly controversial.[2]

I therefore want to be very careful to indicate just what I
mean when I suggest that something about our commitment to
growth seems to be akin to the phenomena observed in individual neuroses. For me the heart of the notion of neurosis is the
occurrence of vicious circles in people's behavior in which their
sense of security is undermined by the very effort they make to
bolster it. In what follows I shall examine how our quest for economic growth has been both a cause of drastic changes in the
way we live and a cornerstone of our efforts to deal with the
anxiety generated by those very changes. Secondly, I shall indicate how the steps we have taken to quell the anxiety have actually exacerbated our sense of insecurity and—by an ironic logic
familiar to the student of the neuroses—have thereby called
forth still more of the same kind of efforts and thus still more
undermining of security and still further acceleration of a one-
sided and self-defeating pattern. The workings of our social
and economic system in this regard bear a remarkable resemblance to the vicious circles one sees in individual neuroses, and
it is for this reason that I think some such term as "social neurosis" may not be inappropriate in describing this process.

The term neurosis is not itself essential in conveying what I
am concerned with. It is just a convenient label. It does have
the advantage of making more explicit the frame of reference I
am bringing to bear in discussing these matters. But it is the
understanding of the ironies of the vicious circle that is most
important, not the term neurosis itself, and those readers who
may be put off by the use of such a term will find that the argument can be followed without it.

Growth and the Decline of Community

In explicating further, I wish to begin not with economic
growth per se but with the sense of community and its decline.
Since the causal sequences I am discussing are circular, any

starting point is arbitrary, and I find it convenient to begin here.

For most of human history people lived in tightly knit communities in which each individual had a specified place and in which there was a strong sense of shared fate. The sense of belonging, of being part of something larger than oneself, was an important source of comfort. In the face of the dangers and the terrifying mysteries that the lonely individual encountered, this sense of connectedness — along with one's religious faith, which often could hardly be separated from one's membership in the community — was for most people the main way of achieving some sense of security and the courage to go on.

Over the past few hundred years, for a number of reasons, the sense of rootedness and belonging has been declining. In its place has appeared a more highly differentiated sense of individuality, implying both greater opportunity and greater separateness. In Protestant countries, this development was symbolized by the view that man faces God, man encounters the infinite and incomprehensible, not through the mediation of (and hence as part of) the mother Church, but as a separate and isolated individual. In the rest of the Western world no symbolic shift quite so vivid emerged, but the relation between man and his social context changed in a similar way. In more recent years this process has been accelerated still further.

This does not mean, of course, that *some* sense of community, and *some* secure ties to others do not remain. We could not survive without such ties. Any society always entails some mix of orientations and adaptations. Neither the sense of embeddedness in a larger community nor the sense of separateness can exclusively characterize the living experience of any society. Thus, to gain perspective by reversing our lens, we may also be sure that in primitive, ancient, or medieval societies some degree of individuality, some sense of separate destiny must have been a part of people's experience and world view. While there is much truth in the common claim that individualism arose in the Renaissance,[3] that claim must be understood as referring to individualism as a vector that began to challenge that of rootedness as the central force in society, not as a new phenomenon altogether. The facts of our separate bodies, our separate pain, our separate deaths, as well as the differences in

look forward with complete equanimity to a future in which we are sure we will continue to be valued, needed, respected, and securely "inside."

All this is not to say that ancient or medieval man, or the member of a peasant community today, are or were happier or more secure than modern Western man. In many respects the opposite may well have been true. Life was certainly harsher and usually shorter then, and the knowledge of how to cope with various natural disasters was obviously far more limited. Moreover, in contrasting, as I do here and below, the sense of community and belonging that were the lot of men born in prior times and the *lack* of connectedness of modern Western man, the *sundering* of ties he experiences, I do not mean to imply that people were necessarily nicer to each other then. Cruelty is not a modern invention. Rather, I wish simply to highlight the degree to which we now look—and must look—in other directions for our sense of security than our ancestors did and to examine the consequences of that difference.

In discussing the new direction we have taken, however, I do intend to stress some of its problems and its ironies. I do this for two reasons. First, I feel we have thus far wasted a golden opportunity. Our enormously greater capacity to predict and control events, to alleviate pain and hunger, to provide leisure and abundance *should* have made us happier. Life now shouldn't be just different, it should be better, much better. We ought to have found a way of establishing a much sounder basis of security, rather than just a different basis. It is not enough to be able to say that things were no better in the old days. With all we have discovered and achieved, there should not even be a question, there should be no ambiguity. That, I think, is not the case.

The second reason I am stressing the negative features of our new adaptation has to do with a different aspect of our technological superiority to previous civilizations. Their errors had their effects on a smaller scale. Ours, by virtue of our prodigious capacity, are writ large. We are now in a position to alter the face of the earth, to change our environment so radically that our entire species is threatened. The quantities of toxic materials we spew into the air and water, the dangers of proliferating nuclear wastes, and all the other consequences of our accelerating technological powers are so enormous in scope, so incomprehensible in their scale, yet so within our power to bring about, that our foibles lose their ancient right to be acknowledged with wry humor. They are no longer innocent. They are deadly.

Wealth as a Substitute for Faith and Community

Our present stress on growth and productivity is, I believe, intimately related to the decline in rootedness. Faced with the loneliness and vulnerability that come with deprivation of a securely encompassing community, we have sought to quell the vulnerability through our possessions. When we can buy nice new things, when we look around and see our homes well stocked and well equipped, we feel strong and expansive rather than small and endangered.

But the comfort we achieve tends to be short-lived. Our efforts to achieve a sense of security and well-being in this fashion have ironic consequences. As I shall describe below, their effect is further to undermine more traditional sources of security and thus to commit us to the pursuit of still further material progress as compensation. We chase around frantically filling up the holes we have just dug, with little recognition or understanding of what we are doing and still less ability to stop. And all the while we tell ourselves that this is simply what we "want."

In all eras people must find means to reassure themselves in the face of their finiteness and mortality. We are all ultimately helpless to a far greater degree than we dare admit. Our fragility before the forces of nature (both those outside us and those within that cause pain, disease, and aging), as well as the certainty that death is our ultimate earthly destiny, are unbearable to face without some means of consoling ourselves and of giving meaning and purpose to our lives. Religion, as well as the sense of belonging to a community, once provided that means for most people. But over the years the progress of science and the development of newer, more efficient modes of production undermined religious faith, as it did the traditional ties between people that, together with religion, made life livable.*

---

*It is interesting to note that for those with a vivid sense of the hereafter, the question "Is this all there is to it?" did not have to be answered in terms of earthly passions and possessions. In our modern, secular culture, such a question haunts us, whether it be addressed to sex or to the goods and gadgets we amass.

These changes were not necessarily intentional, but they were powerful, and they required some response to compensate for the loss. Neither the loss nor the response were discrete events in which cause followed effect in a clear-cut, isolatable sequence. Rather, a complicated set of mutually interacting events led gradually to our current state of affairs. New discoveries and technical developments were prompted by an atmosphere of questioning and critical thought, and in turn these developments contributed to furthering such an atmosphere as a counterpole to traditional ways of viewing the world. The older ways did not disappear. (Even today they are compelling to many, though often in revised form that accommodates to new ideas more than is recognized.) But they ceased to exert the exclusive dominance they had previously.

These technical and intellectual changes led as well to changes in social structure and in the way men lived their lives and related to each other.* New productive possibilities led both to explicit policies—such as the Enclosure Laws, which drove farmers from the land and into the cities—and to more diffuse, yet powerful, social forces, which disrupted traditional agricultural ways of life and presented many with the difficult challenge of living in unfamiliar urban surroundings without the support of either familiar people or familiar traditions and rhythms.

The result was a substantial undermining of the sources of security men had relied upon for centuries. As Karl Polanyi has noted, the industrial revolution was marked both by "an almost miraculous improvement in the tools of production" and by "a catastrophic dislocation of the lives of the common people."[8] Gradually, and often without reflection or recognition, the vacuum began to be filled by the very aims and activities that had begun the process of undermining security in the first place. Deprived of roots, traditions, and secure ties to a community in which a place was guaranteed, men began to try to reduce their anxiety by identifying with our increasing power over nature. The accumulation of wealth and material comforts, rather than secure rooting in a frame and context, began to form the primary basis for quelling the feelings of vulnerability that inev-

---

*They were also, *pari passu*, accelerated *by* the changes in social structure and way of life.

itably afflict us. New theological doctrines began to depart
from the "eye of the needle" warnings about the incompatibility
of wealth and heavenly reward and to stress that those who
achieved material success were manifesting signs of having been
favored by grace, of being part of the elect. Growth in the production of goods came to be the overriding goal of life and of
society, as a religion of progress and success rose to challenge
the prior teachings of stability and submission.

   This new faith and new world view, illuminated for us particularly by Max Weber,[9] was at first a particular comfort to
those at the top and developed largely at their behest. For many
people, despite rising total productivity, life was worse. In England, where the rise in productive capacity was for a long time
greater than anywhere else, widespread misery was a regular
companion of increasing societal wealth. The London of Dick-
ens — or Marx — did not compare very favorably in the life pleasures it provided the average man to the rural society of several
centuries before, at a time when England was less "developed."
Polanyi notes that "writers of all views and parties, conserva-
tives and liberals, capitalists and socialists invariably referred to
social conditions under the Industrial Revolution as a veritable
abyss of human degradation."[10]

   But most people had little choice in the matter. The old
communities and traditions from which they drew sustenance
were being eroded, and they could not go back. It was a time of
turmoil and misery, but inevitably it began to lead to new
modes of adaptation. Many, to be sure, continued to flounder
in despair, unable to find new sources of sustenance, yet deprived of the old. But increasing numbers began to base their
hopes and dreams on the evident progress in our ability to produce goods (a kind of progress that preceded by a very long
time any signs of progress in the quality of life itself for the average man).

   Some were radicalized and felt that if this productive capacity could be used for the good of all men instead of its enriching the few, an earthly paradise could be achieved. The
radicals, while often committed to replacing the steady state of
workers' material existence with one of continuing progress and
increase, also in many cases tried to reappropriate earlier bases
for comfort and meaning: In their emphasis on solidarity and
submerging oneself in a cause, they created to some extent a

new version of community and faith in something larger than themselves.

Others began to hope that even without radical changes the system would begin to yield dividends to those below as well. Sometimes this took the form of what in recent times has come to be called identification with the aggressor.[11] In other instances this attitude was the result of a gradually developing pattern of real improvements in workers' standard of living as the increase in wealth did begin to "trickle down" to the population at large. This occurrence was long in coming and small at first, and it was largely, to begin with, a response by those in power to the agitation of the radicals. After a while however, it became a standard expectation of capitalist societies: A rising standard of living for all (even if unequally distributed) was seen as everyone's birthright. The idea of more became a mainspring of the Western psyche.

This trend was particularly evident in the United States, where the fruits of increased productivity were more evenly distributed than in Europe. It has accelerated enormously in the present century, both here and abroad, and is now the dominant theme in our culture (though, it must again be stressed, still not an exclusive one). By now, the majority of the population has participated in the continuing increase in material output, and their ability to acquire more and more each year has become a basic premise of our society.

At the same time we have experienced yet another vicious circle, which has locked us into a pattern it is increasingly difficult — and increasingly essential — to change. In response to our expanding desires and to our dependence on ever increasing prosperity, a system of production has developed that has further uprooted traditional ties and has replaced traditional patterns of cooperation and a sense of shared fate with an ethos of competition and self-interest. This transition began, of course, some time ago, but it has accelerated greatly since the nineteenth century.

Right or wrong, we have assumed that efficiency is maximized by encouraging each to outdo his compatriots. We have further assumed that individuals must be able to be shifted around in order to be deployed where they will be most useful, and thus that geographic mobility must replace identification with a particular place and community.

The economist Fred Hirsch noted that a decline in sociability and friendliness has been characteristic of modern economies. In a droll yet serious application of the economist's perspective, he noted that friendliness "is time consuming and thereby liable to be economized because of its extravagant absorption of this increasingly scarce input. . . . It has been widely observed, both in casual impression and in some survey data, that concern for the wider family is greater among the lower income groups than among the higher." Hirsch attributed this to both a reduced need for mutual aid among higher income groups and a tendency to set a higher valuation on their time, including time needed for consumption of all that has become within economic reach. Hirsch suggested that both of these factors may "reduce friendliness and mutual concern in society as a whole as it becomes richer in material goods and ever more pressed for time."[12]

In our pursuit of efficiency and productivity, we have promoted the expectation that each will view his home, school, and community primarily as a launching pad for the purpose of rising to his appropriate level, and that he will thus leave many former friends behind (and be himself left behind by still others). We have also developed a pattern of constantly moving around as "better" jobs become available elsewhere (and a corollary assumption that familiarity, ties to a community, and relations with friends and family members outside the nuclear household count for little in deciding which job is in fact better for us). All these things contribute to a further decline in the security that can be gained by being part of a cooperative, closely knit community. They therefore also contribute to the need to gain security in some other way, and hence, for most of us, to the need to rely still further upon (and indeed to define ourselves by) the increase in our material "standard of living."

This means placing even more emphasis on productivity and economic efficiency as the ultimate defining values in making societal decisions and therefore, according to our dominant economic assumptions, still more stress on competition, the pursuit of self-interest, and the stimulation of demand. This in turn means still more decline in the security to be gained via shared ties and a stable, securely rooted place and way of life, still more need to compensate by organizing everything around what enables us to have "more," still more decline of traditional sources of security, and so forth. Thus, the more fully we have committed ourselves to increasing material abundance as our ultimate societal value, the more we have undermined older sources of security and made ourselves dependent on material goods for our sense of well-being to an unprecedented degree.

A similar circular process involving bureaucracy and the sense of powerlessness has evolved in recent years. As part of the quest for efficiency and bigness, we have organized ourselves to an extraordinary degree and wrapped ourselves in an interlocking system on which we have all become dependent. The development of our communications technology and the complexity of coordination required to meet our evergrowing demand for more and newer products has made us increasingly part of a national and even a world culture. Few of us can any longer participate in town meetings or otherwise make our voices heard in public deliberations with any sense of affecting the important issues in our lives. Decisions made by Middle Eastern sheiks, Washington bureaucrats, or corporate executives are likely to have far greater impact on our lives than what is decided closer to home.

As a consequence, we feel increasingly frustrated and powerless, unable to exert any control over our lives. But we tend not to make the connection between the sense of vulnerability and our preoccupation with goods and economic considerations. Indeed, though not always conscious of what we are doing, we try to assuage these feelings of smallness and helplessness in the way that has now become standard for us: by attempting to see to it that if we can't feel really in control at least we have "more"; by reassuring ourselves with the larger house we just bought, or the new car, or the stereo, or the new dress, or whatever our particular economic level allows us to buy in order to declare to ourselves and others, "I'm all right, Jack." And again, the results are sadly ironic. For the consequence of this effort to make the bad feeling go away is to strengthen the forces that create the bad feelings.

Inflation is part of a similar vicious circle in which the competitive, individualistic ethic we have evolved as part of our economic orientation traps us in continuing self-defeating efforts that only make matters worse. Each group tries to pull ahead of the others (often recognizing that it is at best just keeping up), and almost all resist an effort to achieve a consensus of the entire national community to set limits and fix a fair level of wages and prices. This is, of course, hardly an easy thing to do; but it is *impossible* to do when everyone feels that he must continually have more and that it is almost his moral obligation to look out only for himself and to reject as an alien ideology any commitment to the good of the community at large.

Dominance, Affluence, and "Moving Against"

The argument presented thus far suggests that having more and newer things each year has become not just something we want but something we need. The idea of more, of ever increasing wealth, has become the center of our identity and our security, and we are as caught by it as the addict is by his drugs. In the terms developed by Karen Horney, we can perhaps be said to be caught in a societal "moving-against" neurosis.

To characterize the structure of individual neuroses Horney conceptualized three basic directions, which she labeled "moving toward people," "moving against people," and "moving away from people." Now at first this may seem rather arbitrary and more than a little silly. Why just three? And why *these* three? It turns out, however, that there is something very interesting and useful about this particular trichotomy. Horney herself had generated a list of ten neurotic trends in an earlier work and then had reduced it to these three basic ones. What is special about this particular grouping is that strategies for building security that fall into any one of the three categories are almost necessarily in conflict with—and tend to undermine—strategies in the other two categories, whereas strategies *within* any particular category tend to be mutually compatible, even if rather different.

Let us look at these three directions in more detail. Within the category of "moving toward" are all those strategies for enhancing a sense of security that involve closely binding oneself to another person and feeling safer as a result of the tie that develops. Thus, within this category would fall clinging dependency, making oneself likable, making oneself meek and harmless so as not to threaten the other, being faithful, diligent, agreeable, and so on—in short, strategies of niceness, meekness, and dependency designed to make others want to connect with you and help and protect you. The range of such strategies is quite varied, but by and large they are mutually compatible and reinforcing.

It is possible to find potential conflicts within this realm, but in doing so one begins to discern the boundary between this broad trend and the other two. For example, one may try to hold on to a loved one by making oneself very physically attractive or witty in order to appear desirable, or one may attach oneself to a powerful figure by being an especially skillful and effective assistant, and this may conflict with the effort to maintain the tie by being loyal and unthreatening. The lover may begin to get nervous at how attractive you have become to others and intimidated by it, or the powerful boss may see your effectiveness as a threat. If "moving toward" is really the primary dimension of your security-seeking, however, you will then seek to mitigate these disturbing trends, to choose clothes and hair style, perhaps, that make you less disturbingly attractive or to bumble somewhat in your assistance to reassure the boss that you are "his" or "hers" and not about to establish an independent identity and power base.

It is the readiness to give up or mask any skill or attribute that threatens the tie to the other that marks a behavior as part of a moving-toward strategy, not its overt properties.

Consider, in contrast, the person whose security is based on the possession of superior strengths and skills. Such a person would refuse to yield to the other's sense of threat, indeed would revel in that sense of threat, knowing it keeps the other "on his toes." He or she too might strive to look attractive or to be the boss's most skillful assistant. But such a person's aim in doing so would be very different. He would aim to be indispensable not primarily by being pleasing but because he has accrued certain strengths the other dares not do without. The threat that he will take his wares elsewhere would be omnipresent, and the ultimate aim would be to dominate the other. Such people, who rely on a "moving against" strategy, seek security through feeling strong and powerful. They ward off feelings of weakness and vulnerability by constantly striving to be successful, admired, and in charge. Deference and dependence are experienced as painful and are manifested only when they can clearly be viewed — cynicism often being more comfortable for them than sincerity — as in the service of broader goals of enhancement. These people value being tough, strong, hard-headed, and dynamic. Skill, strength, and success are their currency and source of self-esteem. For such individuals to care too much about another is threatening, for it signifies to them vulnerability and helpless dependency. All of the behaviors, in fact, that are characteristic of the "moving toward" strategy are threatening for "moving against" types to recognize in themselves and must be vigorously avoided or denied (much as the person of the "moving toward" type must avoid appearing too strong or independent, lest his protective tie be threatened).

A third way of trying to diminish the sense of vulnerability—our unfortunate birthright as finite, mortal creatures—is to disavow all the ties and needs that are threatening because they make one "care." This includes both the protective ties of the "moving toward" personality *and* the ties of domination of the "moving against." Even the "moving against" personality is needy; he needs others to dominate and competitively to compare himself to. Persons employing a "moving away" strategy try as much as possible to avoid *any* really meaningful ties. They wish their sense of security to be in no way contingent on the reactions of others, whether they be reactions of love and protectiveness or of admiration and deference. Such a person need not be a hermit. He could, for example, be an artist or a mathematician, maintaining some ties with others but none that crucially matter to him, focusing all of his real investment on his solitary work. Work that requires a great deal of collaboration would not appeal to him; and in perfecting his own work his personal aesthetic sense, independent of the reactions of others, would be much more important to him than would admiration or recognition, which are contingent upon others' response.

None of these three basic directions are, of course, neurotic in themselves. They are readily identifiable dimensions of *all* human behavior and are exhibited, in varying combinations, in all people. They are appropriately viewed specifically as "neurotic" trends only when several conditions hold: They are rigid, being exhibited in almost all situations whether appropriate or not; they are motivated largely by the effort to avoid anxiety; and they are as a consequence pursued compulsively and excessively. It is in this respect that the three basic trends are incompatible with each other and tend to undermine each other.

In principle there is nothing incompatible among these basic attitudes. It is perfectly possible for someone to be deferential in one situation — being willing to compromise a good deal in order to preserve a valued relationship with a loved one — and hard-headed and dominant in another. But when they are exhibited in a driven and exaggerated way, they do become incompatible. The person whose self-esteem depends on *always* being dominant is threatened by loving or submissive urges. The person who must *always* be aloof is threatened when he begins to enjoy admiration.[13]

What results is a vicious circle in which the person digs himself deeper and deeper into a hole. The person whose security is neurotically based on a moving-toward strategy will inevitably find that his frantic efforts to submit and defer will ultimately cause his own interests to be dismissed and overridden by others. By continually deferring and submerging his own needs in the name of cooperation, love, or being nice, he will induce others to ignore his real needs, and in some way (not necessarily consciously) he will be enraged at this continuing frustration and deprivation. Rage, however, is unacceptable to such a person, who must compulsively seek after harmony and nonconfrontation, so he tries to suppress and disguise the rage by being even *more* cooperative and self effacing — and thus sets the stage for still more rage to be generated, still more compulsive deference to hide it, and so forth. Moreover, since this style of living does not permit much independent development of one's skills and assets, the person fails to establish a firm alternative basis for building security and so is locked into his moving-toward maneuvers by still another vicious circle involving nondevelopment of skills requiring still more dependence on others, which in turn requires still more efforts to show one's loyalty and connectedness by not branching out in independent directions, and so on.

Similar vicious circles are evident in the operation of the other neurotic trends. And they are evident as well in the functioning of our social and economic system. Today, when our pursuit of material gain no longer brings much satisfaction and threatens to drown and choke us in industrial wastes, we are unable to let go — unable because we have cut the ground out from under us and are afraid to relinquish the one thing that props us up, that gives us some sense of security: our possessions and our productivity. As a culture we are like the moving-against neurotic: afraid to stop throwing our weight around even though doing so isn't working very well for us, indeed even though in many respects it undermines rather than enhances our sense of security and well-being.

In thinking of our own culture as a moving-against culture, a number of considerations are relevant. As a nation we pride ourselves on being strong, big, and successful, and in our heroes we value the same thing. The man of great sensitivity or spiritual depth is not a hero in America. We are terrified of being a "pitiful helpless giant" and will commit unreasonable acts of aggression to ward off that feared image.

The moving-against orientation doesn't necessarily imply hostility, but it is never terribly far away. At times it implies a protective stance toward others, that of a seemingly benevolent big brother. But the phrase "big brother," as transmuted by Orwell, did not just adventitiously come to have an ominous second meaning. As is not uncommon in such cases, the protective stance we have assumed in the world has not been easy on its beneficiaries. It has required that some kind of deference, some sign of dependence, be a regular part of relations with us, and that our decisions be accorded a very special role and our interests be regarded as almost identical with those of the cause of freedom and goodness itself.

In our internal relations too, strength is valued over sensitivity or empathic and cooperative attitudes. We honor slogans such as "nice guys finish last" and "show me a good loser and I'll show you a loser." We promote competition and self-reliance, not mutual support. And the "self-reliance" we demand bears little resemblance to that implied, say, by Gandhi in preaching a seemingly similar virtue. Ours has no humble or spiritual component. It implies for us something far more expansive and cocky, a demand that we be strong and capable enough to do anything and everything and do it well. More than anything else, it is a way of expressing contempt for those who need help. In our public discourse, the term "self-reliance" is intended as the virtuous opposite of the state of requiring public assistance, that black hole of our national fantasies whose gravitational pull is imagined to be so fierce it threatens to suck up everything and squeeze the life out of all of us.

Our attitude toward nature and the environment has been much the same as our approach to each other; we strive for conquest and domination, not cooperative coexistence. Lately we have begun to pay a certain amount of attention to environmental concerns, but our priorities clearly stress the effort to make nature submit to our bidding by brute force. When the economy starts to stumble, environmental laws become "red tape" to be cut through.

Now, in suggesting that it may be useful to think of our society as characterized by a "moving against" neurotic trend, I am not suggesting that every *individual* in the society can be so characterized or even that the majority necessarily can. The range of individual personality types in our society, as in any, is wide. Nor am I implying that everyone in our society is unhappy or "neurotic." As individuals we vary greatly in how rich and fulfilling our lives are. In attempting to conceptualize a societal neurosis, it is necessary to accommodate clearly to that fact. Those social analyses which see only misery and empty self-deception seem to me facile and false.

Moreover, it is important to be clear as well that conceptualizing certain trends in terms of a societal neurosis does not mean that one is dismissing the entire society as "sick." There are, unfortunately, some therapists who use their diagnostic acumen not sympathetically to understand the person's dilemmas but to put him in his place and reveal him in his hidden pathology. Writ large, such a diagnostic orientation reveals a sick and hopelessly compromised society. Good therapists, however, see the strengths and fine points of their patients as well as the self-defeating patterns in which they have trapped themselves. To point to a societal neurosis in this spirit is not globally to dismiss or condemn our society. It is to seek to understand how the vital and valuable features of our social order are being undermined by trends whose significance has not been clearly understood.*

When, in contrast to the diversity of individual styles in our country, I suggest that a *particular* kind of *societal* neurosis can be discerned, I am pointing essentially to two kinds of phenomena. First, there are trends in public policy—actions taken by

---

*I am also, I hope it is clear, not suggesting that the vicious circles described in this chapter are the *only* important problems faced by our society. More "traditional" concerns about social equity and political power remain of obvious and pressing importance. We clearly suffer from a number of very basic political and economic difficulties and inequities. These more traditional sources of social unrest can be ignored only at great peril.

those in a position to affect the overall economic system and its way of functioning: legislative decisions that influence how wealth is distributed and how the society's resources are deployed; trends in foreign policy and military actions; and so on. These are the patterns studied by the macroeconomist or the sociologist, the kinds of phenomena that justify viewing a society as a system rather than as just a collection of individuals. In certain important features of that system, in the behavior of that organism we call society, I am suggesting, can be discerned vicious circles of the sort I have been describing.

A second sense in which a societal pattern can be discerned, despite the enormous variety in the behavior of individuals, is in the more public aspects of most individuals' behavior. We are more distinctive and differentiated in the intimate and private aspects of our lives than in the ways we participate in the larger social order—more so as lovers than as shoppers, more as parents than as voters. Even in the intimate aspects of our lives, we are more differentiated in what we do or profess to those we confide in than in what we profess publicly; as a psychotherapist I hear a far wider range of attitudes and ideas about sex than are likely to be reflected in any debate on public policy. But the more publicly expressed attitudes are not simple falsehoods. They represent a set of shared commitments with a major impact on all of us, for many people existing side by side with other, quite different attitudes, as an equally real aspect of who one is (and they produce institutional arrangements that may well be at odds with our more privately experienced needs but are powerful forces in our lives).

A recent report on research being conducted at the Laboratory of Developmental Psychology of the National Institute of Mental Health described patterns of child training that may help us understand the greater uniformity in public attitudes as compared with more private behavior. The degree to which children are taught to be sensitive to the feelings of others in their immediate family varies considerably from family to family. But apparently, with regard to attitudes toward strangers or in public places, we train children much more uniformly. Babies as young as 18 months of age frequently respond sympathetically to the distress of others—and are taught by their parents to eliminate this response. "Far from conveying intense messages about children's responsibilities [when they are by-

standers to others' suffering], the mothers tend either to ignore
the suffering or—more frequently—to reassure the children
and tell them not to worry about it! This lack of involvement in
others' pain, when their own children have not had a hand in it
is startling."[14] According to Marian Radke Yarrow, head of the
Laboratory of Developmental Psychology, "People have little
use for altruism in this society, except when it's institutional-
ized, as through charities and volunteer service. . . . Parents
generally want their children to be able to compete successfully—and how can they compete if they're altruists?"

This, of course, is not all there is to childrearing attitudes
in our society. Even in more public aspects of behavior, we also
instill attitudes of a rather different sort. Horney, for example,
in her first account of how neurotic patterns in America differed from those in Europe (at a time when she had not yet conceptualized the three-dimensional model of neurotic trends),
placed great emphasis on the conflict between our worship of
competition and our Christian ideals of compassion and love.[15]
More generally, conflict is a central feature of all neurotic patterns; the dominant overt trend is not likely to be all that is important. In our attitudes toward possessions, for example,
though I have argued they fit well into a competitive, aggres-
sive, moving-against strategy of security-seeking, they are also
at times associated with a more moving-away trend, as when
each sibling in the home has his own TV set so the family
doesn't have to negotiate about what program to watch; when
each homeowner has his own washing machine instead of
spending time with others at the laundromat; when lonely individuals drive their cars, listen to their stereos, and use their possessions in ways designed to make them less reliant on the company of others.

Nonetheless, I believe that the concept of the moving-
against neurotic trend captures something important about the
manifest patterns of behavior that most characterize our public
life and the workings of our economic system. Such patterns are
not exclusive to America, but they are particularly marked
here. Other observers have stressed that we are far less directly
competitive than we used to be, that we are now more "other-
directed," that in participating in a bureaucratized society, in
fitting into the culture of the large corporation, our ability to
"get along" with people has become our most important asset.

There is, I think, much of value in such characterizations, and in some respects they may be seen to dovetail with the present analysis. But there are obviously also ways in which I disagree with such accounts, and I shall consider the relation between the present picture and those of other observers elsewhere.*

For the present, what I want to stress most of all is the problem posed by our anxious reliance on the production and accumulation of goods to compensate for the decline in other more traditional sources of security. Whether one wants to describe such reliance, and the vicious circles it creates, as "neurotic," or whether one finds Horney's notion of the "moving-against" style illuminating in this context, is of far less concern to me than the simple recognition that there is something compulsive, irrational, and self-defeating in the way we pursue goods. Our overriding stress on productivity and growth and the toll it takes on our health and well-being are part of a tragically unnecessary treadmill on which we run, ever more desperately, with ever more strain, committing more and more of our lives to the hopeless chase to keep up. The search for a way off that treadmill is what this book is about.

*See, in this regard, the discussion of Riesman and Fromm in Chapter Six.

FIVE

The Cultural Context of the Growth Ideology

Our preoccupation with economic growth is part of a larger pattern of assumptions, part of a mindset that goes beyond the realm of material goods alone. The mental habits that support our commitment to growth are implicated in almost every aspect of daily living. They shape our perceptions in such a way that the choices we make seem not only logical but inevitable. It is necessary to understand this larger web in which we are caught—and which we ourselves continue to spin—if we are to have any chance of extricating ourselves.

Finding a way out of the closed circle of culturally shared suppositions and practices is probably even more difficult than unraveling the skein of an individual neurosis, but some of the same principles may be relevant to both tasks. In working with troubled individuals one quickly discovers that "insights" alone are rarely sufficient for enduring change to occur. Action to change the pattern one is caught in, to produce different feedback that makes new behavior more likely, is also essential. But insight is nonetheless a critical part of the process.

Therapeutic insight is more than just understanding. Often what is entailed is bringing to awareness assumptions and

habits of mind that had been unnoticed and automatic. Sometimes what is brought to awareness is something the person is
actively trying not to notice (in psychoanalytic terminology,
something the person is defending against). At other times
there is nothing particularly threatening about what comes to
light; it simply had become so unquestioningly assumed or pursued that it was no longer part of focal awareness. The socially
shared mental habits addressed in this chapter are of the latter
sort. They are so much a part of our assumptive world that we
barely recognize that they *are* assumptions at all. They seem to
us simply "the way things are." In psychotherapy it is often a
critical first step when the patient is simply able to notice
the assumptions that underlie his actions. In attending to his
thoughts and his behavior in this way, he is also as a consequence taking a certain distance from them and is thus in a position to examine critically what had previously not even been
recognized as a choice. In breaking the stranglehold of broader
social patterns too, it is probably first essential to focus attention on what usually seems so natural it is not even noticed. The
point is not necessarily that one has been wrong but simply that
one can then weigh the consequences of any particular view
and consider possible alternatives.

Linear and Circular Views of Life

The first of these largely unnoticed habits of thought to be examined here is a view of life as a path or trajectory, and particularly as a path with a direction, not just an aimless ramble. To
some extent, of course, all societies show such a structure in
their thought. Certain features of our existence seem to *require*
such a view. We are born, we grow up, we get older, we die.
There is a clear and irreversable directionality to this. In that
sense our life *is* a path, indeed a one-way street.

But not all cultures make this aspect of human existence
such a central image in the way they structure their lives. For
us, the dominance of this view of things has provided fertile soil
for ideas of growth and progress. We conceive of things in a
unidirectional, cumulative way. In many other cultures, a quite
different world view is evident; it seems to be based on a second
basic existential feature of our lives: the rhythm of repeated cy-

cles. Although *individuals* may be seen to tread a straight and
narrow path in which they are born, grow, and die, *nature*
seems to run in circles. The rhythms of day and night and of
the changing seasons are as basic a part of the structure of our
experience as is the unilinear advance from birth to death. Indeed, even the linearity of our individual lives can readily be
seen as but a minor feature of the larger pattern of constant
turnover of generations, a rhythm as inexorable as the changing phases of the moon or any of the other cycles that have captured man's imagination.

For most of human history this cyclical vision of life has
been dominant. In primarily agricultural societies (as most societies have been throughout history), people live much more
intimately with the rhythms of nature. Year after year there is
"a time to sow and a time to reap," and the changing seasons
are both immediate in their impact and the main source of
structure for life. In our society nature's rhythms are muted.
We have learned to imitate the sun and can provide ourselves
with light at will. Now that we can turn night into day, our activities are not nearly as structured by the rising and setting of
the sun as were our ancestors'. Neither the sun nor the crow of
the cock wakes most of us, but an alarm clock (probably electric) set in accord with man-made time, not nature's markers.

The seasons, too, are diminished for us as a source of structure for our lives. The occupations of most of us do not depend
on the seasons in the way that the farmer's work does. Even in
climates that vary considerably from season to season, we have
learned to impose a man-made regularity, which substitutes the
rhythms of the nine-to-five world for the rhythms of nature. Air
conditioning and central heating make the seasons relevant
only for recreation, almost as a kind of anachronistic curiosity.
We wear three-piece suits in the summer and spurn sweaters in-
doors in the winter.*

Even our way of telling time is beginning to reflect our
technological distancing from the cycle of nature's rhythms.
Digital timepieces, which, because they are "new," are perceived by so many as "better," break the perceptual and imagi-
nal link between the flow of time and an endlessly repeated

---

*Energy shortages may be changing these latter practices some, but
the basic pattern persists.

circle. Time becomes instead a linear series of increasing but disconnected numbers. Circularity and continuity give way to linearity and disjunction.[1]

The Culture of Quantity

Emphasis on numbers is a pervasive characteristic of our civilization. We are a culture of quantity, and qualities that cannot be reduced to "more" or "less" are likely to be lost or to recede into the background. As Santayana has observed, our "love of quantity often has a silent partner, which is diffidence as to quality."[2]

This concern with quantitative measures was originally part of a salutary and liberating trend in the evolution of our economy and our culture, but it has by now become a preoccupation that is increasingly dangerous and counterproductive. Central to our emancipation from the cycles of nature—and initially this *was* an emancipation, because in most climes the cycle of nature was a cycle of poverty—was the development of farming methods that yielded a surplus beyond what was immediately needed by the farmer. This permitted more people to engage in activities other than producing food, and greater differentiation and specialization could develop. Efficiency and expertise came to be more prominent, and so too did trade; and in the fashion stressed throughout this book, the process became an accelerating one in which the accumulation of surpluses and the changes in modes of production and social organization mutually influenced each other. This seemingly inexorable feedback cycle has propelled us into a world of plenty, but a world in which many traditional values have fallen by the wayside, and only what can be counted seems to count.

We have been freed from the static and limited world of subsistence that was for so long most men's lot. But our ability to accumulate has infected us with the idea of "more," and like a child who has haplessly grabbed hold of a high tension wire, we are unable to let go. Recognition that what we could have was not necessarily set by what our fathers had—that our surplus could yield us still more surplus, enabling us to have more each year and each generation—was a powerful motivating force. It has brought us a way of life that few of us—myself included — would wish to trade for the more stable but limited life of so many generations that preceded us. But in our celebration of the idea of "more" we have become transfixed. As our simple linear notions begin to seem inadequate — as "more" threatens to become "too much," or even "less" — we stand paralyzed, in thrall to an idea we cannot let go of, cannot take sufficient distance from to see when it, rather than us, has become the master.

Not just the acceleration of surpluses and the process of accumulation but the development of trade as well has pointed us toward our overriding emphasis on sheer quantity. To be sure, trade has seemed to be a feature of almost all societies of which we have any knowledge. Even in the fossil remains of our prehistoric ancestors we have found signs of trade.[3] But, until relatively recent times, trade tended to be only an auxiliary activity. Commerce — and money — certainly existed in prior civilizations, but only in ours, over the past few hundred years, have they assumed the centrality that we now take for granted.[4] We are used to thinking of money as an essential factor in human affairs, as not just the "root of all evil" but even at times the "root of all." When we encounter references to money in biblical contexts and other ancient writings — and they are frequent — we are likely to attribute more or less the same meaning to these references that they would have for us today. But as Robert Heilbroner has documented,[5] until relatively modern times the use of money was confined largely to a rather limited realm of luxury items. In fulfilling the bulk of people's material needs, and even in the majority of economic transactions, money played a rather circumscribed role.

When most production was for use, and when trade was largely in kind, the concrete qualities of things were of paramount importance. People grew primarily what they needed, not what would "sell," and when they traded it was for particular items that filled quite specific needs. But as, increasingly, economic activity and the garnering of the necessities of life came to require *money*, a change of consciousness occurred as well. Both work and its fruits came to be valued less for what was concrete and given and more for their exchange value, for the amount of money they could bring. In this way, an enormous range of things came to be capable of comparison on a single scale. A day's labor, a particular tool, a sack of grain, a gem, a piece of cloth, a completed garment — all could be measured in the coin of the realm. Almost everything that men did and had could be treated as equivalent, differing only in *more* or *less*. Thus, in a very important sense, a man's work, his ox, and the food that each of them required all were *the same*. It might take more than one day's work to purchase a particular item, or more than one item to purchase a day's work, but through the medium of money all could be reduced to a comparable rule.

Such comparisons and evaluations, of course, have always been implicit in human transactions. Any trade implies at least a rough notion of equivalence, and even in allocating effort to produce for one's own use there are implicit judgments as to what is most "worth" one's efforts. But the introduction of money — not just as a peripheral feature of men's lives but as a central and essential feature of how our lives are ordered and of how we get hold of life's necessities — provided a tool for an unprecedented degree of abstraction. The manifest qualities of things, of course, entered into their price and thus were not completely lost; but in a very important sense they were submerged or dissolved in the conversion to quantity.

It seems likely that we have here another of those great circles that seem to dominate human affairs. The development of a predominantly money-focused economy occurred hand in hand with an enormous increase in technological development and organizational efficiency. This, it seems likely, was no mere coincidental parallelism. The ability of men to contribute to and comply with the march of technology seems at least in part attributable to the increased tendency to think abstractly and to quantify that money necessarily implied (while at the same time the increasing role of monetary calculations and abstract thinking was accelerated by the advance of technology and its consequences). In establishing equivalence among such a wide variety of goods and activities, in boiling them all down to a single quantitative figure, modern man brings a highly abstract frame of mind right into the center of his life.

This way of thinking has contributed to the unprecedented wealth and productivity of modern industrial societies. But it has also "captured" our imaginations in a sense that is uncomfortably literal. It has become extremely difficult for us to cast important societal decisions in ways that do not reduce to the one quantitative dimension that we call the "bottom line." Reducing everything to one dimension of quantity, we always seem to be left only with the question of whether we want "more" or "less." Once the question is framed that way, the outcome is, of course, obvious.

We have become so used to counting and to giving meaning to our activities in quantitative terms that it can come as a surprise to us to find that not all cultures share this trait. Ruth Benedict reports that when Hopi Indian boys were taught to play basketball, they quickly grasped its intricate teamwork and learned to play the game very well. But they had great difficulty understanding that each side was to keep track of the number of baskets it made.[6]

It is hard for us to empathize with such a difficulty. Quantitative thinking—as well as competition—is in our bones. In our culture, when important decisions are to be made, we feel on safest ground with graphs or numbers. Qualitative concerns are too vague, too ambiguous, too "subjective" for us. What René Guenon has called the "reign of quantity"[7] gains our willing fealty, and the more concrete experience-near-qualities give way to the abstract and quantifiable.

Perhaps the most revealing cultural phenomenon in this regard is the development of the concept of gross national product (GNP) and the use to which it has been put. Originally the GNP was developed by economists as a technical tool to gauge the aggregate performance of the economy. It was part of a concerted effort, spurred by the Great Depression of the 1930s, to gain some degree of control over the business cycles that have plagued capitalist economies over the years. Its working out was an enormously complicated task, and questions of what to include and how required enormous ingenuity to solve. These efforts brought a Nobel Prize to Simon Kuznets and have engaged others of the best economic minds in one way or another. Whatever the limits of the particular definition of GNP now in use, and despite the current travails of the economy, there is a broad consensus among economists that the GNP measure is a very useful tool.

It was not long, however, before the GNP began to be regarded not just as a tool for economic policy-making but as a measure of economic welfare, of how "well off" we were. Annual increase in the size of the GNP was viewed with pride and

seemed to carry a clear implication that things were getting better and better. Economists repeatedly disavowed this interpretation of the GNP, defending it instead on the grounds of its
more limited, technical applicability;[8] but most of them, like
the rest of us, got caught up in the romance of a large and
growing GNP, which came to be viewed as a worthwhile end in
itself.

The contradictions and absurdities that arise when GNP is
taken as a measure of well-being are manifold and have frequently been commented upon. Perhaps the most classic instance is that the medical costs due to the diseases caused by
pollution are figured into the GNP as *pluses*. To be sure, if the
industrial wastes that end up in our air or water cause me to develop cancer, I would rather receive medical treatment than
not and would regard the money as well spent. But it is even
surer that I would rather not have had the cancer at all. Yet if
less pollution occurred, and as a result less medical treatment
was required, this would show up as a drop in the GNP.[9] Is my
hesitancy to develop cancer for the sake of the GNP, then, a
lamentable lack of patriotism, a kind of desertion on the economic front? At the very least I can console myself with the
knowledge that I am hardly unique in my perverse unwillingness to contribute in this way to the increment in our "total."

There are, of course, good economic reasons—technical
reasons, that is—for defining GNP the way it is defined. The
GNP measure is meant to gauge overall economic activity in order to enable economists to keep the economy going at an appropriate rate, to smooth out the booms and busts. Doctors
(and technicians, orderlies, and secretaries in the hospital bill-
ing department) who are in some way involved in the treatment
of my—or your—environmentally caused cancer are, by virtue
of that involvement, not on the unemployment rolls. The calculation of the GNP reflects this fact. It also reflects our preference—however we might weigh it against another person's pain
or debilitating disease—for having people employed.

The problem with the GNP, of course, is that it makes no
distinction as to *how* the person is employed, *what* it is that he
or she is making or doing. The great strength—and also the
great weakness—of the idea of the GNP is that everything is
boiled down to dollars and cents. And all things that represent
the same number of dollars are therefore treated as equal.

This, ultimately, is also the strategy of all the efforts of economists to construct other indices designed to be more frankly indicators of well-being.[10] These indices do attempt to distinguish between expenditures on what are called "regrettable necessities" and those undertaken for their own sake, which yield real satisfaction. But despite my conviction that we need to gauge the performance of our economy in ways that more genuinely reflect the benefits we do or don't receive, I believe these efforts are really more part of the problem than part of the solution. For they attempt to correct the inherent limitations of a particular way of thinking from within the assumptions of that system itself: However much they disclaim making value judgments and insist on the mantle of the technician, on their efforts being "just" economics, there is excess philosophical freight in their ultimate reduction of all qualities and values to the one dimension of dollars and cents.[11]

In grade school we all learned that we could not add oranges and bananas. To avoid absurdity, the two quantities added must be of the same category. It is true, of course, that by abstracting further, one can meaningfully add the two as amounts of "fruit." But "dollars" do not function in this regard the same way that "fruit" does. When we assign dollar values to everything in order to be able to add them, we bring to bear other assumptions that are highly questionable.

In his authoritative economics textbook, for example, Paul Samuelson states that when we measure the GNP "we are not interested in consumption and investment goods merely for their money value: Money is the measuring rod used to give some approximate figure to the underlying 'satisfactions' or 'benefits' or 'psychic income' that comes from goods."[12] But the amount someone is willing to pay for an item is not really a measure of how much satisfaction he gains from it. I pay 30 cents each morning for *The New York Times* and often 40 or 45 cents for a lousy cup of bitter coffee, bought on mornings when I wish to enhance the morning ritual by having a second cup of coffee "out." Do I really value the bitter coffee more than reading the newspaper? If so, there is no better proof for the existence of the unconscious for every sinew of my conscious experience tells me that reading the paper is the important pleasure to me, and the coffee an unessential adjunct. And this is so even though I might well refuse to buy the *Times* for a while if it suddenly went up to the "outrageous" price of 45 cents, the price I readily pay for the coffee. It is simply a matter of my having gotten used to paying 45 cents for coffee, and its thus seeming "reasonable" or "appropriate" to pay that amount for coffee but not for the *Times*. (It might also be noted that I did not instantly adjust to the increase in the price of coffee either, and that for a while coffee did not seem to me to be "worth" 45 cents.)

The mainstream economist might answer that I happen to value the newspaper more highly than many other consumers do and that its price is low because it is determined by marginal rather than average valuations. I thus receive a "consumer's surplus" because I pay the same price that is required to entice the more ambivalent reader. That the coffee—for which *I* am now the marginal purchaser, teetering at the brink of saying "Too much"—costs more at the margin than the newspaper does is due in some measure to the relative scarcity of the items.

So far so good. But in moving from considerations of price to considerations of value, satisfaction, or "psychic income," a crucial assumption tends to be made by economists: that consumers are, for the most part, able to make the kind of wise choices that do in fact maximize their satisfactions. As put irreverently by Shlomo Maital, chairman of the economics department at the Technion-Israel Institute of Technology, the model which often guides the economist is one of "the exacting consumer matching subjective value and objective price right at the precipice of his budget line, along which he or she skates with Olympic precision."[13] This model, as Maital notes, is "far-fetched." It is subtly skewered by Albert Hirschman of the Institute for Advanced Study at Princeton who, in a graceful, non-polemical way, explores the ubiquitous dissatisfactions and disappointments which are at least as much the rule as consumer satisfaction. Hirschman contends that, far from "carry-[ing] within [themselves] a universe of wants of known intensity that [they match] against prices," consumers often "think they want one thing and then upon getting it, find out to their dismay that they don't want it nearly as much as they thought or don't want it at all and that something else, of which they were hardly aware, is what they really want."[14] Hirschman quotes with approval Shaw's dictum, "There are two tragedies in life. One is not to get your heart's desire. The other is to get it."

For most economists, however, the canny consumer, making rational tradeoffs and translating the oranges and bananas of life into a neat, unitary rule, remains the dominant image. The result, frequently, is to lend a rational patina to actions rooted in denial and self-deception. Lester Thurow, for example, offers the following solution to the problem of how far to pursue environmental protection:

> Imagine that someone could sell you an invisible, completely comfortable facemask that would guarantee you clean air. How much would you be willing to pay for such a device? Whatever you would be willing to pay is what economists call the *shadow price* of clean air. If we added up the amounts that each of us would be willing to pay for such a mask, we would have society's shadow price for clean air. Such a facemask cannot be purchased, but any pollution control program that can give us clean air for less than this price is a program that is raising our real standard of living. What we get in terms of benefits is greater than what we must sacrifice in terms of costs.[15]

Thurow's discussion assumes that our judgments in such a hypothetical situation reflect fairly accurately the real benefits we would receive. But the example in fact seems better suited for illustrating how irrational we can be when important life issues are squeezed into the Procrustean calculus of dollars and cents. Suppose such a mask cost $5000. I myself might hesitate to lay out $20,000 for my family of four, despite a concern with pollution problems great enough to motivate the task of writing this book. I can easily imagine some of the sentences that might masquerade in my head as sober thoughts: "They probably wouldn't really work." "How much difference would it make?" "Is pollution really such an immediate threat after all?"

The last sentence would seem at first to back Thurow's point: I complain about pollution in the abstract, but how much would I really give up for cleaner air? Much more, I believe, it illustrates the irrational overvaluation of money that pervades the lives of almost all of us. Trained from early on to think in a particular mode of thought, we become to some degree slaves to it even when it serves us ill. Perspective is gained when we reverse Thurow's question, putting it in a way that proponents of growth solutions to our problems conveniently leave out: How much money would I be willing to take in return for letting someone blow polluted air into my child's face every day?

Put this way, the benefits of clean air are infinite. There is *no* amount of money I would take in free exchange under such circumstances. To be sure, if my children were starving I might have to wonder if the trade might not be necessary. But the point I have been stressing in this book is that at the level of the American middle class, we have reached an economic position where we can afford to free ourselves of the habits of thought of a deprived society. In desperate straits it may be true that "every man has his price." But it is precisely our luxury that we are in a position to reject such a view.

The way Thurow frames his question, it elicits from us our old, bad habits. Were decisions about pollution control to be cast in the framework he suggests, we would likely have more goods and dirtier air. To some this simply means that that is what we "want." But contrary to the simplifying assumptions that dominate social and economic discourse these days, what we want is far more complex than what is revealed just in acts of buying or borrowing.* The cultural trends I am discussing here shape the structures through which we view the world and funnel the alternatives that are apparent to us. Life holds infinite variety, but if everything is reduced to one number, if how we are doing can always somehow be added up, then the only real value can be "more," and growth in some quantity the only acceptable sign of progress or of doing well.

And so we experience an imperative to grow. The word "growth" becomes for us synonymous with the good and is trotted out in an enormous range of contexts. Economists seek to bring about growth; psychologists help their patients to grow; our presidents are expected to "grow" in office. With "growth" such an omnipresent symbol of the good, it is very difficult for us to accept any idea of a limit to growth as implying something other than stagnation. Our emphasis on growth leads us to equate contentment with complacency. Our more general values parallel the assumptions that underlie the workings of our

---

*To be sure, there are important political and ethical questions raised if we do *not* take people's choices at face value as an expression of what they want. These will be taken up in Chapter Twelve, where a further examination will be made of some of the biased or fallacious notions that dominate our thinking about economic issues.

economy. Even those of us opposed to unchecked growth of industry tend to endorse the broader societal trend of seeking, questing, restlessness.

Faust as a Cultural Exemplar

The Faust legend—especially as it comes down to us through the compelling medium of Goethe's classic—symbolically represents a characteristic of our culture that is at the very heart of what I am addressing in this book. Faust has become for us a positive symbol of the dynamism and daring of Western man. We embrace Faust and his restless, insatiable quest. In this, we manifest particularly clearly the difference between our modern culture of change and turmoil and the stable world that was beginning to break up at the time that the real figure on whom the legend is based was alive. The changing view of Faust, from villain to hero essentially, reflects the changing spirit of the Western world as the accelerating rush of commerce and industry began to shake its foundations.

The real Johann Faustus was an itinerant conjurer, gadfly, and provocateur who accumulated considerable notoriety and not a little trouble as he wandered from town to town, entrancing some and getting kicked out of others. When his story was told in 1587, 46 years after his death, he was presented as an object lesson illustrating the terrible price to be paid for dealing with the devil.[16] As he later took shape in Marlowe, Goethe, and many later versions, the meaning of the legend for us changed greatly. Goethe's presentation of the story was certainly not a simple one, and complexities and conflicts abound. But the overall sense one has of Faust in Goethe is clearly not of a villain but of a struggling hero. Faust is the man who *dares*. His virtue is our modern virtue: restlessness. In his wager with the devil it is the very insatiability of his desires, his conviction that he will never be satisfied, that he counts on above all. This is his great virtue, which God Himself endorses in Goethe's tale. The great sin to which the devil tries to tempt him is to enjoy, to be content, to find pleasure. What he must maintain, at the risk of his soul, is ceaseless activity, unbridled striving after achievement and new experience. He agrees that he should perish if ever to any moment he should say "Tarry awhile, you are so fair."

Goethe's genius articulated early what was to become a core myth of modern culture. The story he tells speaks to a consciousness even more endemic in today's world than in Goethe's. But there is a profound irony in what has happened to the myth in the ensuing years. For the contented bourgeoisie that Faust sought to transcend are today's carriers of Faustian restlessness. In a perverted, materialistic form, that restlessness, that refusal to be contented, that contempt for slothful acceptance of one's lot have become the foundation stones of middleclass culture. And indeed, in a further twist, that very restlessness has become what we are content with, the one thing we do accept as a constant, a given that we endorse unquestioningly with piously slothful self-satisfaction. Our refusal to "settle," our insistence on pushing to the limits, we smugly crow from the rooftops. To this attitude itself, we say "Tarry awhile, you are so beautiful."

Now I hold no brief for the conservative Lutheran churchman who first brought the Faust legend to light as a cautionary tale for those who would question Christian orthodoxy. But in our subsequent conversion of the wretched Faust to a kind of patron saint of Western civilization we have gone too far. Perhaps the sulfurous fumes that rise from our factories and power plants should remind us of the company Faust kept. And perhaps we need to follow Goethe a little farther than we have, beyond the prideful and heedless Faust of the early part of the story. As J. W. Smeed presents Goethe's vision, Faust eventually achieves salvation "by gradually freeing himself from his overwhelming ruthless and subjective impulses and seeking a more constructive and altruistic approach to life, an approach which draws its inspiration from nature and from the classical ideals of harmony and beauty."[17] Harmony, not growth; cooperation, not the individual pursuit of more and everything; a respect for nature rather than a ruthless effort to conquer her—these may well be the path to salvation for modern man as well.

At present, though, we continue to celebrate the "restless spirit" as our hero. I say this despite the common—and partially correct—view that we have become a society of conformists. The conformism that critics such as Riesman and Fromm highlighted in the 1950s certainly represents an important vein in our culture.* Even in the economic realm, as Galbraith has

---

*But see my discussion of Riesman's claims in Chapter Seven.

particularly clearly shown us,[18] the mode is one of cautiously managed enterprises, not of intrepid owner-entrepreneurs. Nonetheless, this system of planned, bureaucratized corporate enterprises depends for its smooth functioning on the stimulation of petty Faustian urges in all of us. Those who rest content, who cease to strive for more, are decidedly against the grain. Hunger for more is promoted as a moral imperative.

Outgrowing and Growing Away

A corollary of the restlessness that afflicts our culture is a hesitancy to stay put. We are not only restless but rootless. In the pursuit of more, in the effort to better ourselves, we must leave behind what we previously had; we must not get "stuck." This is not just a matter of not getting stuck in a particular job or at a particular standard of living. Subtly, but inexorably, the same attitude has pervaded our relations to family and community. Upward mobility has frequently meant not just moving up (in status, in class, in material position) but also moving away (either geographically or psychologically — distancing oneself from the values and tastes of one's parents). Put differently, our culture of growth requires us not just to grow — to expand, to increase, to acquire — but also to outgrow or to grow away

The importance of this dimension in the structure of our lives and its powerful impact upon our experience of ourselves and of others are poignantly illustrated in Philip Roth's novel *Portnoy's Complaint*.[19] In one extremely important passage, Alexander Portnoy recalls the softball games that the men in his neighborhood used to play on Sunday mornings. He recalls his boyhood dream of someday being part of that game. It is a typical childhood dream, similar to those that countless generations have experienced — a dream of being inducted into the world of men, of learning its mysteries and its rituals, of having a place as a full-fledged member of the community. But for Portnoy, as for so many of us in today's society, such dreams are but a dim elegiac memory, evoked only rarely and with great pain. The softball game is mentioned only once in the book. Its significance can easily be overlooked. It is not an obvious leitmotif in the book, as is Portnoy's compulsive and unsatisfying sexuality (which is, in large measure, a defense against the haunting dream). Yet that softball game, that lost ritual of community and simple manliness, is part of the psychic heart of the book and a key metaphor as well for understanding our way of life and its costs.

It is not that he is not good enough that keeps Portnoy from fulfilling his dream. We are told that he was a rather good athlete, an especially good centerfielder. Nor is it that he was rejected by the group. Rather, it is that the game no longer exists. Or, if it does, it is no longer accessible to him because he has *outgrown* it. Playing softball in Newark, New Jersey is no longer a fitting aspiration for the man he has become.

At thirty-three, Portnoy is a "success," an embodiment of the American dream, a sophisticated member of the upwardly mobile meritocracy. He has graduated first in his class at Columbia Law School, has served as special counsel to a Subcommittee of the United States Congress (of "America," as he tells his mother one day, proudly but desperately), and he is currently Assistant Commissioner of Human Rights for the City of New York and a frequent subject of mention in *The New York Times*.

But he is a success at a very high price. He is restless, discontented, unable to love or to commit himself to a woman or a home life. Despite his intelligence, and despite what on one level is a genuine desire to lead an enlightened and ethically exemplary life, he ends up presenting himself as an insensitive buffoon, both contemptuous and pathetic, blindly destructive and self-destructive for all his wit and insight. His situation is, of course, readily accessible—indeed, too accessible—to a Freudian explanation; and such an account would be far from incorrect or irrelevant. But there is another dimension to Portnoy's dilemma—and his dilemma is far more interesting than his complaint—that tended to be overlooked by most of the critics who commented on the book when it was published (a failure of perception that accounts, I believe, for the book's having been taken less seriously than it should have been).

Portnoy is caught in a conflict endemic to modern man: He is drawn to the ladder of upward mobility, excited by the transcendence of the severely bounded world of his parents; but in his emancipation from the limited horizons of their lives he has also lost a framework for ordering and making sense out of his desires and his values. If his opportunities seem almost boundless now that he has really entered the mainstream of

American life, so too are his desires. Portnoy's situation is some-what different from the one I have been mainly discussing thus far; his pursuits are primarily sexual rather than material. But the structure of his life is similar. He too is plagued by an un-quenchable thirst that does not let him rest content. Having outgrown and grown away from the community and traditions in which he was raised—and perceiving that he *must* do so in order to advance into the brave new world of more and more— he is left with an empty, somewhat bewildered cynicism in which nothing means very much to him. His conquests are compulsive and unsatisfying. He is an unwilling Faust, caught in a daily round of new experiences that bring no rest or peace.

Most of the time he does not let us see anything of value in the world he has left behind. The importance of the momentar-ily recalled dream of the softball game he onced hoped to join (and of the family to which he would return afterward) is that it is one of the few places in which he permits us to see his yearn-ing for a world in which he has a clearly defined place and in which—perhaps most importantly—he knows what to want. His more typical descriptions of what he has left behind are far less appealing and portray a world in which constriction is about all that is offered. We must remember that we never see his parents directly, but only through his eyes, only as he de-scribes them to us. Thus we are in the position of the psychoan-alyst—indeed, in the structure of the book we are *literally* in that position, since the entire tale is what might be called a *ro-man-à-couch*.

Because his story is told from the couch, it is tempting to dismiss its relevance, to particularize it as the story of a "neu-rotic." Any interesting character in literature has particularity, and Portnoy's, clearly, is (among other things) neurotic—fla-grantly and hilariously neurotic, and acutely rendered as such. But in the form of his neurosis—in his struggle to live without roots, in his discovery that the kind of freedom and autonomy he has sought bring with them a boundlessness of desire, an in-ability to be content, and a pervasive sense of meaningless—he is a representative figure, even if a "patient."

The same tendency toward outgrowing and growing away is evident in sociological studies of those who make it in the cor-porate world. According to the sociologist Lloyd Warner,

The most important component of the personalities of successful corporate managers and owners is that, their deep emotional identifications with their families of birth being dissolved, they no longer are closely intermeshed with the past,
and therefore, are capable of relating themselves easily to the
present and future. They are people who have literally and
spiritually left home. . . . They can relate and disrelate themselves to others easily.[20]

Elsewhere, Warner characterizes our big business leaders
as "men on the move."

They have left behind a standard of living, level of income, and
style of life to adopt a way of living entirely different from that
into which they were born. The mobile man first of all leaves
the physical setting of his birth. . . . [But] he must leave behind people as well as places. The friends of earlier years must
be left, for acquaintances of the lower-status past are incompatible with the successful present. Often the church of his
birth is left, along with the clubs and cliques of his family and
of his youth. But most important of all, and this is the great
problem of the man on the move, he must, to some degree,
leave his father, mother, brothers, and sisters, along with the
other human relationships of his past.[21]

Throughout the modern world, to greater or lesser degree,
men and women are faced with the push to leave parents and
siblings, home and tradition behind in order to "get ahead."
Empty pieties such as Mother's Day and Father's Day help to
disguise the reality, while a celebration of success serves to disguise the price. That price is one of the central themes of Arthur Miller's play by that name.[22] Miller explores on many levels the psychic costs of both staying and leaving in the face of
the modern world's irreconcilable imperatives; but perhaps the
most relevant passage in *The Price* for our present concerns is
spoken by Solomon, the secondhand furniture dealer. Called in
by the sons to dispose of the furniture of a dead father, furniture which, in the old style, was built to last, Solomon indicates
why it will be hard to sell. "A man who sits down at this table,"
he says, "knows he is married and has got to stay married. 'Dis-
posable' is the word these days. Because what is the main thing
today? Shopping."
The links between the culture of growing and outgrowing,
of throwing away on both the psychic and the material level

and the relentless whirring of our economic machine have rarely been stated more succinctly.

Identity and the Self-Made Man

The rift in community and continuity that so characterizes our lives and the tendency to throw things away—whether posses- sions, relationships or ties to a particular place or community— account in substantial measure for why we are so preoccupied with our "identities." In the modern world we must *make* an identity for ourselves; we do not inherit one. We have outgrown the tradition that assigns one's way of life, one's station, and one's loyalties at birth. And, for more and more of us, we out- grow too the particulars of our backgrounds. That we are from a particular place or class, or even the sons or daughters of par- ticular mothers and fathers, does not determine who we "are." In many ways, of course, this is liberating, but it makes an identity something we must *achieve*. Our ties—such as they are—are so various and changing that it is usually an achieve- ment not gained without considerable struggle.

It is a striking fact that the man who has done the most to articulate the concept of identity and to make the concept part of our popular imagination was himself someone who forged his own identity to an extraordinary degree. Erik Erikson— Erik, the son of Erik; Erik the son of himself—had gone for years under the name of Homburger, the surname of the step- father who adopted him at a very young age. He took on the name Erikson when he became an American citizen in 1939.[23]

America in particular has been a place where people could start a life anew, could cut their ties to the past and create a new identity. R. W. B. Lewis traces this theme throughout American literature in *The American Adam*.[24] In our relatively recent literature we have F. Scott Fitzgerald's particularly vivid image of James Gatz who became Jay Gatsby, perhaps the best known literary character of an earlier era of affluence; Gatsby, we are told by the novel's narrator, "sprang from his Platonic conception of himself." On a rather different level, we find Jack Rosenberg, who in the course of leaving his wife and children to find fame and fortune became Werner Erhard and founded est, whose extreme notions of self-determination I shall discuss in the next chapter.

Superman and Leaving Home

One further figure—whose true identity, if not unclear, is at least hidden—casts a particularly interesting light on our culture of growing and outgrowing: Superman is a hero who in one sense has a pedigree going back at least to Hercules and Samson but in another is a uniquely modern figure. The supermen of earlier myths tended to derive their strength from their parentage, from the gods and titans from which they were descended. In one sense this is true for our modern Superman as well; his strength derives from his being born of a people who live on a planet of vastly greater gravity than Earth's and who therefore have vastly greater muscular development than us. But what is highly significant about his story is that his extraordinary powers are only manifested *once he has left home*. It is only far away from the world of his fathers that he is super. Indeed, his only vulnerability is the possible encounter with a piece of home: Kryptonite, material from his home planet, is deadly to him.

One should not, of course, examine too closely the pseudo-scientific foundation of the Superman story. It is intended as entertainment and presupposes a good-natured suspension of critical faculties. But it does seem interesting that contact with a piece of home does not just render him an ordinary mortal, with powers commensurate with its gravitational force (even putting aside that it takes only a little piece, which would not recreate Krypton's gravity—or that earthlings seem entirely unaffected); rather, even a little bit of home is a deadly poison. It is as if Alexander Portnoy had found a way to escape Sophie completely, had developed his talents to an extraordinary degree, and then encountered a swatch from her dress—or a piece of her underwear. Or if Lloyd Warner's successful executives suddenly were subject to the gravitational pull of family and community and became unable to wheel and deal in glorious executive free flight. In a culture of outgrowing, one can rise to extraordinary heights, but the pull of home is deadly.

It is also noteworthy that Superman must be a loner. For all his power—and the sex appeal one would expect would emanate from it—he cannot let himself get too close to anyone. To do so would limit his effectiveness, his ability to accomplish his self-assigned mission. To care too much for any particular other—even if one is a superman—makes one vulnerable. So like many of his real-life contemporaries, who also strive to go "up, up, and away," Superman must assure that he is not too vulnerable to emotional blackmail or to ties that might prevent him from pursuing the tasks that are his destiny. Moreover, there is always in the unspoken background the sense that he is a stranger, an alien—again like so many moderns who have left their homes to conquer in other worlds. Superman can no more fit in among the lesser mortals of earth than could Portnoy among the softball players of Newark. The latter's loneliness is perhaps worse, though, since it is his own original world in which he is the alien, able to leap to heights they cannot reach but not to share their simple cameraderie.*

The Artist in a Culture of Outgrowing

Our view of the artist has similar echoes of outgrowing and growing away. The modern view of the artist is as the perpetual outsider, the one who refuses to fit in, who defies and disrupts all categories and breaks all molds. We forget that many of the greatest artists of former times had to court favor with the establishment and were literally "patronized" by the great princes; moreover, that they saw their role as one of expressing the highest ideals of their culture, of affirming rather than opposing the social order. To us the artist is in a natural, almost inevitable, opposition to the social order. He is a revolutionary, an adversary. As Lionel Trilling puts it, "Any historian of the literature of the modern age will take virtually for granted the adversary intention, the actually subversive intention, that characterizes modern writing—he will perceive its clear purpose of detaching the reader from the habits of thought and feeling that the larger culture imposes, of giving him a ground and a vantage point from which to judge and condemn, and perhaps revise, the culture that produced him."[25]

---

*That the recent movie versions of Superman have broken his isolation and let him respond to Lois Lane's charms instead of being strong, silent, and aloof, a John Wayne in cape and tights, is a hopeful sign. Perhaps—to anticipate a theme of the second part of this book—we are beginning to see the limits of attempts to achieve invulnerability through strength alone, without the leavening of human contact.

Moreover, even within the artistic world itself his role is seen as one of uprooting and challenging traditions not affirming them. It is a quite significant fact about our cultural life that it is essentially impermissable for a serious composer today to write a sonata in the style of Mozart. I am not referring to a sheer *imitation* of Mozart, the individual. We may rightly reserve our highest accolades for those who do more than imitate, but find instead their own distinctive voice. But Mozart had contemporaries whom we do take seriously, composers who if not his equal in genius were nonetheless not imitators but fellow creators working within the same musical tradition and style. We regard their efforts as legitimate artistic endeavors, whereas a contemporary effort along the same lines would be viewed as an anachronism. It might accord its composer some notoriety as a curiosity but would not be treated with genuine critical respect—regardless of how "good" it was. In our contemporary view, artistic creativity must manifest itself in something "new," something that "breaks new ground."

Sometimes this imperative is justified by the claim that the old vein has been thoroughly mined, that no more real creativity can be expressed in that form and that therefore it was necessary to move on and to invent new forms. For this reason, any new work in the older form is not a genuine creative effort but merely a clever imitation. Yet if a previously unknown work—or even an unknown *sheaf* of works—written by Mozart himself were to be discovered, it could readily be hailed as a masterpiece; the theorists of the worked-out-vein school (which dominates contemporary thinking) could easily accommodate to the idea that the vein did after all have one (or two, three, or even many) more gems still in it. A contemporary work, however, simply could not fit the bill. If it were discovered that the newly discovered masterpieces were actually written in 1979 by a living composer, they would instantly be transformed into mere curios, skillful examples of *ersatz* art but not entitled to the reverence that a "real" Mozart composition deserves.

There is another common justification as well for the snarling mastiffs that guard the forms of the past against their appropriation by contemporary artists: the idea that each form expresses the spirit of the times. Thus for a contemporary artist to employ an older form is to fail to be true to the reality in which he lives. It means that he is not fully in touch with and expressive of modern dilemmas and experiences, and it means as well that his effort to write in the style of a different age will lack the full depth of feeling that could come only with true immersion in the life and the problems of that age. However technically skilled his effort is, it will be hollow; it will be an attempt to imitate from outside rather than to express from within.

There is, I think, considerable truth in the idea that particular forms express the spirit of the age. The fragmented, tortured forms of so much contemporary art, music, and literature, for example, are no accident. They do indeed reflect something important about contempory life. But—writers like Christopher Lasch notwithstanding—fragmentation, dissonance, and pain are not the sum total of modern experience. The artist who seeks to express the spirit of the times can, if he is successful, enable us to grasp and symbolize emerging experiences and to achieve a valuable coherence in our vision of our lives. But if that coherence becomes too dominating and centripetal, if it pulls everything into it and leaves nothing free to roam in other directions, if we insist on a monolithic consistency, then we have perverted the value of the artist's gift; we have turned a blazing star into a frightful black hole. We best understand an expression of the spirit of an age if we don't insist that it is "the" spirit of the age.

Human experience—in any age—is too extraordinarily diverse to be captured by any one form. Moreover, however useful it is to understand how different values and dimensions predominated in different times and places—and even how they combined into unique configurations not quite replicated anywhere else—it is essential to recognize as well the enduring continuities in human experience. The classical sonata form indeed seems better suited to symbolize the predominant features of its age than of ours, but it is simply not true that it cannot express and convey emotions of the kind we experience today. We would be able to take little pleasure in Mozart's music now were this the case.

The reasons for what amounts to a prohibition on the use of earlier musical forms must be sought elsewhere. The prohibition does not reflect a rational recognition of the inability of earlier forms to serve the purposes of artistic creativity in our own day; rather, the prohibition itself (quite apart from the particular forms that at present do get accorded some degree of legitimacy) must be understood as an expression of the spirit of our age. Ours is an age in which a linear view of history (whether of art or of anything else), a preoccupation with progress, an insistence on change for change's sake, a rejection of traditional ways of doing things, and an expectation that newer will be better are all distinguishing features. The most characteristic of contemporary art forms is not any of the particular musical, artistic, or literary forms currently in vogue but the quest for the new itself, in whatever form that expresses itself. It is the effort to break with the past, the incessant striving not to sound, feel, or look like anything that has come before, the insistence that the entire way of life of each generation must be different from those before that most express the spirit of our civilization.*

This trend, of course, is not evident just in music. How often have we heard that "the novel" is dead? And how much museum space would be accorded to a contemporary painter — no matter how talented — whose works resembled Rembrandt's as much as did those of other venerated masters of his time and place whose works do find space in museums?†

The issue is, to be sure, a bit more complicated in the realm of the visual arts. The invention and perfection of photography does seem in some respects to have introduced a discontinuity which shut the trap door and made it impossible to "go back." The very meaning of painting in a "realistic" vein does seem to have been altered by the camera. The restless quest of painters to find new expressions for their talents, to represent their peculiarly visual insights and discoveries in a way that legitimates them as art, to assure that their unique gifts have not been made superfluous by technological developments — this questing and probing does seem to be in large measure a response to the peculiar dilemma posed for their art form in our time, and not simply an expression of our general cultural imperative toward progress, change, and emancipation from all tradition. Perhaps this is why the various forms of

*Consistent with what I said earlier, and with certain counterposing themes I will shortly be introducing, I do not want to be taken as saying this is *the* one true spirit of our age. That it be recognized as a powerful and central feature of our civilization is sufficient.

†I express it this way to defuse the argument that the similarity *per se* implies that the present-day artist's work is merely derivative or that it represents mere craftsmanship and not distinctive artistic creativity.

modernist experimentation in the visual arts have found so much wider an audience than equivalent efforts by writers and composers; to a far greater degree, the experimentation of visual artists is rational or meaningful, rather than an acting out of the premises of a throwaway culture.

For that is what we have — a throwaway culture; not just in our material lives but artistically as well. Like bottles, cans, newspapers, and countless other material artifacts, modes of artistic expression are readily discarded, cast upon a scrap heap whose very mass seems to convince us of the richness of our enterprises. The same spirit that lies behind the wrecker's ball laying waste to an architectural treasure in the name of economic growth can be perceived in the attitudes of contemporary artists and critics about the imperatives of newness. This is not to say that no works of art produced today are of enduring value, or that what has been of value in the past is totally rejected; we can still play or hear a classical sonata, even if we dare not compose one. But the breaking of forms and traditions has become a compulsion eating at the foundations both of art and of society. Whether new notions of creativity or new notions of economic well-being will appear first I do not know, but I expect that when they do, they will appear together.

Growth and Stagnation

It is difficult enough, in the face of American assumptions, to argue the case for a vital, fulfilled life without economic growth. In most of this chapter, however, I have gone even farther. Not only am I questioning economic growth, it seems, but also a number of more general cultural assumptions that have accompanied it — assumptions about progress, about outgrowing the strictures of the past, about the value of perpetual striving and the restless spirit. Is there an alternative to these features, which have seemed so central to the dynamic quality of Western culture, that does not imply stagnation? Or is there at least another way of defining and understanding these properties of our collective life that permits us to partake of its vitalizing waters without drowning in its ecological consequences?

In some form, this problem is an old one. An important concern of Aristotle was to prevent the realm of trade and

wealth-seeking from becoming independent of the constraints
of the traditional way of life of the city-state. What he feared
has in fact come to pass: an incessant expansion of needs that
leaves people both unable to be satisfied and too preoccupied to
participate in the public life of the community or to engage in
the intellectual and spiritual pursuits that are the real foundation of living well.[26]

But Aristotle's solution is not tenable today. Despite the
prescience of his warning about the unchecked expansion of the
economic realm and the individualistic pursuit of wealth, his
contemporary relevance is compromised by his profoundly conservative assumptions about "natural aristocrats" and "natural
slaves." Our own pursuit of the good life cannot rest on the
backs of others, nor can it justifiably be limited to an elite. The
possibility of *universal* access to a fulfilling way of life depends
on the very expansion of economic activity that Aristotle opposed. The success of our liberated economy has made universal well-being a realizable dream; the progress we have made in
multiplying our powers of production has introduced the possibility of leisure for higher pursuits for the populace at large.
Nonetheless, if the solution offered in an earlier and simpler
age is not viable today, the warning that echoes through the
centuries must still be heeded.

Our contemporary insistence (half-hearted though it is in
the mouths of many) that everyone must be enabled to live lives
of vitality and opportunity would have been unthinkable without a great deal of economic growth and progress and without
the supporting structures of thought that made it possible. But
today we are at a point (at least within this country and other
modern societies) where further "progress" of the sort we have
become used to may be beside the point. We face other problems today, though we persist in framing them in familiar
terms. Today our problem is not to produce more but to learn
to enjoy what we have produced. Inflation and OPEC are real
problems, to be sure, but they would be minor (and soluble)
ones were we to come to terms with the more basic ones. "A
chicken in every pot" used to be a slogan that implied a satisfying abundance. Now, in a *New York Times* article on how
Americans cope with inflation, we find quoted, with no apparent intent at irony, the plaint of a Long Island schoolteacher,
grown used to steak and roast beef, that "if I see chicken or
hamburger once more I'll scream."[27]

This schoolteacher and millions like her are victims not of economic deprivation but of a way of thinking that has pervaded our lives and made it extremely difficult to keep any perspective on what we want and have. We have by and large achieved the economic miracle of the chicken in every pot. We have made an end run around the limitations that Aristotle would have imposed on our economic life and have established an economic base for the masses well beyond that which Aristotle reserved only for his natural aristocrats. But now we must return to the serious questions he and others have raised through the ages, questions of the purpose and use to which we will put our abundance and our possibilities for leisure.

If we continue to multiply our desires and cultivate our discontents, we will have wasted our achievements. Hundreds of years of economic progress will leave us far less fulfilled than the Athenian of antiquity, whose possessions were meager compared to those of the average American slum dweller.* I do not suggest we return to the way of life of the Greeks. That is neither possible nor desirable (and togas would be hardly adequate in New York or London or Moscow in the winter). But I do think we need to question seriously our automatic valuation of restlessness, discontent, and striving. We need to explore the implications of the steady state, to find a new set of guiding images and metaphors suited for a culture that has *achieved* affluence rather than one that is pursuing it.

A steady state need in no way imply stagnation. As John Stuart Mill has written, "It is scarcely necessary to remark that a stationary condition of capital and population implies no stationary state of human improvement. There would be as much scope as ever for all kinds of mental culture and moral and social progress; as much room for improving the art of living and more likelihood of its being improved."[28]

We have learned to associate vitality with growth, but life is often characterized by a dynamic equilibrium. Early in our lives, of course, growth is dramatic; but for many years our bodies do not expand, nor do our powers. There is growth *within* the body, a constant replacement of new cells by old;

---

*H. D. F. Kitto points out that the Athenian citizen's leisure, rooted as it was in systematic inequality, depended as well on the limited material expectations of the Greeks. They valued social intercourse and the life of the mind more than material comforts, and did without one to gain the other. H. D. F. Kitto, *The Greeks* (Baltimore: Penguin, 1957).

there is continuous activity—building, rebuilding, assimilating nutrients, and so on—but the overall dynamic equilibrium serves to *maintain* the body for many years, not to promote further growth. Indeed, the body provides us with a metaphor for unchecked growth, and it is our most feared disease—cancer.

But we need not starkly pit growth and the steady state against each other, as the basis either for an economy or for our culture generally. We do, I think, have a great deal of work ahead of us in forging vital images of the steady state or of dynamic equilibrium, and it is essential that we wean ourselves from our *compulsive* allegiance to growth, change, and progress. But there is no reason we could not continue at the same time to pursue progress in certain delimited—but critically important—areas such as medical research or scientific research in general. Nor need we even completely abjure the search for new products and new material comforts. The point is not to put a lid on progress but simply to avoid making a fetish of it; to learn to be more content with what we have while still imagining what might be.

PART II

Beyond the Consumer Society

SIX

Economic Growth and Personal Growth

THE VALUES AND STRIVINGS associated with economic growth have brought us to an impasse. Their implications for the achievement of personal satisfaction, for the maintenance of an ecological balance, and for the body politic are discouraging. I wish here to begin to consider how we can extricate ourselves from the habits and assumptions I have been describing.

When I first began thinking about the issues addressed in this book, I was attracted to the idea that personal growth might be an alternative to economic growth as a guiding image both for individuals and for society as a whole. Striving for personal growth—the development of what has come to be called "human potential"—seemed more likely to accomplish what we seemed to be trying to do via economic growth: provide a fuller and more satisfying life for ourselves. Personal growth, moreover, seemed to have fewer harmful side effects. And the balanced, almost Manichaean opposition between economic growth and personal growth was aesthetically pleasing.

After a while, however, I began to feel uneasy. Playing off the two kinds of growth seemed a bit too glib. Gradually my thinking began to shift, and a notion almost the opposite of what I had originally intended took hold. I began to see that in many respects the idea of personal or psychological *growth* was but one more manifestation of a growth-obsessed society. The emphasis on growth, change, and self-betterment that one sees in much of Western psychology at least since Freud's time seemed to me part of the very thrust that had created our environmental crisis and our endless discontent. Rather than an *alternative* to economic growth, this psychology began to seem like a psychology *of* or *for* economic growth, filled with the same images of conquest and expansion, and the same highly individualistic assumptions that characterized the rest of our culture.

Several more years of wrestling with the deceptively difficult notion of "growth" in its varied contexts and guises has persuaded me that there is merit in both of these opposing views: Notions of psychological growth are at once an alternative to the destructive features of our culture and but one more expression of them. I shall focus in this chapter primarily on the latter, as a prelude to considering in the next chapter the more positive question of how a psychological orientation can be part of a system of values and orienting assumptions that can lead us in a more fulfilling direction. It is necessary to see how insidiously the growth ideology has intruded into what were thought of as efforts to challenge it if one is to have any hope of transcending it successfully.*

A Flawed but Significant Model

In the 1960s large numbers of young people engaged in an effort that is extremely relevant to the concerns being addressed here. Youths from the most privileged sectors of society seemed to be turning their backs on their birthright. The very people whom one would expect to be most eager to sustain the system in which they had grown up were withdrawing or opposing the system instead. Much of their protest and resentment was di-

---

*Other criticisms of the human potential movement and of the turn toward psychology as a framework for values and social change efforts, by Philip Rieff, Christopher Lasch, and others, will be addressed in Chapters Nine and Ten.

rected toward traditional political concerns such as civil rights and the war in Vietnam. Increasingly, however, they also expressed resistance to the values by which they were brought up and to the prospect of following in their parents' footsteps. The blandishments of the consumer society seemed to them pale stuff, and they felt an urge to seek a way of life that was richer, more meaningful, more deeply experienced. To many of them, life in middle class America seemed to be experienced through gauze. Their successful parents seemed sadly limited, out of touch with themselves and other people, object lessons to avoid following at all costs rather than models to emulate.

Their efforts were at once personal and political. The evils of war, racism, and oppression and those of the dulling and constricting of experience even among the supposedly advantaged were two sides of the same coin. In changing society, they wanted to save themselves; and in saving—in revitalizing—themselves, they sought to change society. The highly privatized version of personal growth and expanded consciousness that came under attack in the 1970s was—to use in a different context the apt phrase of psychoanalyst Heinz Kohut—a "disintegration product"; a fragment of a potentially integrated whole which has become misshapen and problematic as a consequence of frustration and of a hostile or unresponsive environment.

The offshoots today of the struggle in the Sixties to change and expand our consciousness have mostly lost their social and political cutting edge; they have become recreational activities to pursue *within* the present culture rather than challenges aimed at founding our lives on a different basis. Our bookstores today are still filled with self-help books and sections labeled "new age," "new consciousness," or "personal growth," but these offerings sit comfortably next to *How to Make a Killing in Real Estate*.

It is essential, if we are to find a way off the self-defeating treadmill described in the previous chapters, that we get back to the original impulses that motivated the various countercultural and personal growth efforts. For however much they were sidetracked, and whatever flaws they incorporated even from the beginning, they also did represent a serious effort to imagine and live out a modern alternative to the consumer way of life.

Though currently masked by the increased preoccupation with economic concerns that inflation has spawned,* the structure of discontent to which young people responded in the Sixties still underlies the organization of people's lives in our society. The personal and social change efforts launched then still provide a sounder guide to a workable and fulfilling way of life than do present genuflections to the bottom line and the supply side. Understanding how these efforts were hampered by flawed psychological assumptions can help us to see how something similar might be achieved on a more lasting and more widely appealing basis.

The Greening of America

The spirit of much of what was being attempted by the young rebels of the Sixties was captured well by Charles Reich in his best-selling ode to the movement, *The Greening of America*:

> There is a revolution coming. It will not be like revolutions of the past. It will originate with the individual and with culture, and it will change the political structure only as its final act. It will not require violence to succeed, and it cannot be successfully resisted by violence. It is now spreading with amazing rapidity, and already our laws, institutions and social structure are changing in consequence. It promises a higher reason, a more human community, and a new and liberated individual. Its ultimate creation will be a new and enduring wholeness and beauty—a renewed relationship of man to himself, to other men, to society, to nature, and to the land.[1]

The Greening of America had many flaws, which both reflected and exaggerated those of the movement it described. It was in many ways naive even at the time it was written and seems even more so from the present perspective. But for all this it is an extremely valuable document, both as a statement of the mood and minds of the young people who were struggling to transcend the culture in which they were raised and as

*As I will discuss in Chapter Eight, the present difficulties which the economic growth machine has encountered have actually strengthened the growth mentality that powers it. This reimmersion in materialism is, I think, a temporary state of affairs, the more complete elimination of which this book is attempting to hasten.

a guide to the errors that led that struggle to collapse into self-caricature. It is also worth examining as one of the most explicit statements of the idea that a change in consciousness can change society — an idea that is in some respects at the heart of this book, but that when pursued without an understanding of the *reciprocal* influences of consciousness and social structure on each other can be puerile and even dangerous.

Part of the impact of Reich's book was due to his impressive credentials. After graduating from law school, he had been a law clerk for a Justice of the Supreme Court, the most prestigious and sought-after position a young lawyer could attain. At the time of the book's writing he was a respected professor at Yale Law School. His book was widely criticized, but also widely read and discussed. It was serialized in *The New Yorker* and subsequently sold more than 2 million copies. It was a continuing topic of controversy in the Op Ed pages of *The New York Times* and other newspapers, and at least one other book appeared consisting entirely of commentaries on Reich's book. The title itself became one of those catchwords that are the nodal point for the intersection of numerous complex questions and controversies.

The basic theme of Reich's account of what was happening in America, reflected in the quotation above, was that a new kind of consciousness was developing out of the contradictions of the consumer society and that this new consciousness was destined to sweep over our society and bring with it a new and far better way of life. Reich called this new way of thinking and experiencing "Consciousness III," in contrast to Consciousness I (the rugged individualism of the frontier and of nineteenth-century capitalism) and Consciousness II (the mind-set of New Deal liberalism and its later permutations).

The terms "Consciousness I, II, and III" are Reich's, and the criticisms I shall make are directed toward his particular formulations. But it is well to keep in mind that one of the strengths of Reich's account is that it articulated the underlying assumptions of a large number of people who — without making their assumptions as explicit as Reich did — were engaged for a period in an important and massive social experiment. In this sense, the weaknesses of his arguments are as interesting as its strengths, since they are the shared weaknesses of a great many — and weaknesses which caused the premature dismissal of an effort that was closer to being sound and sensible than the present conventional wisdom.

NEW CONSCIOUSNESS AND OLD INDIVIDUALISM

Most of the flaws in the social and personal change efforts of the Sixties can be traced to an unwitting incorporation of many of the mainstream assumptions of the growth and consumer society these efforts were meant to transcend. Of particular significance in this regard was the persistence of highly individualistic modes of thought. As we saw in Chapter 2, examining Hirsch's account of the social limits to growth, a key element in the continuation of striving after economic growth beyond the point where it brings any real benefits is the tendency for each person to think only of what he can do to better himself as an individual in the competitive struggle. The cumulative effect of these individual decisions is negative for almost all, but when thinking in an individualistic, piecemeal way we cannot grasp the larger picture and fail to see alternatives. As a consequence we remain chained to the wheel of economic growth.

Reich and other proponents of the personal growth alternative wished to change this state of affairs, but to a far greater degree than they recognized they incorporate closely related individualistic assumptions. Reich states, for example, "Consciousness III starts with self. In contrast to Consciousness II, which accepts society, the public interest, and institutions as the primary reality, III declares that *the individual self is the only true reality*."[2] He does try to temper this rather bold statement, adding that "to start from self does not mean to be selfish" but rather implies "a radical subjectivity designed to find genuine values in a world whose official values are false and distorted."[*][3]

But selfishness is only part of the problem with thinking individualistically. Also at issue is the assumption, repeated again

---

*In this latter phrase he sounds like Herbert Marcuse and other members of the Frankfurt school of social analysis. Marcuse, however, called Reich a "revolutionary ostrich" and *The Greening of America* "the Establishment version of the great rebellion." See H. Marcuse, "Charles Reich as Revolutionary Ostrich," Philip Nobile, ed., *The Con III Controversy: The Critics Look at the Greening of America* (New York: Pocket Books, 1971), p. 17.

in Reich's very next sentence, that "human life is found as individual units." This is, of course, the classical assumption of liberal social theory, from Hobbes and Locke, through Adam Smith, to contemporary liberal and conservative economists. Apparently, in this respect, Consciousness III is precisely the sum of I and II, as our grade school arithmetic might have led us to expect.

Reich does try to complement this atomistic vision with a concern for community. " '[H]uman nature,' " he says, "was not necessarily always privatistic, grasping, competitive, materialistic. The 'average man' is descended from people who had the capacity to put community ahead of their immediate wants."[4] But his discussion of the relation between the individual and the community is problematic, a mixture of valuable insights and facile evasions. There is no real sense of sacrifice in Reich's account, no inner struggle over what to forgo for the sake of others or for the cause. No picture of immediate wants being put aside ever really emerges.

In fairness to Reich — and to those in the movement he describes — there are good reasons for this contradiction, and some of it is more apparent than real. He and they were aware that old-style radicals often dedicated themselves to their cause in ways that made them "puritanical, sour, righteous," and that the fruits of their sacrifices were often not a humane society but a further chain of still broader sacrifices. Bitterness breeds bitterness, and a revolution achieved at the expense of twisting the personalities of its leaders will twist those of the populace. Reich was essentially correct, I think, when he insisted that "dedication to the community is not to include means that do violence to the self" and that "to make [oneself] an object to serve the cause would be to subvert the cause."[5]

But where does meaningfully endured sacrifice end and "violence to the self" begin? When does sacrifice, dedication, or channeling one's desires and ambitions into a socially meaningful goal strengthen the personality and when does it make one "an object" to serve the cause? Reich largely evades these issues. In the euphoric glow of his rhetoric (again symbolic of the times and of the movement) age-old moral questions dissolve. There is for Reich no conflict between one's immediate desire for pleasure and one's dedication to a social cause; one's whole-hearted enjoyment *is* what one owes society, for that is what will lure others away from the destructive path they are following, a path based on an artificial and erroneous view of human needs. As the reader will sense, I am actually in sympathy with much of this view. But things are just not that simple. If we ignore the difficult and complex questions, then the valuable contribution such a perspective can make will be lost, as it partly (and, I think, temporarily) was in the 1970s.

Oddly, though Reich plays down too much the potential for conflict between one's commitment to social ends and one's duties to oneself, he at the same time sets apart the individual and his community or society to an excessive degree. The individual is portrayed as *influenced* by the society in which he lives, but he is not really perceived as an organic part of it. The "community" Reich envisages is a temporary and voluntary association of separate individuals. There is an implication that precisely because one's relationships and commitments are chosen, and not pursued in an automatic, half-sleeping trudge through a well-worn groove, they will be vital, deep, and meaningful. But the question of whether such thoroughly contingent commitments can really be so deep—or indeed whether individuals are ever quite as independent of their context as Reich assumes—is never really addressed.

Reich does seem to be searching for a vision of community in which each individual is related to each other in an organic and mutually enriching way. His intention is to describe a new kind of individualism that is not the opposite of commitment to the group but the natural outcome (and foundation) of such commitment. But the greater strength of the pole of traditional individualism is evident in his attitude toward political activity. "From the start of this book," Reich says, "we have argued that consciousness plays the key role in the shaping of society. . . . For culture controls the economic and political machine, not vice versa."[6] Reich has no real conception of a reciprocal influence between consciousness and context. As he stated earlier, the individual for him is ultimately the only reality, absolutely primary as a category of analysis. Change occurs only from inside out; change individuals and you change society. The causal relation is unidirectional. Radicals must see "that their real target is not a structural enemy, but consciousness."[7] Indeed, for Reich social structures hardly exist. Though he spends much effort articulating the psychic costs of our social

and economic systems ultimately the system is for him really a
phantom, a shared illusion that will disappear as soon as we all
stop hallucinating it.

Reich's emphasis on the consciousness that underlies political effort is in part a useful corrective to the purely institutional
emphasis in much political writing. But in shedding light on
one facet of a complex reality, Reich is led to misleading conclusions and foolish evaluations and predictions. Bob Dylan,
for example, according to Reich, "did what he wanted to do,
lived his own life, and *incidentally* changed the world; that is
the point that the [political] radicals have missed"[8] [italics
Reich's]. From the present vantage point it is clear that Dylan
did not change the world, intentionally *or* incidentally; he became very rich, like a good capitalist "superstar." Dylan did
have a political influence for a while—so long as he concentrated to a substantial degree on frankly political topics. When
he began to focus his efforts solely on himself, when his personal mystique became his primary preoccupation, the "greening" of Bob Dylan was the color of money.

CONSCIOUSNESS III AND THE ETHIC OF OUTGROWING AND GROWING AWAY

Reich also echoes mainstream American values—the values discussed in the past few chapters—in his emphasis on continual growth, change, uprooting, and rejection of tradition:
The "new generation constantly tries to break away from the
older, established forms which, in a changing society, must for-
ever be obsolete. . . . Accepted patterns of thought must be
broken; . . . Personal relations are entered into without commitment to the future; a marriage legally binding for the life of
the couple is inconsistent with the likelihood of growth and
change; if the couple grows naturally together that is fine, but
change, not an unchanging love, is the rule of life."[9] Reich advocates "escape from the limits fixed by custom and society, in
pursuit of something better and higher." In the continuing
search for personal growth, Consciousness III "lives in a never
ending state of tentativeness and uprooting."[10]

To be sure, some attitudes of this sort are essential if any
kind of radical change is to occur, especially a radical change in
consciousness itself. But Reich—like most of those who have ar-

gued that "personal growth" alone can change the world—does not recognize the tensions between such an outlook and the attitudes that make for a community that binds men and women together. He does not appreciate the contribution made toward our runaway materialism and fragmenting me-first individualism by the thoroughly negative attitude toward traditions and social structures he so easily endorses. As a consequence, the quotations from Reich in the paragraph above are almost indistinguishable from the picture in the last few chapters of the values that characterize the consumer society. Little wonder that in an entire book devoted to comments on Reich's work, the most favorable review came from an editorial in *Fortune* magazine.[11]

Probably one reason we can so readily accept the degree of mobility—both social and geographic—that characterizes our society is that we don't think of ourselves as rooted in a matrix of ties and relationships. Our view of the self is that it is "portable"; it can be carried around from place to place, fully intact, and then plugged in whenever necessary. In many societies, people have thought of their identities—if they thought of their identities at all—as inextricably bound up with their role and their context. They were part and parcel of the soil and the community from which they came. Our image is rather different. We feel society's influence but conceive of it nonetheless as something clearly external that impinges, much as a ball is influenced by a bat or a racquet, but remains a thing apart.

There is no dialectical tension in Reich's vision, no struggle to resolve the contradictions between the need for freedom and liberation and the need for links to a tradition and to values sunk so deep they are not optional, not obsolete simply because our feelings change. The growth Reich wants us to seek constantly, and to turn over everything in the quest for, is, to be sure, not simple material growth but a growth of consciousness. To a far greater degree than he recognizes, however, Reich's new consciousness demonstrates a structure of mind that is the essence of the capitalist spirit he thinks he decries. The cultivation of discontent, the worship of the "new and better," the throwaway attitude toward what has until this moment seemed serviceable—these are the mental structures that have supported our unprecedented industrial growth. Whether they are also—without a good deal of modification and tempering by other casts of mind — the structures whereby we can transcend the imperatives of material growth is questionable.

Psychoanalysis and Mainstream Assumptions

The errors of Reich and of the movement he depicted derived in large measure from the psychological assumptions on which their efforts were based. It was at root a *psychological* revolution that was being sought, a basic change in values, desires, and habits of thought. Its primary objective was not the gates of the White House, but the gates of perception. But far more than they recognized, Reich and the youth of the counterculture incorporated in an unexamined way the basic psychological tenets of the culture they tried to oppose. If a future collective effort to organize our lives in a more psychologically satisfying way is to have a chance of succeeding, we must take a closer look at the psychological assumptions that now prevail in our culture.

There are many psychologies in America, both implicit and explicit: the traditional and religious psychology of sin, duty, and obedience to authority; the academic psychology of stimuli and responses or of cognition and information processing; the rationalistic, calculating psychology of the economists; and others. But clearly no account of how we think psychologically can leave out the enormous impact of Freud and his followers. For most Americans, this is what is meant by "psychology," and it is this kind of psychology that almost all commentators have in mind when they say that we have become an increasingly psychologically oriented culture. Freud's influence has by now so pervaded our thinking that it is difficult even to be clear precisely which of our ideas are of specifically Freudian origin. What we take for everyday common sense is, far more than we recognize, a specifically post-Freudian common sense. (Indeed, it sometimes seems that the only people in our society who remain resolutely uninfluenced by Freud's ideas are the economists.)

Any effort to consider a psychologically oriented alternative to the culture of growth and consumerism must therefore come to terms with Freud. There is much in Freud that points to possibilities for a more satisfying alternative, but much also that can be used to affirm the status quo or that can lead astray the would-be explorer of new paths. In order to begin the task of sorting out what might be thought of as the transformative and the conservative possibilities in Freud's thought, it is important to consider how Freud's theorizing was shaped by some of the reigning assumptions of modern Western culture, even as it altered those assumptions in important respects.

It has been common to point out the influence on Freud's thought of the contemporary science dominant in his day—the emphasis on forces and energies, the commitment to explanations that were ultimately material, and so forth.[12] More important for present purposes, and less commonly remarked upon, was the influence of broader societal assumptions and values, in particular the influence of the prevailing economic assumptions in a society in which the economic dimension had assumed an unprecedented centrality. Freud did, of course, greatly alter the vision that was handed down to him. The rationalistic individualism of the economists became a very different kind of individualism in Freud's hands, and it goes without saying that much of Freud's work took a critical stance toward accepted cultural values and assumptions. But I wish to examine how certain features of Freud's thought nonetheless reflected prevailing conceptions and lent themselves to being used as an affirmation rather than a challenge to the evolving society of consumerism.

Freud's intent, of course, was not to affirm this trend in our culture—which was at any rate only slightly evident when he began his work; his career spanned a period of transition from an economic system based on restraint and delay of gratification in the service of capital accumulation to one based more on spending and the generating of desire. Nor was Freud's intent particularly to challenge this trend, though he may well have found distasteful those aspects of it that had already emerged in his lifetime. Rather, it is simply that the structure of some of his theoretical assumptions muted the challenge that a psychological orientation could have presented to the prevailing economically dominated value system. Moreover, his promethean stature, as well as the compelling imagery in his writing, made it difficult for later critics to escape the gravitational pull of his powerful ideas and reach a position outside the orbit of individualistic assumptions that characterized both Freud's work and the underpinnings of the growth and consumer society.

ECONOMIC AND PSYCHOLOGICAL INDIVIDUALISM

One of the key ways in which Freud's formulations paralleled the prevailing economic paradigm was in the highly individualistic cast of his thinking. Freud implicitly incorporated the atomistic vision that economics had bequeathed to us, but he essentially modernized it, putting it in a form that extended its scope and that had appeal even to many who were rather negatively disposed to related economic conceptions. The individualistic emphasis previously noted in Reich and the youth of the counterculture, for example, was an individualism that owed much more to Freud than to the earlier individualism which Freud transformed.

To see how Freud's thinking replicated changes in society that were rooted in the development of the economy, it is necessary to note an important contrast between modern industrial society and all those which came before. In previous societies, economic activities were always constrained by a broader set of guidelines and policies, implicit and explicit, spiritual and secular, but always subordinating the individual quest for profit to the goals and values of society. As numerous observers have described, this relationship has shifted in the modern era. Now, as the noted social and economic historian Karl Polanyi put it in *The Great Transformation*, "instead of economy being embedded in social relations, social relations are embedded in the economic system."[13] By the nineteenth century the legitimizing of the unconstrained pursuit of private gain had reached proportions that completely reversed traditional views of the rules and ideas by which life was to be conducted. The new society, Polanyi says, "was economic in a different and distinctive sense, for it chose to base itself on a motive only rarely acknowledged as valid in the history of human societies, and certainly never before raised to the level of a justification of action and behavior in everyday life, namely gain."[14]

As part of this transformation, a new conception of the individual developed as well. Over time, people came less to be perceived in terms of their context and their roles in society and more as autonomous actors who made independent decisions regarding personal gain and loss. By now, this view pervades not only economic activity but personal life as well. If the gains of marriage, for example, do not exceed the drawbacks, we are far more likely than people in prior eras to go our separate ways. Marriage for us is not primarily a matter of fulfilling a social role but rather a contract between two people, to be terminated when it no longer brings its expected rewards.

Society, from this perspective, becomes simply the sum of many separate decisions; rather than individual choices being understood as following from the rules of society, society itself was conceived of as the product of the choices of individuals. Whether it be the early social contract theories of Hobbes and Locke or the "primal horde" theory of Freud in *Totem and Taboo*, we are presented with a picture that at least hypothetically presents individuals as prior to society and an understanding of the nature of society based on an understanding of the choices or dynamics of individuals.

This conception of individual choices of profit or loss is evident in much of contemporary psychological thinking. B. F. Skinner's theories of reinforcement are variations of it, as are other learning theory accounts of instrumental behavior.[15] So too are the more rationalistic "exchange theories" of social psychology, which look at how interpersonal behavior is determined by the expectations of gain or loss of the participants in the interaction.[16] For these theories, understanding the separate decisions of individuals faced with varying consequences for different courses of action is—as it was for the classical economists—the methodological keystone.[17] Individuals separately responding to the possibilities of gain or loss occupy center stage.

This was true in important respects for Freud, too. HIs conception of the pleasure principle was, in effect, a biologically rooted version of this basic economistic paradigm: Each individual seeks to maximize pleasure and minimize pain by reducing the tension of drives whenever they build up. Other people, in this view, are conceived of as "objects" of the drive, resources as it were for the improvement of the individual's mental economy, rather than as participants in a shared pattern of interaction. At the center of Freud's analysis was always the single individual seeking his individual gratification.

To be sure, what the individual wanted was more complex for Freud than for the economists. We want many things at once, many of them in conflict with each other. The choices we make are compromises that tend not to embody fully *any* of the manifold particular desires; the motivational structure behind them is not revealed in any simple one-to-one way by the manifest choices themselves. And, of course, Freud did not believe that we made most of our choices either consciously or rationally. Self-deception was at the heart of Freud's theorizing. The "sovereign consumer" of the economist was in important respects not even master of his own house, according to Freud.

These features of Freud's analysis lend themselves to a powerful critique of many of the dominant assumptions that shape the consumer society and legitimate its institutions. At the same time, however, there are ways in which Freud's individualistic perspective blunts the critical possibilities that psychoanalysis potentially offers. The two sides are well illustrated in considering how psychoanalytic structures of thought bear on a key question in attempting to alter our present way of life: how "natural" or inevitable are the desires that characterize the consumer society?

CONSUMER DESIRES AND HUMAN NATURE

Defenders of growth and consumer values frequently argue that it is "human nature" always to want more, to want the kind of consumer goods we seem to find irresistible, and to resent taxes and other efforts to direct our resources toward communal needs and the needs of the less advantaged rather than toward private gain. In some ways the ideas of psychoanalysis present an important challenge to these assumptions. The psychoanalytic emphasis on the multiplicity of our desires, for example, and on the "compromise" nature of the final choices we make suggests that consumerist and growth-oriented choices are hardly the inevitable expression of a singular human nature that their proponents imply. So too does the psychoanalytic emphasis on self-deception undermine the claim that our choices in the market place are a clear expression of what we "want." Moreover, psychoanalytic insights into our vulnerability to anxieties about our bodies and our social selves reveal starkly the manipulations employed in advertising messages.*

---

*Unfortunately, though, those in the advertising industry have used psychoanalytic insights as shrewdly in their endeavors as the critics have in theirs—and thus far to greater effect.

Other aspects of Freud's thought, however, seemed to lend support to the idea of the naturalness of consumer desires. In his focus on the single individual and the vicissitudes of his desires, Freud implicitly minimized the role of others in shaping the nature of those desires and pointed instead to their being spontaneous upwellings from within (or at least "derivatives" of such spontaneous upwellings). Parents are, of course, powerful influences upon their children in Freudian theory, but their impact is largely described in terms of excesses in either gratifying or frustrating the child's desires, not in shaping the desires themselves. The desires that *get* gratified or frustrated are essentially "independent variables" in the theory. Thus a basic structure of Freudian thought, homologous to the mainstream assumptions of the growth and consumer society, is to view desire itself as a kind of prime mover, emerging from within one person rather than from transactions with others.* Such a structure of thought undermines or at least limits the potential Freudian critique of the manipulative role of advertising.

Implicit affirmation of our present social and economic arrangements as reflections of "human nature" also seemed to come from Freud's Hobbesian assumptions about our deepest instinctual urges and characteristics—that we are at root selfish, brutish, concerned with our immediate pleasures, and that concern for the welfare of others or the pleasures of joining with others in common purpose are secondary or derivative in our nature. To be sure, Freud valued highly these "derivative" characteristics, and much of his work—both in the therapy of individuals and, implicitly, as it bore on broader societal concerns—can be seen as in the service of strengthening them. Nonetheless, Freud's pronouncements about our instinctual depths seemed to provide scientific support to those who equated selfishness and the profit motive with "human nature." In the light of these pronouncements, those who challenge eco-

---

*There is some impact by other people on the content of experienced desire in the psychoanalytic account; they influence just what "derivatives" are able to rise to consciousness, and in that sense they affect the content of experienced desire. This is somewhat equivalent to the "substitution-effect" of the economists, in which external constraints such as higher prices lead to a substitution of tea for coffee or of a subcompact for a large gas-guzzler. In both views, however, the underlying structure of desire is untouched; the real world affects only the degree and kind of compromises that must be endured.

nomic growth assumptions can appear to be naive or unwilling to face facts.

Most laymen, however, are not aware of the highly speculative nature of Freud's instinct theories. On many matters Freud ventured well beyond what could in any way be determined by scientific inquiry. Alternative theories were offered by later psychoanalytic thinkers that were just as consonant with careful observation and that did not make grasping selfishness seem so inevitable and natural.*

No doubt the ascendancy of Freud over his challengers was to a substantial degree a function of both his priority and his consummate powers as a thinker and a writer. But part of the triumph of Freud's version of psychodynamics, I would suggest, is attributable to the way in which—however much he also challenged comfortably held assumptions—he presented a powerful new version of what were in large measure well-rooted cultural myths of original sin and primal, individualistic selfishness, myths even more central to maintaining the status quo than were the myths of conscious and rational choice that he did challenge.

Is "Self-Actualization" an Alternative?

The human potential movement was to a substantial degree conceived out of critical responses to psychoanalysis, which tended to be seen by human potential proponents as conservative and needlessly pessimistic.† The movement is of particular relevance to our concerns here, because it was closely associated with a conviction that a middle-class consumer society produces a constricted and psychologically impoverished way of life. Although the work of some of its leading figures can be traced back several decades, the movement coalesced and gained momentum in the 1960s and overlapped in many ways with the youth movement Charles Reich described. But the human potential movement was not just a youth movement. Some of its

---

*Some of the implications of these "neo-Freudian" theories will be considered in Chapter Nine.

†Human potential proponents are also opposed to behaviorism and describe themselves as a "third force" in psychological thought, in contrast to both psychoanalytic and behavioristic traditions.

leading figures—Carl Rogers, Abraham Maslow, Fritz Perls, and others—were people of middle age and more, with advanced degrees and often established reputations. Many who flocked to the various "growth centers" that sprang up or who participated in marathon sessions or sensory awareness groups were also "established" in jobs, marriages, and middle-class communities. Some were looking for a way to reconstitute their lives rather totally, others had a more limited interest or commitment, but they shared at least some sense of seeking an alternative to a way of life that, for all its material comforts, had become gray and uninspiring.

Clearly there was a strong thread of social criticism woven into the theorizing and the practices of the human potential movement. Yet in important respects its critical potential has been limited by its adoption of many of the same mainstream assumptions that seeped into psychoanalysis. The human potential movement too has succumbed to an individualistic imperative that has narrowed its possibilities for social renewal and at times has led it into absurdity and self-caricature. It is necessary to be clearer about how this has happened if we are to extract the liberating possibilities in the search for personal growth or self-realization.

Abraham Maslow seems an exemplary figure to consider in this regard, in both the positive and negative senses of exemplary. A psychologist of substantial reputation in the academic world as well as a leading theorist of the movement, Maslow was universally perceived as sincere and dedicated. Unlike the self-styled gurus or the profit-seeking franchisers of personal growth packages, Maslow was a serious researcher who offered not quick cures but reflections on the process of achieving maximum self-development. He had pursued his inquiries long before they became fashionable, and his ideas continue to be influential both in the academic world and in the continuing personal growth movement. At the same time, Maslow's writings reveal very clearly the pervasiveness and the limitations of individualistic assumptions even as he struggled to free himself of them (and thought he had).

Maslow claimed that his ideas were misunderstood by his critics. The term "self-actualization," he lamented, had the

. . . unforeseen shortcomings of appearing (a) to imply selfishness rather than altruism, (b) to slur the aspect of duty and of dedication to life tasks, (c) to neglect the ties to other people and to society, and the dependence of individual fulfillment upon a "good society," (d) to neglect the demand-character of non-human reality, and its intrinsic fascination and interest, (e) to neglect egolessness and self-transcendence, and (f) to stress, by implications, activity rather than passivity or receptivity. This has turned out to be so in spite of my careful efforts to describe the empirical *fact* that self-actualizing people are altruistic, dedicated, self-transcending, social, etc.[18]

For Maslow, as for other growth movement leaders, there seemed to be little conflict between the ethic of self-actualization and the necessity of human beings to cooperate, to find ways to dissolve their individual strivings in the imperative of group life. Yet their own descriptions suggest that matters are more complex than that. The authentic person, says Maslow, "resists enculturation. He becomes more detached from his culture and from his society. He becomes a little more a member of his species and a little less a member of his local group."[19] Now, in some respects this is a good thing. Identification with the species as a whole rather than just with one's own society may well be a prerequisite for lasting peace. Erik Erikson has described how "pseudo-speciation" contributes to international violence precisely by disrupting our identification with the entire species.[20] But whether such an identification can be achieved *in place of* identification and involvement with the immediate and concrete human beings of our everyday life seems to me rather questionable and hardly a simple empirical finding of Maslow's investigations. Maslow suggests about his description of the authentic person that "most sociologists and anthropologists will take this hard."[21] Indeed they might, for it reveals the degree to which Maslow denies the importance of being rooted in a culture (at least for those whom Maslow regards as demonstrating the "human potential" we should strive to release for all). This acultural, individualistic point of view would make sociology and anthropology historical curios from the era when we thought that people lived in cultural contexts.

According to Maslow, there is "uniform agreement among biological theorists in considering increasing autonomy and independence of environmental stimuli as *the* [his italics] defining characteristics of full individuality, of true freedom, of the whole evolutionary process."[22] Here again, Maslow views the world through extraordinarily individualistic lenses. The study of evolution as a process of adaptation to specific environments, the ethological perspective in the study of behavior, which stresses that real understanding can be attained only by understanding behavior *in context* — apparently these and other evidences of the importance to biologists of *not* viewing individuals as independent of their environment fail to get through Maslow's perceptual net.

It is not surprising that many of those who read Maslow's descriptions of self-actualization have difficulty in seeing how his conception of it is consistent with a deep concern for and interest in others, a commitment to the improvement of society, or a willingness to view oneself as rooted in an ecological context that requires care and restraint. Notwithstanding his disclaimers that his critics misunderstand him, the radically individualistic, acultural cast to Maslow's thought does repeatedly point to his holding an ideal for people that, despite good intentions, implies a loosening of the bonds of affect and mutual need crucial for the functioning of a humane social order. Maslow fails to recognize the degree to which we depend upon each other for our well-being. The growth of the personality, for him, is achieved by permitting behavior to be emitted from deep within, "radioactively."[23] The behavior of self-actualizers is "unlearned, created and released rather than acquired."[24] In the later stages of growth "the person is essentially alone and can rely only upon himself."[25] Consciousness III circles back to join Consciousness I, as it were, and Maslow becomes (like other leaders of the human potential movement) a kind of Adam Smith of the senses, a psychological proponent of laissez-faire and radical individualism.

Self-actualizing individuals are depicted as autonomous, self-directed, heeding a call from within. "Far from needing other people, growth-motivated people may actually be hampered by them." They have a "special liking for privacy, for detachment and for meditativeness." They are "self-sufficient and self-contained."[26] Their perception of other people, based on "desirelessness" and "choiceless awareness," is, says Maslow, "the kind of untangled and uninvolved, detached perception that surgeons and therapists are supposed to try for and which self-actualizing people attain *without* trying for" [italics Maslow's].[27]

I would seriously question whether the psychotherapist should really try for the same kind of detachment as the surgeon; but even the therapist's degree of detachment—much less the surgeon's—would hardly be pleasant in a spouse or a friend, or indeed in anyone with whom one must engage in ordinary social intercourse. Attaining detachment without trying is an occupational disease of some therapists, but it is hardly an ideal for which the human race should strive.

The failure to appreciate the degree to which our behavior is always in relation to a context—and the view that to be so rooted is equivalent to being conformist, "other-directed," and so on—leads Maslow to a fallacious dichotomy between the authentic person and the person who is a slave to the environment. It leads him as well to an unsound (though extraordinarily widely cited) notion of the hierarchy of human needs. According to Maslow, the needs for safety, belongingness, love relations, and respect are lower needs, deficiency needs, and produce considerable dependence on the environment. When all these needs are satisfied, then the "higher" needs, the growth needs, come to the fore. The person becomes markedly less dependent on others, and his pursuit of self-actualization proceeds by simply letting all the creativity within emerge untrammeled. Such a view of what is "higher" and "lower" in human nature—in which belongingness and love relations, for example, are mere "deficiency needs"—can encourage an ethic that is markedly asocial. If adopted by large numbers of people, it could contribute—as our present less idealistically packaged individualism does—to a lack of concern with such mundane things as returning cans or bottles for recycling or checking the emission controls on one's auto.

Even for the single individual who attempts to live by such a view, serious problems are likely, because the hierarchy as Maslow presents it is really fallacious. To begin with, in distinguishing between "deficiency needs" and "being needs" Maslow asserts that the person motivated primarily by the former must change "himself to fit the external situation. *He* is the dependent variable; the environment is the fixed, independent variable."[28] This description is in fact strikingly consonant with those of the behaviorists, so derided by Maslow and other human potential proponents. For that small minority who have supposedly reached the level of growth motivations, this description is said not to hold true, but for the vast majority of us mired in the mundane search for belongingness, love relations, or respect, apparently Maslow thinks that radically environmentalistic theories are quite sufficient. In fact such descriptions are not at all adequate for describing the everyday behavior of most people.[29]

Maslow's failure to recognize the way in which people mutually determine each other's world — along with his basic vision of people as isolated monads to whom other people and the environment are radically external — leads him as well to another error. Maslow seems at times to assume that the lower needs are filled once and for all, that one satisfies them and then simply goes on to bigger and better things. The self-actualizing individual, "by definition gratified in his basic needs, is far less dependent, far less beholden."[30] It is as if lower needs were a hole or vessel to be filled up and then ignored. Though occasionally noting (for the purpose of making invidious comparisons to growth needs) the periodic nature of many of our needs, the cycle of seeking, of satisfaction and rest, and then of renewed desire and seeking, Maslow seems to forget this when discussing his *Ubermenschen*. But their "lower" needs are not in fact taken care of and no longer an issue. The needs for love, respect, and belonging — and all the more for food or shelter — can *seem* in the background so long as they are continuing to be satisfied. But they will continue to be satisfied only if the conditions for their satisfaction continue. The person who decides he already *has* love, respect, and community, and who therefore feels no longer "dependent" on others and able to pursue his inner promptings, may discover that if his relations with others are not continually attended to he develops again a press of deficiency needs and must forgo his place at the top of the hierarchy to return to the basics with the rest of us. It may not be *literally* true that "we never outgrow our need for milk," but symbolically at least it seems to be.

EXTREME NOTIONS OF SELF-DETERMINATION

Throughout the human potential movement, emphasis is placed on such concepts as the natural urge to grow, innate self-actualizing tendencies, and other notions which present change as a spontaneous upwelling of something from within the organism. One has the sense that if one just removes certain blockages it will pour forth like vintage champagne. There is little room in such a vision for the shaping role of culture and society. Society may be seen as *blocking* these spontaneous processes—and thus some critique of society may issue from such assumptions—but once the presumed block is removed, social variables recede far into the background. There is little sense of the continuing feedback and interplay between person and social context that is so crucial in determining our sense of ourselves, our goals, and our values.

Stephen Appelbaum, a respected psychoanalyst who has written a sympathetic account of his explorations of the human potential movement, observes that in that movement "people are the sole creators of their own destiny; they are as they choose to be."[31] The consonance between this extreme notion of individual responsibility and the right-wing rationales for cutting back on welfare, national health care, and other forms of assistance to the needy seems ironic. So much of the impetus for the human potential movement came out of the atmosphere of criticism of American society engendered by the Vietnam War and by concern over racial injustice and poverty. The tendentious claim that helping people is crippling and that "self-reliance" is essential; the view of people on welfare as lazy and shiftless—this harsh, ungenerous vision seems a far cry from the sunny pronouncements of the growth movement. In the structure of its assumptions, however, are some surprising (and almost certainly unintended) parallels.

Perhaps less surprising is the parallel between that ethic—an ethic, after all, strongly encouraged by an Administration cozily tied to big business—and the views promulgated by est, the McDonald's of the human potential movement, with thriving branches from coast to coast. There is much that is troubling in the actual practices of est. One demonstration session I attended out of curiosity looked as if it was scripted by George Orwell. But what is even more disturbing—because it is likely to permeate a wider audience than is willing to submit to est's abuses, and indeed is likely to become part of our language and reinforce already strong cultural trends without even being identified as originating in est—is an extreme individualism that might make even Ayn Rand blush. This philosophy is effectively dissected by Michael Rossman in his chronicle of radicalism and the growth movement, *New Age Blues*.

Rossman's picture of est is particularly interesting both because he has studied it closely and because he initially approached est with a quite positive bias and came to his critical
conclusions painfully and reluctantly. Taking as an example a
woman holding a menial job in a sexist organization, Rossman
contrasts the est approach with one in which the woman, realiz-
ing her dissatisfaction and the role into which she had been
cast, not only complains to her superiors but shares her feelings
with other women in the firm and attempts to organize for collective action:

> An EST woman would instead be more likely to see herself as
> responsible for whatever she experienced; and set out positively
> to prove that *she personally* could be trusted to do the more cre-
> ative and rewarding work, and were worthy of this as well as of
> lesser evidences of respect. So much, so good: admirable, neces-
> sary. But it stops here. In this task she would be competing,
> perforce, in a male-dominated system and its terms, and if suc-
> cessful, would indeed set a quiet example of nominal desexism
> . . . but she would also be leaving her old share of the shitwork
> to be done by some other woman, less talented, responsible,
> and enlightened, for whom she of course would bear no respon-
> sibility. Nor would she bear responsibility for changing this *sit-
> uation*, as distinct from any particular employee's state, if she
> rose to be among its administrators, since her very rise would
> testify that the situation was okay as it was.
>
> All very neat: no fuss, no furor, no action undertaken on
> any basis other than through private initiative and means and
> with private intents; no challenge to the basic scheme that di-
> vides work and workers into superior and inferior classes, nor
> indeed any questioning of any social arrangement that might
> help people *together* to be conscious of and govern their collec-
> tive condition and work. Instead, the myth of society as a col-
> lection of separate atoms, preserved and reinforced by follow-
> ing the basic rule: *get yours*. Get whatever you can however you
> can, but get yours and get it first.[32]

Est has been described by Peter Marin, in his influential essay on "the new narcissism," as "the logical extension of the human potential movement."[33] The preceding discussion of the
movement in this chapter suggests that in certain respects this is
sadly true. But est is also a miscarriage of the movement, in
which all the socially regressive features have flourished and the
truly valuable parts have atrophied. If the original hopes of the

movement are to be realized, it will require going beyond the limiting perspectives highlighted here.

A Note on Individualism and Conformism

Throughout this chapter I have stressed the limiting effects of individualistic assumptions both in society at large and in psychological theorizing. I have suggested that ours is a problematically individualistic culture and that the incorporation of like assumptions into our thinking about psychological matters has prevented the effective establishment of an alternative to a life geared around consumerism and economic growth. This conclusion seems at odds with a number of important critiques that have appeared since the 1950s. Represented perhaps most significantly in the work of David Riesman[34] and of Erich Fromm,[35] the claim has been made that we have in fact shifted from a society of rugged individualism to one characterized by other-directedness and conformism. Riesman, for example, says that the other-directed child, which he saw as the emerging personality type in our culture, "is taught at school to take his place in a society where the concern of the group is less with what it produces than with its internal group relations, its morale."[36]

I believe that this characterization was premature and remains today largely unrealized. Our present national preoccupation with "productivity"—contrasted with the failure of Jimmy Carter's attempt to characterize our difficulties as a "malaise," that is, a *psychologically* rooted problem—indicates where our underlying priorities remain. To be sure, the world of the corporation (as the world of the small town before it) does require a certain conformity. But it is a superficial conformity, which is simply the *vehicle* for effective individual advancement and competition.

Even in the university world in which Riesman was immersed, loyalty to the group and group goals was hardly the norm. The readiness of academics to move from one university to another as better opportunities presented themselves; the eagerness with which professors ran off to conferences, conventions, or various sojourns in Washington instead of teaching their classes; the clear priority they gave to their own efforts to publish over spending time with their students; the competition and vying for status among faculty members—these things were widely complained about by students or commented on in novels and journalistic accounts. It is only the tightening job market in the academic world, the drying up of grants, and the pressures of university administrators for greater "productivity" in processing students through the system that have for the moment reversed these trends to some degree.

In the less idealistic world of the corporation, what I am pointing to is even clearer. Self-interest remains the very religion of the corporate world. As Walter Prescott Webb has cogently put it,

> The rugged individualists of the late nineteenth century . . . were in perfect harmony with the society in which they operated because every individual in that society was acting as they were, and hoping to follow their examples. The rugged individualist has now disappeared within the business corporation; the little fellows have before them no such living examples, and have given up all expectation of being giants. Personality has been submerged by organization on all sides. But what remains in the business corporation is the old motive of profit, the old method of competition, the old philosophy of a free and unfettered world. In a sense the business corporation has *institutionalized* the old individualism and is seeking to preserve it especially for itself as a survival from an extinct period.[37]

The milieu in which corporate employees are immersed, the goals and actions they must support, represent the most primitive kind of blindered individualism. It is not larger purpose that they encounter, not a concern with goals beyond the self or with the kind of self-enhancement that involves mutuality and cooperation; it is narrow self-interest itself writ large. From Love Canal to the army of lobbyists seeking to restrain health and safety legislation what is evident is (not even terribly enlightened) self-interest.

Even in the many instances where the imposition of restraints on *all* producers would leave the corporations in a similar competitive position to what they currently experience without the regulation—and where the health of workers or the air and water that even the executives breathe and drink would be greatly improved—the ideological commitment to an atomistic, asocial vision leads to opposition. With even a shred of understanding of the need for *mutual* efforts to produce many important individually enhancing results, corporate leaders would positively *crave* legislation that required all manufacturers to dispose of wastes properly, to protect workers from cotton dust or other hazards, even to provide genuine opportunities to women and minority workers. The social bonus in each case is enormous, and the consequence for each corporation in terms of its ability to compete with other corporations (facing similar requirements) is practically nil. Yet such legislation, if it is achieved at all, is usually done so only in the face of enormous resistance (which may then turn to apparent advocacy at the late stages in order to turn a defeat into a "public relations" victory).*

To be sure, some degree of cooperation within the corporation is needed to pursue effectively these anti-cooperative efforts in the world outside. But one would not expect the sensitive employee to miss the contradiction between what is being asked of him and what his cooperation is supposed to be in the service of. And there is much evidence that in fact the message has come through loud and clear—from the executives who change corporations when a tempting offer arises to the workers who manage always to be "sick" just before or after the weekend.[38] Indeed, even the pervasive pattern of moving out to move up within the corporation—from the Dallas office to the Denver office to the Atlanta office—reflects the same structure of commitments; here one stays within the abstraction called Gulf or Coca Cola or Westinghouse, and even is doing what is deemed to be in the best interest of the corporation, but one severs one's connections to those who have actually been one's co-workers. So much for internal group relations and morale.

VARIETIES OF INDIVIDUALISM

"The term 'individualism'," Max Weber noted, "embraces the utmost heterogeneity of meanings."[39] Steven Lukes, in a recent book-length review of the concept, portrays more than a

---

*Regulation is, of course, sometimes actively sought when it is perceived to be in the interests of the corporation (e.g., airlines that fought deregulation). But again these interests tend to be defined very narrowly—in terms of "the bottom line," not of being able to carry on business while sharing in a social bonus of cleaner air or greater racial harmony.

dozen basic conceptions of individualism, with many variations within each.[40] He notes that the term has been used by the right as a critique of the left and vice versa. Clearly it is necessary for me to place my own use of the term in the context of these varied uses.

Some of the ways in which the term "individualism" has been used are quite consonant with the value system for which this book argues. Others are rather close to the opposite, pointing to assumptions very closely linked to the untrammeled pursuit of economic growth, the vain pursuit of happiness through buying, and the destructive social consequences of such pursuits.

It seems to me, however, that despite the multiplicity of meanings, one can distinguish between two broad classes of referent for the term whose implications are rather divergent. In this I follow Lukes to some degree, but with a somewhat different intent and organization. On the one hand are such notions as self-development, the dignity and worth of the individual, the valuing and attending to our uniqueness and personal qualities and—particularly relevant in the present context—a concern with the subjective experience of individuals as the primary criterion for evaluating personal choices and social policies.

These meanings of individualism are not the ones I have criticized. They seem to me not merely harmless but positive and essential. Individualism in this sense has been responsible for a number of things I hold precious, such as the defense of civil liberties and the commitment—however incomplete it still is in our country—to assuring that the elderly, the handicapped, and others who are disadvantaged have an opportunity to lead full and enriching lives. Moreover, the very ideas of the inviolable dignity of the person or the full development of each individual's capacities and experiences are at the core of what I value and at the heart of what this book is about. In the sense of embracing such ideas and commitments, it would be correct to say that I am an individualist.

But there is a second cluster of meanings to the term that are what I refer to when I object to individualism and relate it to the social trends I am criticizing. These are the meanings that are often referred to under the rubric of competitive individualism or possessive individualism.[41] The idea that each individual should pursue his own private interests without regard to the needs of the community, that community needs will be taken care of automatically if that occurs; the idea that people's wants are self-generated and autonomous, not shaped by social forces; the idea that people have a right to keep what is "theirs" and the denial that differentials in wealth are a function of particular social arrangements rather than a simple matter of hard work, initiative, or capacity; the effort to solve social problems by an accumulation of separate individual choices and a suspicion of collective efforts; the failure to recognize how much individual well-being or individual commitments depend on a social matrix and on feedback from others—it is these kinds of individualistic thinking that I find troublesome, not a concern with individual liberty, fulfillment, uniqueness, or intrinsic worth. In some respects it might be best if the same word were not even used for the two clusters, if perhaps the first were designated as a concern with *individuality* and the second as *atomism*. Years of usage, however, have made it difficult to avoid using the more ambiguous word "individualism."

Moreover, there is a sense in which the two divergent clusters do seem to be related and in which the problematic kinds of individualism have frequently pervaded our understanding of individual fulfillment and individual rights. Alisdair MacIntyre has argued that

> . . . the essence of individualism is not so much to emphasize the individual rather than the collective—whether methodologically or morally—as to frame all questions according to an ostensible antithesis between the individual and the collective. Those who continue to base their thinking on this false antithesis even if . . . they champion the claims of the collective against the individual, remain within the basic categories of individualist thought and practice.[42]

MacIntyre's remarks are directed toward Durkheim, but clearly this "false antithesis" is characteristic of Freud as well, and of the other thinkers discussed in this chapter. So long as our conception of individuals stresses autonomy, self-generation, and internal dynamics—and so long as we conceive of these notions as the only alternative to seeing people as the helpless product of social forces or mere slaves of stimuli or class positions, we will fail to understand the real basis of fulfillment and integrity. Without a transactional understanding that integrates our existence as separate individuals and our membership and participation in a web of social relations, and that sees them as but two aspects of the same unity, we are likely continuously to alternate between equally unsatisfactory solutions without achieving what we seek.

SEVEN

New Alternatives

THE CONSUMER WAY OF LIFE is deeply flawed, both psychologically and ecologically.* It fails to bring the satisfactions promised and its side effects are lethal. In the last chapter I considered some of the efforts to find an alternative way of life that emerged in the 1960s, and I found them unsatisfactory in important respects. I wish here to indicate at least the outlines of what I regard as a more promising alternative.

The basic thrust of what I am trying to point toward is probably already evident to the reader, both from my criticisms of our present way of life and from my dissatisfactions with the alternatives of the 1960s. I would like to see less emphasis on the economic dimension of our lives—growth, productivity, the creation of needs for more and more goods, the "bottom line"—and more on the psychological: the richness of subjective experience and the quality of human relationships. But I believe that a psychological emphasis can succeed only if the psychological premises on which it is based are less individualistic,

*As discussed at numerous points throughout this book, our present way of life is unsatisfactory on ethical grounds as well; those fruits it does provide are distributed unevenly and unjustly. In focusing here on the psychological and ecological I am not slighting the ethical. The changes I would like to see bear on issues of distribution as well.

Most of us are aware of feeling one way about ourselves with some people and quite differently with others. Meeting someone who laughs at our jokes can change very radically how we feel about ourselves when with that person. Many theorists concerned with personality development and psychological distress and well-being pay lip service at most to this obvious and crucial characteristic of human experience, presenting instead a picture of our fate as sealed in our early years and largely impervious to everyday experiences. By overestimating the effect of "internal" factors in determining our proclivity to experience pleasure or distress, they discourage us from giving serious attention to crucial influences upon our experience.

It is often noted that the superego is soluble in alcohol. Its supposedly "internalized" influence also can diminish enormously simply by being away from all the various signals and sanctions that are in fact required to maintain it. That is why so many Americans experience being in Paris as a liberating experience while the French they envy find more freedom in New York.

But it is not simply a matter of "away is better." There are also variations in the mores of different cultures and subcultures that make some more likely than others to be facilitative for most people. Some firms, university departments or neighborhoods seem to have a warming esprit de corps, offering a much greater likelihood that someone *will* laugh at your jokes, regard your effort as valuable and tell you so, or be interested in what you have to say. In other settings you feel less witty, somehow everyone else seems to be doing something more important than you are, and things that come to mind to say seem boring. Often those immersed in one or the other of these situations are not even aware of its properties until they move to another and experience the difference, often a difference not only in how one is treated but in how one finds oneself treating others.

The Centrality of Values and Basic Assumptions

Neither the individual's values nor those of the system are primary; each determines the other in continuous reciprocal interaction. People in a system with competitive values tend to become competitive, and in so doing they keep the system competitively oriented. Similarly, when people are accepting or act cooperatively they help to create or maintain a warm or cooperative system, which in turn brings out in them further accepting or cooperative behavior.

In a large system, such as a society or a corporation, the properties of the system predate the participation of the individuals currently part of it. These individuals' behavior in the system is largely shaped by the prevailing climate as they are inducted into it. But it is nonetheless the case that the properties of the system cannot be maintained unless the *people* in it maintain it. If, because of whatever experiences they encounter — a shortage, a common experience of disappointment, even a persuasive book — they begin to change their values and assumptions, they will perforce begin to change the system as well. In mutually prompting each other and in interacting with others who have not yet changed their view, they can begin to create and to stabilize a new structural arrangement with different consequences for everyone within the system.

Throughout this book I have focused most of all on values and basic assumptions. In my approach to change, too, I am most concerned with these ideational or psychological influences. I am pleased to notice that even hard-headed economists of widely differing persuasions have also recognized the importance of the ideational element. Milton Friedman, in one of the few passages where I find myself in agreement with him, pointed out "the importance of the intellectual climate of opinion, which determines the unthinking preconceptions of most people and their leaders, their conditioned reflexes to one course of action or another."[1] And John Maynard Keynes wrote that he was "sure that the power of vested interests is vastly exaggerated compared with the gradual encroachment of ideas."[2]

For all the concrete changes I would like to see in our society, it is in many ways values and modes of thought that I wish most to address. This is not to argue, as Charles Reich and others did in the 1960s, that changing the consciousness of individuals is sufficient; traditional political efforts and the creation of appropriate institutions and structures is crucial if a change in consciousness is not to be merely an ephemeral change in style while the substance remains unaltered. But I do believe that *without* a change in values and grounding assumptions political and institutional changes will themselves be superficial and leave the basic structure of life unchanged.

There do seem to be a number of features of contemporary capitalism that are particularly closely linked with the problems addressed here—for example, the preponderant emphasis on the profit motive; the deliberate generation of needs; the apparent requirement of growth to keep the system running at all well; the encouragement of greed and the rationalizations about self-reliance that discourage mutual aid. These characteristics are hard to reconcile with the kind of life I would like to see. But socialism alone—that is, a change in who owns the means of production without a concomitant change in values and consciousness—is clearly not a panacea.* Developments in the Soviet Union and in Eastern Europe demonstrate rather unambiguously that ending private ownership alone does not in itself change values and consciousness. Without the latter kind of change, the growth and consumer way of life persists, perhaps less efficiently and effectively, but not for want of wanting.

As Philip Rieff has put it, "Both American and Soviet cultures are essentially variants of the same belief in wealth as the functional equivalent of a high civilization. . . . The answer to all questions of 'what for' is 'more.' "[3]

I do think that some shift in the direction of communal ownership will have to occur, as well as a rather substantial turn away from the profit motive as the main guiding force in the economy and in the decisions of responsible individuals. Some of the changes I am advocating in this chapter clearly would not be possible under our present market economy without rather substantial modifications in the system. But I want to be clear that most basically I am addressing assumptions that will be important in *any* political or economic system. Questions of just how much socialism is desirable or just what kind are obviously not unimportant, but they are not my focus here. Rather, it is with what Seymour Sarason has called "hidden axions,"[4] basic values and assumptions, which, if not addressed quite directly, can silently undermine any effort at changing the manifest institutional structures of society.

---

*Some have essentially *defined* socialism as including a change in values and consciousness. For them, the distinction I am making here is not a meaningful one. But clearly the *institutions* of socialism alone, or more specifically, the institutions of ownership alone, do not in themselves automatically define consciousness. Such a view is not tenable this late in the twentieth century.

What Might Change?

The results of a societal shift in values are a bit like the changes that accrue from psychotherapy: One doesn't know just what choices will be made, but they are likely to be sounder and more life-affirming than those made previously. Nonetheless, it is possible to suggest at least some of the changes, both in mode of thought and in practice, that might come to pass. In a variety of ways, the seeds of an alternative to the growth and consumer culture are beginning to emerge. Based on a number of national surveys of attitudes—both by his organization and by others—Daniel Yankelovich has argued that a large shift in values has begun which in many respects is quite consistent with what is being called for here. Increasing numbers of Americans have reported a greater concern with "self-fulfillment" and "quality of life" than with such things as bigger cars and higher incomes. To Yankelovich, the data point to "nothing less than the search for a new American philosophy of life . . . a new way of conceiving life and its meaning aris[ing] spontaneously from the great mass of the population."[5]

Yankelovich documents an increasing trend toward rejection of traditional social roles in an effort by people to be truer to their "real selves." He argues that this

> . . . resort to psychological justification marks a sharp break with the past. In other eras people have changed the course of their lives because they could not make a living or achieve the social status, wealth and power they sought. Politics, religion and war have also uprooted people and transformed their lives. But ours is the first era when tens of millions of people offer as moral justification for their acts the idea that an inner and presumably more "real" self does not fit well with their assigned social role.[6]

Yankelovich criticizes the asocial aspects of the self-fulfillment ethic in terms consonant with my own criticisms of the human potential movement's individualism. He highlights as well recent more mature and promising visions of self-fulfillment that center on commitments and on community rather than on a duty to self alone or on notions of inexorable, multifarious needs that must not be denied. From the changes Yankelovich describes, as well as from developments described by a host of other observers, one can see the outlines of a pattern of changes that give concrete content to an alternative to the culture of growth and consumption.

I shall try to convey in what follows some of the chief characteristics of the emerging alternative. It is important to be clear, however, that although the forces pointing toward change are substantial, they are not inexorable. New perceptions and new values now exist side by side with growth and consumer values, and the latter continue to create conditions that threaten to undermine the positive changes or make their further development impossible. The balance is shifting, but we are in a race against time — and against the momentum of our own errors.

Deployment of Resources

When considering further what sorts of changes are developing or need to develop, it is useful to consider just how resources of time, money, and effort are currently deployed and how that would change in a more psycho-ecologically oriented culture. Today, for example, an astounding total of well over $100 billion a year is spent on advertising and sales promotion in the United States.[7] Clearly the ascendance of psycho-ecological values would eliminate such enormous expenditures on efforts to induce people to buy more and more.

Another enormous amount of effort and money is spent in the production of products with planned obsolescence. They are of two sorts: products that will break in a relatively short time and products that, as part of a societal pattern, are rendered no longer appealing or even acceptable by changes in style. Changes in hemlines, lapels, and so forth in clothing and annual model changes in automobiles are both instances of the latter type of obsolescence. Auto model changes have amounted over the years to about a quarter of all that we have paid to buy automobiles,[8] and a substantial proportion of the $45 billion[9] we spend on clothing is the result of perfectly good clothes having "gone out of style."

In a psycho-ecologically oriented society, expenditures of this sort would be drastically reduced. At present the meeting of social needs is for most enterprises an indirect rather than a

ige environmental effects in the workplace; irresponsible
mping of chemicals into our soil, lakes, and rivers (both le-
ly and illegally); resistance to adequate emission controls
l air bags in cars; routine use of antibiotics in cattle that
eatens to create drug-resistant strains of bacteria; efforts to
se permissible levels of smoke and other pollutants; and so
th. These various policies, all motivated by the wish to save
ney, actually cost us all an enormous amount.

Our annual medical costs are now up to 250 billion dol-
s.[13] A very substantial proportion of this is due to environ-
ntal factors. Samuel Epstein, a medical authority on cancer,
tes that "a series of epidemiological studies have concluded
it environmental factors cause from 70% to 90% of all can-
s."[14] Many other illnesses are similarly attributable to man-
de factors or factors potentially within our control. The sum
al of our various efforts to save money by cutting corners on
lth, safety, and environmental standards may well yield a
national loss — without even taking into account the more
portant consideration of pain, suffering, and premature
th. When one considers the totals for excess medical bills
l the productivity lost to missed workdays resulting from en-
nmentally caused illnesses (not to mention such nonmedical
cts of pollution as higher bills for cleaning clothes or main-
ing buildings), our "bottom-line" oriented policies require
earsighted accountant.

An important part of an alternative to our present
rse — and again an alternative that is already beginning to
erge — would be an emphasis on prevention of illness instead
a primary commitment to treating illnesses after they de-
p. The result would probably be better health at a lower
t.

New Assumptions about Health

er changes in our attitudes and assumptions about health
ild also be part of the new outlook. Many recent develop-
its reflect an increasing awareness that the consumer society
important negative effects on our health. The most obvious
ct, of course, is that due to pollution. The growing influ-
e of the environmental movement indicates that large num-

direct aim, the direct aim being profits.
greater if there is a high turnover of people
large sales each year. If people can be induc
cars frequently or buy new clothes each seas
items built to wear out, sales are large and
rangements) jobs are more likely to be plent
more durable and remained desirable longe
to be replaced less often; annual sales would
ple would have similar stocks of goods wi
each year. The resources now deployed in]
replacements would be available elsewhere.

There are indications that such chang
occur. Ninety per cent of the American p
would be willing to do without annual mod
mobiles,[10] and recent policies from Detroit i
ever reluctantly—the auto makers are beg
Similarly, American auto makers are begi
number of years their cars last instead of ju
year's dream machine."

It is not unreasonable to speculate tha
from the growth and consumer emphasis th
by the defense budget, currently upwards o
a year,[11] would also decline substantially. M
that the profit motive, as much as any actu
rity, influences the enormous size of the
Moreover, with a different conception of (
ests" the numbers and kinds of our interna
would change. Getting involved in a war in
example, would be less likely if our conce
needs were more modest. Similarly, less ex]
policies would engage us in fewer internatio

In place of these various unproduct
sources could then be devoted to such thin
tion, scientific research, the arts, and recre
the case of medical costs, though, expendi
be less, despite—or really because of—grea
health. Our present system encourages eac
cut corners in ways that have numerous a
our national health: cutting corners in wor

*But see Chapter Eleven.

bers of Americans are beginning to be concerned about the effects on our health of such things as air and water pollution, chemical dumping, and radiation. Abroad, this trend seems in some ways even more advanced, as attested to by the pivotal influence the various "Green" parties are beginning to have.

Other trends as well point to a growing recognition of the mixed blessings our consumer society provides. We have become so surfeited with labor-saving devices, for example, that the sedentary existence of many of us has become a very real hazard to our health. The great increase in jogging and other forms of exercise is an important statement as well as a healthy response. Tibor Scitovsky puts it wittily in the economist's argot:

> When a person spends his day surrounded by power-driven equipment and vehicles to help him save effort on his every move, at work, at home and at play, and he then proceeds on doctor's orders to squander the energy he has so carefully saved on jogging around the block or riding his exercycle in the bathroom, he gives clear evidence that he realizes the irrationality, if not of his personal behavior, at least of the pattern of behavior society imposes, the pressure of which he is not strong enough to resist.[15]

Jogging and other such activities have come under attack in recent years as examples of the so-called narcissism that affects us.* It is true that jogging—or eating health food, which has been similarly criticized—do in themselves represent individual efforts to save oneself rather than political efforts to join with others to eliminate the social causes of the dangers to our health. But there is nothing to prevent people from doing both—eating health food *and* working politically to alter the conditions that make some ordinary supermarket food suspect. Only an old-fashioned Freudian hydraulics would imply that one "drains" energy from the other. I know of no survey that compares the level of political activity of people who jog or eat health food with that of people who do not, but I suspect that in fact the former group would turn out to be *more* engaged.

---

*See Chapter Ten for a more detailed critique of the claims that we have become a culture of narcissism. See Daniel Callahan's *The Tyranny of Survival* for a more interesting and balanced picture than Christopher Lasch presents.

They are, after all, the people who have most explicitly recognized that our mainstream way of life has drawbacks to our health.

Notwithstanding whatever "narcissistic" or trendy qualities can be found in the various pursuits of better health that have engaged people in recent years, they reflect an understanding that illness is not just something that "happens" to people but is very much a function of the kind of life we lead. The problematic features of our way of life include more than just external dangers such as air and water pollution or insecticide sprays in food. They include as well matters of habit, customs in the society that are not obligatory but exert powerful shaping forces. When people begin to cut back on red meat or eggs and to eat more fruits and vegetables, they are not committing a social act (except in the minuscule degree to which their actions contribute to signaling the market to switch somewhat from the one to the other). But they are implicitly reaching a conclusion — however close or far from consciousness its full implications are — that calls into question whether more of what we've been taught are the rewards of our affluence (say, red meat) is really such an unqualified good. Such questioning is a crucial first step in any effort at broader changes in values and institutions.

Interacting Solutions: An Illustration

In envisioning a further, more societally oriented approach to a healthier way of life one can begin to see how various solutions can interact. We suffer, for example, both from insufficient exercise and from air pollution caused by autos. Both problems could be greatly alleviated at once if large numbers of people biked to work instead of driving. That is an individual alternative even at present, of course. But biking to work on city streets or on highways, breathing the fumes of cars or fearing being hit by them, is not most people's idea of a pleasant, relaxing way to get exercise.

In New York City dividers were recently built along certain streets to provide bike lanes separated from auto traffic. This did attract a greater number of bikers, but insufficient attention was given to how our entire system discourages such an alternative. The program was done poorly and half-heartedly, and public preparation was minimal. Before long it was declared a failure, and the dividers were ripped up.

Imagine instead an elaborate system of bike lanes segregated from auto and pedestrian traffic, with glass or clear plastic overhead protection from the rain and moderate amounts of heat for cold winter days (not much would be needed, because the exercise itself would warm people). Imagine as well an elaborate campaign to introduce the public to the benefits of such an alternative mode of transportation and to encourage enough people to use it so that reduced automobile-produced pollution would redound to the public at large, benefiting even those who did not bike to work as well as providing individual health benefits to each biker (and providing further benefits even to those who, because of health, age, disposition, or the number of packages they had to carry that day, drove on the now much less crowded streets and highways). Imagine as well greatly expanded parking facilities for bikes in all business centers and perhaps even the provision of showers for employees to freshen up after their exercise and before a day's work.

To most of us, such a scheme might evoke the adjectives *healthful, invigorating, pleasant* — and *ridiculous*. Our present mindset makes such things seem impossible. Immersed in our habitual assumptions, we cannot see past or around them. But an alteration of values and assumptions along the lines suggested here would make such a scheme seem both appealing and practical. The resources it would require to implement it are far less than the resources we have devoted to our present transportation system, with all its negative consequences for our health. Whether, ultimately, reduced hospital bills for heart disease, lung cancer, and emphysema would completely offset the costs of constructing such a system, I can't say. But it is clearly a combined health and transportation solution that is well within our means and prevented at present only by our assumptions and habits.

Another scheme, which could complement the above one nicely, has already begun to be tested in Europe. Developed by Angelo Dalle Molle, an Italian enterpreneur, it centers on electric cars and would greatly reduce energy consumption while diminishing noise and pollution.[16] The limiting factor thus far in the use of electric cars has been the long time it takes to recharge the battery and the relatively short distance between necessary rechargings. Dalle Molle's plan, which seems well suited for urban transportation, provides for an integrated system, utilizing computers, in which many garages have the facilities to recharge batteries. Recharging time is relatively short if a partial recharge is given every 40 or 50 miles. Most trips within a city are no more than that, and the system is set up to provide drivers with an incentive to leave the car off at their first destination for a quick recharge and pick up another when they are through with their shopping, visit, show, or whatever.

Customers unlock the cars with a special credit card and are charged for the time the car is out of the garage; thus it is to their advantage to return the car to the garage when any leg of their ride is finished for a while. (Garages are distributed in such a pattern that any destination within the system's area is very close to a participating garage.) This arrangement enables a much higher percentage of the cars to be in use, since particular cars are not tied up for hours just sitting parked, as they are under a system of individual ownership.

Another potential advantage of such a system, if expanded and elaborated, is that it could enable drivers to be using exactly the appropriate vehicle for any of a variety of uses. Instead of owning a particular car, used on all occasions, a participant in the plan would take out a station wagon when he had something large to transport, a small two-seater for the trip across town, and perhaps a convertible for a trip in the country. Since only as much car would be used as the purpose required, energy and pollution costs would be further minimized; and since, again, cars would not be kept out of circulation when their sole owners weren't using them, fewer cars would be needed, resulting in lower costs and a further reduction in energy use and pollution (that associated with the process of manufacturing the cars). At the same time, drivers would have the convenience of driving just the kind of car they need for any situation.*

THE PSYCHOLOGY OF OWNERSHIP

Such convenience is not available under the present common versions of car rental. These reflect the "ownership psy-

---

*Similar schemes, some of them already in use on a trial basis, have been described by Emma Rothschild in *Paradise Lost: The Decline of the Auto-Industrial Age* (New York: Random House, 1973), pp. 212-20.

chology" that characterizes our society. A large portion of what is formally described as rental is in fact akin to ownership: The customer has a long-term lease, which provides some services not usually associated with outright ownership, but essentially it is "his" or "her" one car for a year or several years. When the owner (renter) isn't driving it, the car is parked in his garage or driveway or on the street, sometimes at an expense to the owner (renter), and is unavailable for use by others even if a period of several weeks or more goes by when the owner (renter) doesn't use it. Short-term rentals, by the day or week, are different but are still really variants of the ownership model. You still rent a particular vehicle for the period, have to find parking space for it when it is not in use, and keep it parked waiting for you instead of available for general use. Part of why short-term car rentals are as expensive as they are is that one is paying not just for time of use but for "owning" it over that period—that is, for the exclusive right to it whether using it or not.*

Psychologically, a key feature of ownership is precisely the nonuse by others. Indeed, as Philip Slater has shown, exclusiveness of access is sometimes a more significant subjective meaning of ownership than access *per se*.[17] In some limiting conditions—e.g., the purchase of stolen art works by certain collectors, who must hide the illicit objects and can see them less readily than when they were in the museum they were stolen from—exclusivity of access actually *reduces* the owner's opportunity to use and enjoy the object (except for the pleasure of knowing that it is "his" or "hers"). The preoccupation with owning that our present system breeds is expensive in both an economic and a psychological sense, and it points, by contrast, to a major difference between our present psychology and way of life and that potentially emerging one to which I am pointing.

It is important to be clear that Dalle Molle's approach, like all the ideas and developments I am describing here, does not turn its back on the modern world. These approaches instead aim at substituting real pleasures for illusory ones and at assur-

---

*Short-term rentals are also very inconvenient in that there is usually a good deal of paperwork for each rental and often substantial amounts of waiting time and/or requirement for reservations. In Dalle Molle's scheme, in contrast, one's credit card gives the same instant access that keys now do for car owners.

ing that the pleasures we take do not destroy the legacy for our children. They are not antitechnology. In many instances they depend heavily on technology, as Dalle Molle does on computers and electrical circuits, but they maintain a critical perspective on the assumptions under which our technology has tended to be employed.

The Meaning and Nature of Work

Central to the changes that a new set of values would bring about would be a different view of work. When income or production is our primary concern, other things are sacrificed in the effort to maximize this one abstract dimension. When the quality of subjective experience is the criterion, things look very different. Work, from this standpoint, is not just "input," to be manipulated in the service of some higher aim, but a part of life experience in itself, to be examined as an activity that occupies many hours of the day. Any gains in available consumer goods must be weighed against the extra pressures and deprivations undergone during the heart of the day when we are at work. The real nature of the choices we are making is often obscured when dollars and cents—instead of concrete experience thorughout the day—become our defining criteria.

A good illustration of how traditional economic thinking leads us astray is unwittingly provided by the Nobel economist Paul Samuelson in a discussion of the setting of prices in an ideal planned economy.[18] Samuelson is concerned in this discussion with the proper allocation of resources. He introduces a hypothetical paradigmatic situation in which two twins of equal capacity are each working an acre of land, but one acre is better than the other. Samuelson's analysis leads inevitably to the conclusion that some of the labor "must be shifted" onto the more productive land. "Most important of all," he says, "the socialist production manager must try to minimize the combined labor and land cost." Note, though, that Samuelson addresses himself only to the efficiency of production, not to the experience of the worker. What is left out, for example, is that people can feel attached to the land or—by extension from the artificial example to more realistic situations—to a particular community, a particular workplace, or a particular job in that workplace.

To be sure, we should know the costs in lost production that are entailed in preserving the experiential values, and we may assume that some number of people would adjust well to being shifted to where their productivity is maximized and might prefer the transfer if greater purchasing power were provided as a compensation. But Samuelson, thinking like an economist, does not really address such issues, despite his claim that even "the most finicky humanitarian" [*sic*] will have nothing to complain about. So immersed is contemporary economics in a value system in which greater product and more efficient production is the be-all and end-all of life that this highly intelligent man does not even notice that he has left something extremely important out of his equation.

In a culture less monolithically concerned with maximizing material product, very different choices might be made and very different considerations brought to mind. Both in the formulation of social policy and in the decisions made by individuals, considerably greater weight would be given to the value of remaining in a community where one has friends and a sense of belonging relative to the weight given to increasing income or production. There are indications that this is already beginning to happen on an individual basis. Increasing numbers of individuals (and their families), for example, are refusing to accept promotions that require them to move to another city.*[19]

A number of other changes would follow as well from a greater recognition that we have made poor tradeoffs by overestimating how much increased income and production contribute to our well-being. With less emphasis on criteria that maximize *economic* well-being alone, the choices we make might be very different.

I recall vividly a cab driver who proudly told me of having bought his daughter a Buick when she started college—and who also told me, during the same ride, that he had to drive 14 to 16 hours a day to make ends meet. The values that led him to try to be a good father by buying things for his daughter, at the

---

*Samuelson might well respond that a benefit of the price system for allocating resources is that people *are* free to choose not to move. If values shifted in the way I am suggesting, enormously high incentives would have to be offered to lure people away, and employers would be motivated to provide work for people in the places they wanted to stay. The point of offering the Samuelson example, however, was not to argue that the mechanism could not be adapted to a different set of preferences but rather to highlight the hidden value biases that permeate the discussion.

direct expense of actually being able to spend time with her, may well have been a product of marital discord or personal conflicts; but his tale made an impression on me because it was not really so at odds with mainstream American experience. He was perhaps an exaggeration of that experience, but his behavior is immediately recognizable. Few people would explicitly endorse the idea of being away from their children and then making it up to them by buying them things, nor did this man, in fact. The way it is experienced is that there are things which, because of economic necessity, one simply "has to" do. There is no experience of having made a choice. The tradeoffs between economic criteria and personal, experiential criteria are not really in our awareness. To a considerably greater degree than we realize, with differing contents at different economic levels, economic criteria usurp our consciousness, as it were, and feel somehow natural or God-given. Other values recede without the explicit sense of a decision.

It is just such consciousness of choices and tradeoffs that a heightening of psychological values implies*—asking oneself such things as which will *really* feel better, a new car and a stereo or an extra hour a day with one's son or daughter; or being aware that when one says one *needs* a new car it in fact can have more to do with one's learned sense of what one is supposed to have than with how reliably the old Ford handles the daily commute. Finally, what is entailed in the awareness of choices I am describing is that organizing one's life to meet such needs can have psychological consequences that we are usually encouraged not to notice.†

---

*Typically it is economists who think they are highlighting the tradeoffs. Their discipline is concerned with the apportioning and untilization of scarce resources, and resources are always presumed to be scarce—there is no such thing as a free lunch, and every gain has its price somewhere. But the gains, prices, and tradeoffs of the economist do not usually include the considerations discussed here, as we saw in the example from Paul Samuelson. To show why those (still rather exotic) efforts that have been made to cast into economic equations such things as leisure, health, and love are not sufficient would take us too far afield.

†Economists tell us that people rationally and calculatingly *choose* in such circumstances; that they weigh the subjective utility of leisure and work more only if what they buy is worth more to them than the leisure is. Self-deception is left out of this picture. Each party to the exchange is tautologically defined as better off (else he wouldn't have chosen as he did). Clearly the present view differs. See also Chapter Twelve.

With a different set of assumptions, we might well conclude that we would all be better off if less were produced and if
the workplace, where we spend so much time, were a more
pleasant place to be. Among the changes along these lines that
might be sought — depending on particular workers' desires and
on the particular deprivations that currently exist in different
workplaces — are greater opportunity for workers to engage in
relaxed conversation on the job or more breaks to permit this;
more recreational facilities attached to the workplace and provision of time to participate during the workday; and greater
opportunity for workers and groups of workers to take responsibility for how things get done.*

This latter change in traditional working conditions has
been of particular interest lately and has begun to be tried in
some of the most productive factories in the world. There are
indications that — in addition to making work more interesting
and enjoyable — it actually increases productivity as well.[20] But
it is important in the present context to emphasize that even if it
led to somewhat lower productivity, such a change might appear desirable in terms of the value orientation being discussed
here.

When the result is lower worker output per day — as it
probably would be if greater recreation time, greater break
time, and other amenities were what was at issue — people
would have to be willing to choose these compensating pleasures instead of more material goods. This is not to say that distribution issues could not also be negotiated. There is nothing
in what I have said that would preclude those at the bottom of
the income distribution from demanding a more proportionate
share of the pie. But overall it is certainly true that an emphasis
on greater leisure, chatting, recreation, and other workplace
pleasures and amenities would require some sort of tradeoff.

For many people this remains an unappealing prospect at
this point. Moonlighting to gain extra income is very common,
and the cab driver I described earlier is in some respects only an
exaggeration of what is still the American mainstream. But
there are already signs that many Americans — and not just the

---

*I omit here health and safety factors in the workplace, obviously not
because they are unimportant, but because they are discussed elsewhere in
this chapter.

upper middle classes who have more goods than most and who
are so often the focus of reporters looking for trends — are beginning to sense that there is an imbalance in our values, that
extra consumer goods do not compensate for what has been
lost.

In the auto industry, for example — where once the deployment of human beings in machinelike fashion for the purpose
of efficiency of production was the pride of our economic system — increasing numbers of workers are no longer choosing to
maximize their income regardless of the personal costs. Mon-
day and Friday absences are becoming common, as a strange
affliction seems to strike only on days contiguous to a weekend.[21] And in a G.M. plant in Tennessee, thousands of men
holding jobs with higher pay and higher status applied for a
small number of lower-paying custodial jobs. The jobs were
thought by management to be appealing to only a small number of worn-out men approaching retirement age, but to the
great shock of both management and union officials, a great
many young, vigorous workers found less tiring and stressful
work more appealing than a higher wage.[22]

A Synthesis of Old and New

It is important to be clear that what I am pointing toward is not
just a matter of working less hard and taking less income. Nor is
it a "going back," a simple return to some hypothetical good
old days when people were poor but happy. I do believe that we
have lost some things of great importance in our frantic pursuit
of economic growth. But we have also made significant gains in
human welfare that I wish neither to deny nor to give up. The
citizens of today's industrialized nations live longer and
healthier lives than people did in the past; fewer of them are
plagued by poverty and fewer still suffer malnutrition; they
have greater opportunities for education and for entertainment
than any whole population has ever had.

What I and other like-minded people are seeking is a synthesis of old and new: not a simple *return* to older amenities
and patterns of living, but an *incorporation* and *transformation* of them so that they can be combined with the best of the
new. As in Dalle Molle's plan for a computerized electric car

system, the aim is not to reject the benefits of modern technology but to use them properly, with a better appreciation of human needs than has recently been evident. Gearing up for greater efficiency was, in the long run, in the service of human needs (though for a long time at an enormous price for the poor and working classes). Even as severe a critic of capitalism as Marx could say:

> The bourgeoisie, in its reign of barely a hundred years, has created more massive and more colossal productive power than have all previous generations put together. Subjection of nature's forces to man, machinery, application of chemistry to agriculture and industry, steam navigation, railways, electric telegraphs, clearing of whole continents for cultivation, canalization of rivers, whole populations conjured out of the ground — what earlier century had even an intimation that such productive power slept in the womb of social labor?[23]

But the very advances in our productive capacities have changed our needs, and if we fail to recognize this we will fail to capitalize on the potential for human well-being these economic advances have put before us.

What many people are beginning to realize is that now time is more precious than goods, that indeed we hardly have time to consume what we already can afford. Even for many children the effective life of their possessions has become very short. They have no time to play with the toys that fill their closets, because there are always new ones to be played with. For a growing number of people, it is too little time to use their goods rather than too little in the way of goods to fill their time that is the problem. This is put most wittily by the Swedish economist Staffan Linder, who depicts the modern affluent man as "drinking Brazilian coffee, smoking a Dutch cigar, sipping a French cognac, reading *The New York Times*, listening to a Brandenburg Concerto and entertaining his Swedish wife — all at the same time, with varying degrees of success."[24]

Linden is clearly depicting the life of a particular class, but his description captures a state of affairs that holds already in many segments of society, simply with different contents. Taking the surplus that modern technology offers in leisure rather than in goods would provide benefits both psychologically and ecologically.

Many, however, continue to opt for goods, at least in part because they are unsure how they would use the extra time. As Tibor Scitovsky has noted,[25] it takes certain skills to enjoy our panoply of consumer goods, and many people vaguely sense that they lack these skills. So despite a surfeit of goods they occupy their time seeking after more—spending time not only on earning the money but on making the purchases as well; the shopping center provides much of the structure for many Americans' lives.

Even more fundamental is a deeper inability to enjoy life fully that is kept out of awareness by focusing on dollars and cents and on goods. The lives of all of us—not just those who are ordinarily labeled as in need of psychological treatment— are limited both by restrictions and inhibitions that reflect social custom and by a key feature of human development: our prolonged dependency in childhood. This dependency, added to the fact that for years our cognitive capacities are so much more limited than they will be when we grow up, has a profound impact on our development. Our view of the world and its possibilities is largely shaped when we are helpless and uncomprehending, and this view is then acted out in our adult years, when many more possibilities are in fact available to us. Indeed, the differences between the cognitive capacities and life situation of the human child and the human adult are far greater than between many species. It is as though we learn how to live as one creature and then apply that lesson when we are something quite else.

If we are to take more of the fruits of our technological progress in the pleasures of play and leisure, rather than in accumulating still more material goods, we will need, among other things, to overcome the constrictions that derive from our early fears and fantasies. One valuable contribution of the human potential movement has been the development of therapy-like techniques that are directed not at those limitations we ordinarily label as neurotic but at the psychological forces that make "normal" people's lives less free or exciting than they could be. Such a therapy for the healthy, as it were, would hardly be the sole or defining feature of a more psychologically and ecologically oriented society, but it would have an important role to play.

Experience and Technique

Notwithstanding the criticisms made in the last chapter, the ideas and methods that have arisen from the human potential movement — if recast in a less individualistic form — can help make possible the changes that can lure people away from a consumer orientation to life. Even more than Freud, these new therapies alert us to the blinders and distorting lenses we wear and evoke in us the question of whether society has exacted an excessive and unnecessary tribute. They hold out to us the tantalizing image of a life lived more fully, sensually, alertly, and humanely. Moreover, unlike the romantic abstractions of Herbert Marcuse and Norman O. Brown,[26] which are based on (and, in the bargain, distort) Freud's most speculative and dubious writings, these approaches are rooted in concrete techniques and experiences.

The variety of these new methods is bewildering. Some of them are the serious products of therapists with years of training in conventional approaches, who have reached out for more dramatic or effective techniques. Others are the progeny of opportunists, instant gurus, or prescient businessmen — three categories that are not necessarily mutually exclusive. It is not easy to sort out the trendy chaff from the more nourishing stuff, especially because they all loosely constitute a movement with countercultural roots, and so many of them have shared the same California locales. Nonetheless, it is possible to highlight a few recurrent themes that hold out promise.

One is an emphasis on the body. Change, it is suggested, cannot occur just in the head. We are embodied creatures, and our constrictions and inhibitions are as much in the stubborn set of our muscles as in anything that can be put into words. Most of these notions have their origin in the pioneering work of Wilhelm Reich,[27] but a considerable variety of methods have developed that supplement Reich's original techniques. The strategies range from direct manipulation and massage to interpretations of and constant calling attention to posture, gestures, facial expressions, and so forth, in order to break up chronic, locked-in patterns. More recently biofeedback techniques have been added to the repertoire, offering the possibility of a quantum jump in our control of bodily and mental

states. At this point sober analysts of the successes of biofeedback techniques tell us that the original near-miraculous reports were greatly overselling what has been accomplished thus
far,[28] but continuing progress is being made, and developments
in biofeedback technology may still point us toward new methods of overcoming constricting and deadening modes of
thought and experience.

A second important feature of many of the human potential approaches is the use of "marathon" sessions. For periods
ranging from several hours to several days, participants encounter nearly continuous challenges to their customary patterns of relating, until their social façade is eroded and new
perceptions and experiences are enabled to break through.
These techniques, which often tend to include a relentlessness
on the part of the leader and deprivation of food, sleep, and familiar social supports, have a real element of risk.[29] But they
also do have the potential, especially if pursued wisely and humanely, of revealing to people possibilities in their lives that
have been unrealized in the constraining net of convention and
habit. They have been limited, however, as have most of the
human potential approaches, by the individualism noted in the
last chapter. Not only are the values implicit in many of these
approaches problematic, but so too are the assumptions about
what makes change enduring.

People who go off on marathon weekends often come back
high, experiencing the world in a fresh, exciting way. But usually it is not long before old patterns reassert themselves. The
missing link is the person's context. He returns to an environment in which the expectations he encounters and the behavior
of other people toward him is the same as it was before the marathon. His new behavior does alter this somewhat, but the pull
of other people's ingrained patterns is strong, and their behavior, like his own, is not readily modified by just one or two new
experiences. Consequently, in thousands of interaction sequences each day, he encounters a force pulling him back to
old patterns, and before long the effect of the marathon has
dissolved.

This analysis suggests that for psychological change techniques to be maximally effective they should address whole networks of people, who can mutually support the changes that

come about until they become more stabilized. Such a contextually oriented approach—in contrast to individualistic strategies that attempt to change "the person" essentially regardless of context—has affinities with the emphasis on interdependency that characterizes the science of ecology. It is another way in which the point of view being advocated here might be viewed as a "psycho-ecological" point of view.

Some psychological change techniques do take into account the importance of context and interdependency. Family therapy techniques, which have become increasingly important in recent years, have been developed, in part, as a direct challenge to the individualistic assumptions that had predominated in the field of psychotherapy.[30] Thus far, however, these methods have not tended to be employed in the service of expansive, human-potential kinds of goals but rather in the treatment of specific distressing symptoms and/or in the effort to return a family to a prior equilibrium.

The human potential movement has made use of groups a great deal and thus to some degree has made use of contextual influences. But even the use of groups has tended to be influenced by individualistic assumptions: Frequently, each person in the group is regarded as individually responsible for what his own experience is. Moreover, even where the group's contextual effect is recognized—as when it is understood that certain kinds of behavior or experience are possible only with group support or possible for each only when all do it—there tends to be the lack of follow-up mentioned before in the context of marathons. Each individual in the group is assumed to have been changed by it, and each separately goes back to his or her original context, to face its powerful conservative influence alone.

It is understandable that such an approach would have been taken by human potential practitioners. Dealing with the continuing contextual influences and/or working only with functioning networks of people is enormously more complex and demanding and often, in present circumstances, simply not practicable. Moreover, many of the human potential practices derive from work with patients, where distressing symptoms or undeniably thwarting ways of life produce motivation for change strong enough to enable some individuals to change with less attention to context than is required for the kinds of changes—at once more subtle and more extensive—that human potential work with relatively healthy people attempts.*

The latter kind of change, however, will require considerably more attention to context, to support groups, and to the mutual sustaining of values and assumptions. It is also, for similar reasons, much more likely to be useful as an adjunct to more generalized changes in values throughout a substantial segment of society, rather than as an isolated attempt to change people one by one, or even in twos, threes, or tens. Changes in broad societal values, changes in social institutions and structures, and changes in individual psyches are best viewed as mutually facilitative levels of change. As the one emerges, it is best pursued and amplified by working on the other two as well. Powerful psychological techniques can help to accelerate the changes—both by making alternatives clearer and simply by demonstrating that a shift in emphasis toward more intense and satisfying experience instead of accumulation of goods and income really does feel better—but these techniques *per se* hardly define or delimit the kinds of changes toward which the present analysis points.

The Renewal of Community

If we are to fashion an alternative capable of luring us away from the attractions (and the concomitant costs) of the consumer way of life, clearly restoration of the sense of community and of connectedness to others must be at the heart of it.

Jeremy Seabrook presents a particularly vivid picture of the decline of community that seems to be part and parcel of the consumer society. "Why hasn't having more made people happier?" he asks in the subtitle of his book, *What Went Wrong?*[31] Seabrook interviewed hundreds of older working-class people in

*Psychotherapy with patients also is often practiced in the context of an ongoing relationship rather than one or a few sessions, and this relationship provides continuing support for the change. Moreover, it too probably works best when explicit attention is paid to how feedback from other people either sustains or undermines the changes achieved in the sessions. See, for example, Paul L. Wachtel, *Psychoanalysis and Behavior Therapy: Toward an Integration* (New York: Basic Books, 1977).

England, examining the changes they had experienced in their lifetimes. Most were considerably better off materially than their parents or grandparents had been or than they themselves had been earlier in life. Yet Seabrook did not find them, or their children, to be happy. As Studs Terkel puts it in the foreword to Seabrook's book, "Lost values are what it's all about; a broken sense of belonging; an abandoned sense of place; a mutilated sense of self."[32]

Far more than joy or contentment with their present materially comfortable status, Seabrook found disillusionment, a sense of hopes betrayed. A sense on the part of parents that they had lost touch with their children; a sense on the part of the children that they had been set adrift; a fear of muggers, rapists, vandals; a diminished sense of being able to count on others for help—these were some of the things that seemed to accompany and to spoil these people's increased affluence. "It cannot be without significance," Seabrook says,

> that when you talk to the old about their poverty, the great consolation in all that suffering was the quality of human relationships; now that things have been so well perfected, the only thing wrong is seen to be people. That is not a gain for humanity.[33]

Seabrook paints a particularly grim picture of life in the consumer society. The child, he says,

> . . . tends to be stripped of all social influences but those of the market-place. . . . The individual is denuded of everything but appetites, desires, and tastes, wrenched from any context of human obligation or commitment. It is a process of mutilation; and once this has been achieved, we are offered the consolation of reconstituting the abbreviated humanity out of the things and the goods around us, and the fantasies and vapours which they emit. A sense of self has to be sought in the parade of images and products; and this culture becomes the main determinant upon morality, beliefs, and purpose, usurping more and more territory that formerly belonged to parents, teachers, community, priests and politics alike.[34]

Not all of this book's readers will resonate with the passionate intensity of Seabrook's biting account, but most will acknowledge that the loss of community is one of the great problems we face as a society and one of the great burdens for a very

large number of individuals. In our politics we see a growing influence of fractionated interest groups and difficulty in uniting
in a broadly consensual way. In our personal lives loneliness is
increasingly being described as a virtual "epidemic" by sociologists and mental health experts. A recent cover story in *The
New York Times Magazine* presented example after example
from every walk of life and every segment of society. In that article Thomas J. Peters of the Stanford Business School refers to
the "unbelievable and deep-felt need to be part of something"
and suggests that the economic successes of Japanese business
have more than a little to do with the strong sense of community in Japanese companies. Those few American corporations,
he notes, that manage to convey a genuine sense of community
and belonging to their employees are thriving as a consequence.[35]

Competition is certainly not absent in Japan, where scores
on one crucial examination can influence the entire course of
one's life, nor is there by any means an absence of desire for
more and more consumer goods. But these influences are kept
somewhat in check by a unique and long-standing cultural tradition of strong ties of mutual obligations and expectations.
Observers have differed as to how benign this arrangement really is or how much longer it can contain the centrifugal forces
of materialism and comeptition, but few disagree that, within
the industrialized world, Japan and the United States are on
opposite ends of the cultural continuum with regard to the
sense of community. In the United States the anticommunal
forces of the competitive market place are reinforced, rather
than checked, by prevalent cultural values. As the University of
California sociologist Robert Bellah puts it, "Personal freedom,
autonomy and independence are the highest values for Americans. You're responsible for yourself. We place a high value on
being left alone, on not being interfered with. The most important thing is to be able to take care of yourself. As soon as possible, we believe, a child should take care of itself. It's illegitimate to depend on another human being."[36] Not surprisingly,
Bellah's research also revealed "an element of loneliness not far
below the surface" and a sense of community as being "brittle,
fragile, with a tremendous turnover."[37]

Such deeply held cultural values are not readily changed.
But many, including Bellah, have also noted a nostalgia and a
deep longing for the tight-knit communities and close family

ties that, at least in myth and perhaps in reality, were once also part of our cultural tradition. It is difficult to sustain such ties in the face of the "launching pad" image of family and community discussed earlier in this book or in a cultural milieu in which we are encouraged to think of people as "winners" or "losers."

A recent ad for *Popular Mechanics* magazine shows a lone figure with the caption "The New Achiever. He depends on himself and *Popular Mechanics*." The body of the ad begins, "I'm an industrial designer. And whether I'm at my drafting board or sailing my catamaran, I'm out to win. So I'm always looking for a competitive advantage." Note that this paragon is not completely self-reliant; as the ad later says he can rely on *two* things: himself, and the product being hawked.

Few of us would explicitly avow that we have chosen to rely on products instead of other people, and, fortunately, the bonds of community and of interdependency are too important to be severed completely. Friendships, family ties, and sometimes even a genuine sense of community remain realities for a great many of us. But the widespread yearning for greater closeness to others suggests that for many there is a sense of superficiality about these connections, even when things look good "from the outside." In my own practice as a psychotherapist, such complaints predominate substantially over specific anxieties or symptoms.

A key to developing a realistic and satisfying alternative to the culture of growth and consumerism is to help clarify and channel these vague longings and to make clearer the links between our present discontents and the goals we have embraced in both our public and our private lives. The task will not be easy. The kind of community feeling that is suited for our affluent and technologically oriented culture will probably be quite different from the ties we nostaligically remember or imagine. Moreover, we are faced with having to learn again about interdependency and the need for rootedness after several centuries of having systematically—and proudly—dismantled our roots, ties, and traditions. We had grown so tall we thought we could afford to cut the roots that held us down, only to discover that the tallest trees need the most elaborate roots of all.

In this sense, the modern version of an age-old human task—reconciling ourselves to the finite limits that frame our lives, and to our dependence upon each other—is peculiarly difficult for us. Having unlearned and rejected much of what we will need to deal with the task we confront, we are less well equipped than were our ancestors. In another sense, however, what is new in our situation is just cause for hope. The state of our technology is such that we in fact can expect a good deal of progress; we are not bound upon a wheel that revolves but goes nowhere as generation after generation used to be. But to make use of our technology in a way that enhances rather than degrades our lives, we must take account of our new understanding of ecological limits and interdependence. Most of all, we need to learn how to use the efficiency of production our technology has achieved not merely to produce more but to provide us with the luxury of time to examine our lives and time simply to enjoy ourselves and enjoy each other.

The Spiritual Dimension

In recent years there has been a great upsurge of religious seeking, both in the developed countries and in the Third World. The manifestations of this religious resurgence are diverse, as are its causes, but it is clearly a powerful force to be reckoned with. How does this religious yearning bear on the prospects for the changes pointed to here?

Much of what is happening seems to be a response to both the excesses and deficiencies of the industrial society. The Nobel laureate physicist Dennis Gabor has described our civilization as "based materially on the solid foundation of scientific technology and spiritually on almost nothing."

Religion, of course, has persisted throughout the modern era. Some intellectuals may proclaim that God is dead, but He lives for many, many millions. But religious doctrines and practices have accommodated to the forces of industrialization, sometimes losing their spiritual core in the process. Observers from Max Weber to Karen Horney have noted how religious ideas have been put in the service of production or how religious practices have been encapsulated from the mainstream of daily life.

Religious doctrines and practices today frequently stray from the inspiration of the great religious founders. "These religious founders," says Arnold Toynbee, disagreed with each other in their pictures of what is the nature of the universe, the nature of the spiritual life, the nature of ultimate reality. But they all agreed in their ethical precepts. . . . They all said with one voice that if we made material wealth our paramount aim, this would lead to disaster. They all spoke in favor of unselfishness and of love for other people as the key to happiness and to success in human affairs.

This is not the voice of much of the current religious revival. Clearly the upsurge of fundamentalism in this country has not put the fear of God into General Motors. Piety and materialistic grasping have seemed perfectly capable of proceeding hand in hand. Some of the same voices that call for devotion to God's ideals and a commitment to the "right to life" push for government funds for price supports for cancer-causing tobacco and for the active promotion of this deadly habit. (That they are at the same time, when it suits them, advocates of minimal government intervention is but one more contradiction. On all levels, it seems, it is profits before prophets.)

A genuine revival of spiritual and ethical yearnings is to be welcomed. To be sure, the changes discussed here do not require a traditional religious commitment; an ethical commitment to secular humanism would also provide a supportive framework. But they are in no way antithetical to a belief in God. Those who see religion only in its distorted forms, which relegate compassion to some minor corner of the moral universe and stress instead submission, the evils of sexuality, and the virtues of business as usual, mistake a corruption of religion for its spiritual core. A turn to the psychological is a turn away from the materialistic, not the spiritual.

EIGHT

Strategies and Pitfalls

THE CHANGES IN VALUES and assumptions that we need will not come easily. Notwithstanding the promising beginnings I have just described, there are powerful forces that tend to reinforce our present way of seeing things and doing things. We are enveloped in a web of our own making: Given how we see things, continuing as we have seems only natural; and given the steps we therefore take, we are again induced to continue to see things just as we have.

But the web of ideas and consequences is not seamless. There are frayed edges where the possibility of its being untangled can be glimpsed. The very sense of crisis and distress at large in the world is a potential ally in the effort at change, even if it also creates the danger of our digging ourselves into an even deeper hole by an even more intense effort to do more of the same. In this, the parallels noted in Chapter Four between our present societal dilemmas and those of individual neuroses are again relevant. Neurosis too consists of vicious circles in which each (false) step we take seems just what is required by our view of things and in turn keeps that (false) view alive. In neurosis too the consequences of prior choices face us as an objective reality which constrains subsequent choices, as institutions do on a social level. And, importantly, in neurosis too the sense of dis-

173

tress is often a hopeful sign that at least the possibility exists of turning things around.

The parallel, moreover, seems to me to go still one crucial step further. In working with the vicious circles in which individuals are trapped, I have become persuaded that what works best is a multiple approach, confining itself neither solely to changing overt behavior nor to promoting insight alone, but rather attempting to weaken a number of links in the causal chain simultaneously.[1] In our present, more broadly societal dilemma, a similar strategy seems called for. Since our beliefs and values shape our institutions, and our institutions shape our beliefs and values, a multifaceted effort is required.

The efforts at social change that came to prominence in the 1960s were the closest approximation thus far to what I have in mind. In some respects these efforts still provide a useful model for how to proceed in the present. In other ways they clearly failed, and their failures are instructive. In this chapter I shall consider some of the strategies and tactics that were characteristic in that most recent period of social activism. My hope is that a new such period will emerge before too long and that understanding both the insights and the errors of the past will enable the quest for change to be pursued more wisely and more effectively.

The efforts of the Sixties are particularly relevant in the present context because—notwithstanding the particular historical circumstances represented most of all by the Vietnam War—the context for those efforts was similar to the present. The aims of the rebellious youth of that era were not confined to ending the war or even to the still larger task of establishing a more just and equal social order. They included very centrally as well the transformation of personal life, the substitution of new values, ideals, and models of the good life for ones that had begun to feel stale and constricting. In many respects the movements of the Sixties can be seen as the first large-scale effort to establish a post-consumerist society. As such, they particularly merit our attention here.*

*The term "post-consumerist" should not be taken as implying an end to the availability of consumer goods. *Post*-consumerist and *pre*-consumerist ways of life are as different from each other as either is from what we have now. In a post-consumerist world, affluence would persist. What would change is the compulsive insistence on growth and the tendency to define our lives in terms of goods rather than in terms of experience and human relatedness.

The Politics of Experience

The most important insight of the Sixties centered on—to use Laing's evocative phrase—the "politics of experience." In a sense broader than Laing's particular usage, there was a greatly increased recognition of the ways in which our consciousness shaped our social institutions and vice versa, and an emphasis on changing not only manifest political arrangements but modes of thought and perception as well. Using a somewhat different terminology, Marshall Berman referred to these efforts as a "politics of authenticity," by which he meant a politics centered on "a dream of an ideal community in which individuality will not be subsumed or sacrificed, but fully developed and expressed."[2] Berman traces this dream back to before the French Revolution but notes that subsequent defeats of revolutionary efforts "generated a disenchantment and despair so deep that the very memory of the dream was lost." Instead, radical efforts were directed toward a "collectivism" that submerged and negated individuality, while the prerogatives of the individual were stressed within the competitive culture of capitalism. Political thought, he says, "was frozen into this dualism until the cultural explosion of the 1960's redefined the terms."[3]

The social historian Eli Zaretsky has similarly noted both a split in the aims of radical reformers and then a coming together of themes of personal and political liberation in the 1960s. In Zaretsky's account, an earlier synthesis was attained for a brief period at the beginning of this century but was disrupted as a consequence of the Russian Revolution. The Bolshevik victory, says Zaretsky, "helped refocus the political attention of European and American socialists exclusively on the question of state power just as 'personal' questions were assuming widespread significance. Following the Russian example, the goal of socialism came to be presented purely in terms of economic development."[4] Only in the 1960s (and then all too briefly) was this split healed.

Unlike earlier generations of radicals, the generation that came to political awareness in the Sixties began its political education at a time when all but the most dogmatically committed could see that the Soviet Union and the regimes it created elsewhere were not the fulfillment of the socialist dream. As the Frankfurt school of social criticism developed because the predicted revolution didn't spread despite the supposed "objective" conditions for revolution, so too was this later turn to a radicalism infused with subjectivity rooted in a failure of orthodox socialist thought—in this case the failure of the Soviet Union to become a humane society.

Despite much rhetoric that sounded rather thoroughly rejecting of all things liberal and Western—and despite an unfortunate tendency to succumb to their own rhetorical excesses— most of the Sixties radicals were struggling with a recognition that different did not necessarily mean better. This was one of the reasons there was so much hesitancy to formulate concrete programs: The Soviet Union had achieved (in at least some respects) the *letter* of socialism; the young dissenters of the Sixties sought its spirit.

According to Christopher Lasch, "the radicalism of the Sixties failed to address itself to the quality of personal life or to cultural questions."[5] The present analysis suggests a rather different picture. Certainly there were some Sixties radicals whose vision was dark and monolithic, who saw concern with emotional life and personal relations as a corrupt bourgeois distraction from the cause of the revolution. But there was nothing new about that segment of the "new left." It was essentially old vodka in new bottles. What *was* new in the Sixties—or at least a *re*discovery of what had been lost for many years—was, precisely as Zaretsky describes, the coming together of political radicalism and personal, experiential liberation.

The Vietnam War, of course, was the galvanizing central event of the period. It was both monstrous and stupid, and it mobilized the moral sense of a generation. But the protests of the period were not merely protests about what "we" were doing to "them"; they were protests as well about what we were doing to ourselves. The superego played a role in those protests, but so too did the ego and the id. It was not just guilt that motivated the young; it was a sense that the lives toward which they were being programmed seemed so empty and unappealing.

The tactics of the Sixties rebels matched their aims. Their desire for change was expressed not just in formal protests or political organizing but also in their rejection of the style and role that were expected of them. Although more overt and traditional political activity was common as well, it was a time when every facet of personal life was fraught with political significance. The clothes one wore; how one wore one's hair; the music one listened to; the phrases one did or didn't incorporate in one's speech; and, most significantly, the kind of job one projected oneself ahead to (and the anticipated role of work and career in one's life altogether)—all these were political statements. All indicated "which side" you were on.

Sadly, it did turn out that much of the political commitment and disaffection from materialist, competitive values was not as deep as it had seemed. Many of today's rising young professionals and executives are people who as youths looked so "different" from either their parents or the "teenagers" of the 1950s that it was hard to imagine what they would grow up to be. Many people disapproved of what they were up to, but only the most cynical pictured them simply fitting in, becoming basically indistinguishable from previous cohorts of "kids" who "grew up."

The cynics' prediction seems, on the face of it, to have been so correct that it is already difficult to remember just how "different" the youth of the Sixties seemed to be. But I think they really were different, if not quite as different as they seemed; and they were different because they were responding to a different set of conditions. The war was the catalyst, but more basic was a failure of identification, a recognition on the part of many young people that their parents' affluence did not bring the satisfaction and contentment they were led to expect it would. The vanguard of the movement in the Sixties was from the middle class rather than the working class, because it was there that so many had reached the point of diminishing returns, the point where further affluence did not bring further satisfaction, and thus where some of the assumptions that had structured American life began to lose their legitimacy and power to compel. Preoccupation with the quality of personal life was a natural consequence of disillusionment with received values and an inability to identify with and commit oneself to them.

As it turns out, the effort to promote a new way of life was pursued ineffectively, but the perception that such an effort was crucial was sound and still is. The central point of this book is that our values and our way of life are at the heart of our discontents, not our political and economic arrangements *per se*. But an equally central point is that this does not mean traditional political and economic concerns are irrelevant. A crucial

error of many who in one way or another concern themselves
with the kind of shift in values and life-style I am addressing—
both among those who advocate it and those who oppose it—
has been to assume that psychology or personal growth implies
an individualistic calculus that ignores the social context. I
have argued that our best understanding of the roots of personal contentment and fulfillment points to a broader and
more far-sighted perspective, one in which our interdependency and need for cooperative action are highlighted.

The Re-splitting of Radical Aims

Many things contributed to the inability of the social movements of the Sixties to sustain the joint commitment to political
and personal transformation and to the decline of the exuber-
ant and idealistic spirit that infused the lives of so many in those
years. Certainly one important factor was the sense of discouragement that followed the failure of the antiwar efforts in the
1968 presidential elections and the sense of shock and horror
generated by the assassinations of Martin Luther King and
Robert Kennedy. Leaders who stood for humane ideals were
being murdered, while the effort to unseat Lyndon Johnson
gave only the choice between Hubert Humphrey and Richard
Nixon—one a man so compromised by his association with the
war that his earlier good work paled by comparison, the other
perhaps the most cynical and soulless man ever to hold the pres-
idency. Following that, those who still felt the strength to fight
had to witness a policy of alleged disengagement from the war
that in fact extended it into Cambodia and kept it going—even
reckoning only from the time Nixon took office with his "secret
plan" to end the war—for a longer period of time than all of
World War II.

The McGovern campaign essentially marked the end of
Sixties politics. One final effort was made to use the electoral
system not only to end the war but to transform society. It is important in the present context to recognize that McGovern was
not just an antiwar candidate; his was also a politics of compassion and transformation, responsive at least implicitly to many
of the issues I have raised here. McGovern made many errors,
to be sure, from his handling of the Eagleton situation to his

proposing of (essentially enlightened) economic policies before he had prepared sufficiently to defend them. But history, I suspect, will be far kinder to McGovern than were contemporary journalists and party hacks. He lost an election — perhaps even lost an election he could have won — but what he stood for was what needed to be stood for, and still needs to be. Though in retrospect the triumph of a sincere antiwar candidacy would certainly have been preferable to what actually happened, to have trimmed his campaign of the "social issues" that subsequently contributed to his defeat would have been to abandon half of what made his campaign a source of hope for those who supported it.

But defeat did take its toll. Already in 1968, but almost completely after 1972, the synthesis of personal and political concerns was shattered. Many of those who maintained an overt political commitment turned away from a politics of personal life to a sober, unsmiling fanaticism. Others, gradually but inexorably, were led into a retreat to apathy and a decline in political interest altogether.

The retreat from politics became clear only gradually. Many of those who retreated continued to talk of liberation and to experience themselves as in a struggle to oppose the dehumanizing values and institutions that they saw (largely correctly) lying behind the war, racism, abuse of the environment, and other social and political phenomena they abhorred. Only gradually, as the 1970s wore on, did it become clear how much the political thrust of these countercultural revolts had been eroded and how much they had been absorbed into the commercial mainstream of American life, as one more thing the quick-witted might find a way to sell and one more way our impulse to think only of our own comfort could be encouraged.

The insight that life-style could be revolutionary was a valid one, indeed an essential one at a time when the limits of traditional revolutionary activity were so painfully obvious in the Soviet police state and when we were beginning to recognize the environmental costs of our compulsive consumerism. But it was a mistake to pretend that politics, in the usual sense of that word, could be abandoned altogether.

To be sure, there was initially something "political" about taking psychedelic drugs or turning to an exploration of Eastern and mystical religious traditions. Certainly there was a political impulse behind the movement to communal living; and in the context of the times, dropping out of school and pursuing sandal-making or even panhandling could be viewed as political as well. These were all protests stemming from a dissatisfaction with the world as it was, and frequently they were at least thought to be part of an effort to change it. Much of it looks silly to us now. (Much of it looked silly even then.) But there were a sincerity and a commitment behind these efforts that are already hard to recapture as the hucksters have taken over and packaged all of it.

CONSUMERIST STRUCTURES OF THOUGHT

The falling apart of the Sixties synthesis and the particularly powerful discouragement that contributed to it, were in substantial measure due to the difficulty in transcending one's point of origin. Our upbringing is not our destiny in any linear or monolithically constraining way, but it will have its due.

As I noted earlier, it was the children of the affluent—the children of the consumer culture—who were in the vanguard of the effort at change. One of the central features of that culture is its preoccupation with the new, the different, the "revolutionary." When the latter adjective can be used so casually for laundry detergents and the like, when the children who huddle before the TV set are bombarded with so many such claims well before the age of critical reflectiveness, what does this do when, in their first ventures into adulthood, they are thinking about real revolutions, about turning society upside down? Why should they not think that there is far more room for change in a society, or in an individual's way of life, than in a detergent? If the latter could be revolutionary, what might we expect on this far broader field? When the basic schemas by which reality is apprehended are infused with the idea that everything made last year is now hopelessly outmoded, this cannot but influence one's thinking about society and about the course of one's life.

The young rebels of the Sixties sensed that the life they were being groomed for was hollow at its core. But they *had* been groomed for it, and their very way of rejecting it reflected that grooming. In addition to the expectation that total newness could be achieved, they showed their grooming in their expectation that achieving it would be easy—and fast. The culture of instantaneous gratification, of buy-now-pay-later, produced rebels against that culture who expected fundamental social change to be instantaneous as well. As many have noted, when that did not happen, they became discouraged rather easily.

Social change, many of us have learned since the 1960s, is a slow and uneven process. To an earlier generation, shaped by the Depression rather than an era of TV and stereo, this was obvious. The expectation by my generation of change at the flick of a switch seemed naive to our elders — and it was. But it was not simply the naiveté of youth. It was as well the inevitable homage we had to pay to the place where our feet were planted when we began our leap.

CAPITALISM PRESERVES ITSELF

Ironically, the failures of the present system may, for the moment, be maintaining it in a way its successes (at least in its own terms) could not have. The inflation and disruption of economic growth that today are of such concern have the effect of countering the disengagement from economic preoccupations that had begun to take hold in the Sixties. Americans had no more (in material terms) in the Sixties than they do now, but many *felt* more affluent. For that reason a certain degree of questioning of the sufficiency of wealth as a life goal and as the chief source of one's life satisfactions could occur. It was simply harder to attribute one's dissatisfactions to not "having" enough.

We still live well, but fewer of us see a continuing prospect for "more" each year, and consequently fewer think of themselves as affluent or comfortable.* This makes it easy to revive the "if only I had" kind of thinking that attributes one's discontent to economic rather than psychological factors. Many of the young today, responding to their parents' subjective sense of being economically strapped, have returned to the quest for higher income as the royal road to security and the good life.

---

*As noted earlier, this feeling is also a result of our having created a way of life in which we actually do need more all the time. Families who some years back experienced their one car as a luxury are now enmeshed in a way of life that requires them to support two or three cars, with no sense of luxury about it at all.

Thus there is an unwitting conservative genius in our social arrangements that neutralizes the prospect for change. The success of our economic efforts threatened to undermine the commitment of a new contingent of young people in the 1960s, but the ebbing of growth in the 1970s brought the young people of that decade back into pledging allegiance to the GNP. What success could not achieve, failure did handily.

So for the moment the economic vision of life is again ascendant. But the custodians of this economistic *revanche* face a ticklish task. To succeed they must fail. To keep our eyes glued to "the bottom line" they must convince us we are in the red. If they dare to let us see our affluence, we must seek the source of our discontent elsewhere, and our vision of the good life can be liberated from its economistic blinders, as it was in the 1960s. The conservative tide that seems to be sweeping not only the United States but some other Western nations as well is not insubstantial, but it is nonetheless fragile. It is natural for people, when they are confused and troubled, to wish to reaffirm what they have organized their lives around. But as described in the last chapter, there are ample signs that, quietly and with much less notoriety, many of the trends that began in the 1960s are in fact continuing. Whether a successful and enduring transition to a post-consumerist way of life can be achieved will depend on whether we can avoid the errors that have brought us our present regression.

Structures and Illusions

One of the central errors of the Sixties was a failure to appreciate the importance of structures in maintaining any way of life or cast of mind. In some respects the *negative* implications of structures were in fact grasped; the way, for example, that roles can trap us and make it almost impossible to live out values that one held before immersion in the role's demands. Recognizing that taking a job that was part of an ongoing social structure might dull their idealism, many young people delayed entering careers and similarly put off traditional commitments to marriage and family. But in many cases they failed to appreciate sufficiently that they had to live in *some* structure, that an autonomous existence guided only by the lodestar of their inner promptings and true selves is a myth. As a consequence, they failed to create alternative structures that could sustain them in their desire to work for change.

The momentum for change was generated largely from the campuses because the campuses did provide such a structure. Daily contacts with others who shared the same aims and values helped activist students to sustain each other in their efforts. Group support was a crucial element in each individual's ability to persist. (So too, of course, were the opportunity for large amounts of unstructured time and, in many cases, the lack of a necessity to earn a living.)

Efforts to develop support groups that would sustain their evolving set of values certainly were made. The commune movement is the most obvious example. The communities of hangers-on that accumulated in university areas, with their own hand trades and shops, are another instance, less explicitly planned but effective for a while.

But the next step—that of creating structures and paths that would enable them to retain their new values and ideals as their student days began to recede—proved more difficult. As the need arose to earn a living and, particularly, to support children and provide them with an education and with opportunities of their own, more and more of the Sixties rebels found themselves feeling forced to enter the very structures against which they had protested. At first many tried at least to enter human service jobs, even if within traditional structures. As the economy became more problematic,* the decline of support for human services forced many into jobs still farther removed from what they would have expected just a few years before.

The hesitancy of Sixties activists to put forth concrete plans for the new society they desired is understandable in light of the perversion of ideals that resulted from the overly planned structure of the Soviet Union. But the refusal to attempt to articulate some new, potentially more humane set of guiding structures was a serious error. The romantic notion of just letting the revolution happen, without encumbering it with premature designs, was ultimately a formula for erosion of the thrust for

---

*I use this ambiguous word intentionally here because, as I have argued elsewhere in this book, the problem was at least as much one of people's *perception* of their economic situation as of actual difficulties in obtaining needed goods.

change. Lacking alternative structures, the majority of dissi-
dent young people were inexorably edged into the only structures there were—those of the economic mainstream. I do not
believe that their conversion thereby to the values they had resisted was as complete as the media have sometimes implied. A
potential for the participation of many of them in a new effort
for change still exists. Even those who entered Wall Street law
firms or corporate hierarchies did in many instances remain
different from their older colleagues. But clearly the cutting
edge of their dissent began to dull as they entered their new
roles.

STRUCTURES OF TRANSITION

Given the obstacles our present system poses, it was probably not possible to create alternative structures on anything like
the scale of, or anywhere near as comprehensive as, those of the
mainstream of the economically dominated society. A counterculture is by its very nature relatively small. It is not realistic to
think that a whole generation—or even the entire progressive
portion of a generation—could escape the necessity of employment within and dealings with large corporations. But it *was*
possible to conceive of a far more extensive set of support structures than was actually developed. If a total alternative to
mainstream institutions could not be achieved, middle-range
efforts—efforts neither individualistic nor pointed specifically
toward state power—could have been attempted more than
they were.

The effectiveness of such efforts was evident in the one
place where it was extensively tried: the women's movement.
Consciousness-raising groups provided mutual support that sustained women in a way that more individualistic efforts would
not have. The leaders of the women's movement recognized
that it was not enough to educate women as separate individuals; to stay changed, they needed to help each other not fall
back. There is certainly still a great deal more to be achieved by
the women's movement (at this writing the ERA is still unrati-
fied, and a powerful backlash has developed toward the movement as a whole). But it is nonetheless true that in a rather
short time profound changes in the social fabric have appeared, including changes in the most intimate realm of per-

sonal interactions, a realm where change is not achieved very easily.

In general, the social movements of the Sixties did not utilize in a sustained fashion mechanisms equivalent to the consciousness-raising group. (Teach-ins, for example, tended to be one-shot affairs rather than ongoing groups with a stable membership and the possibility of airing—and receiving reassurances about—doubts of a personal nature.) There was potentially a sufficient critical mass to sustain the movement through difficult times, but there was insufficient creation of mutual support groups, which are essential if people are to be able to risk both temptation and humiliation and to press on with moral suasion despite the lack of immediate results. What distinguishes a movement from a fad is the creation of sustaining structures that keep people bound together in their commitments. The larger socioeconomic system creates powerful negative feedback that sustains the present equilibrium. It is extraordinarily difficult for the individual to resist those forces for very long. In order to do so, continuing mutual encouragement and mutual reaffirmation of commitment are essential.

Because of the individualistic assumptions that Sixties youth brought to bear on their change efforts (discussed in a different context in Chapter Six), they failed to appreciate how crucial structures like those provided by the college campus were to the movement they were part of. The inhibiting effect of present structures was perceived, but the need for alternative ones was befogged by a neo-anarchist rhetoric that confused premature *closure* of structures with structure altogether. It is particularly tempting, having achieved the insight that what is most essential for us now is a revolution of *personal* life, to assume that that can be achieved individual by individual. As I have tried to show, the irony is that that way of thinking is very much at the core of the system they were trying to change.

Generational Politics and the Dangers of "Us–Them" Thinking

The slighting of sustaining structures was closely related to another feature of the Sixties movements that contributed to their at least temporary dissolution: the emphasis on youth. This emphasis itself reflected the power that sustaining structures do play when they are available: the importance of the campus as such a structure shaped a vision that was generational rather than ideological or class-oriented — and this despite evidence that many of the activists of the Sixties in fact shared values with their parents (and of course differed with many of their own "under-30" generation).[6]

The problem is poignantly illustrated by an Op-Ed article that appeared in *The New York Times* after the election of Ronald Reagan.[7] The author had been a member of the Sixties generation, had worked for Eugene McCarthy and other peace candidates, and had "never missed a peace march." When she married in 1968 she vowed never to abandon her commitments and never to be like her parents. Writing in 1980, she lamented the life-style she was living. She was "furious" with herself but felt "trapped in the labyrinth of our consumer-oriented society" and a "slave to [her] possessions."

In trying to understand what had happened, she points to the new economic needs brought on by the birth of her children, to the culture she encountered when she moved to the suburbs to give the kids more room, and to the death of her mother, which forced her to grow up. She concludes as well that she was naive in expecting her generation would change the world, because for everyone like herself there were 50 who couldn't care less about war, injustice, or anything but property values.

Her story struck a chord in me. Though she in some ways fitted the media image of the Sixties activist who had sold out to the consumer society, she clearly was still struggling with the choices she had made, as are, I suspect, the great majority of those now being written off as safely settled in suburban conservatism. I felt sympathy for her and hope that she might still rejoin the effort to make it a better world. But most of all I felt that like so many of her (my) generation, she still didn't understand what had happened. She berates herself for not keeping the three promises her husband asked of her when they married: "Promise me we'll never be bourgeois; promise me we'll never be bogged down by possessions; promise me you'll never grow up."

The reason for the failure to keep the first two promises, I submit, was the thinking that underlay the third. It equated the keeping of their ideals with not growing up and thus made it almost certain that when they (inevitably) did grow up they would be unable and unprepared to sustain their commitments in the face of the pressures of the consumer society. In making such a promise they were evidencing a failure to think through how they *would* maintain their ideals as they grew up, or even to anticipate that that would happen. The hopeful side of her story is that, for all her immersion in a life organized around possessions, she still holds to the first two promises as an ideal; the discouraging side is that she still does not see the flaw in the third. One of the most crucial lessons we must pass on to the generation now coming of age is that they must not equate idealism with youth. For they too will grow up, and anything they achieve in working for a better world will be ephemeral if it must disappear with their youth.

An equally important, and related, lesson that today's youth must learn is not to dismiss a whole generation as hopelessly compromised, as did many of the Sixties generation. People like the writer of that Op-Ed article are now bourgeois, they are part of the problem; but they are also sensitive human beings who recognize how they have been lured onto a false path and who might again be recruited as allies rather than inevitably locked in opposition. Generational politics is inherently futile; it inevitably means that you will grow up to be the enemy of your own ideals. It turns serious social and political analysis into a fad that can last no longer than the time until the present generation in revolt has children of its own. (In this sense it is symptomatic of the faddist proclivities of the consumer society as a whole.)

But it is important to go beyond just avoiding generational politics in order not to box oneself into a corner or to leave room for oneself when one grows up. It is necessary as well to avoid the kind of us-them thinking that dismisses a substantial proportion of the human race as beyond redemption and views it essentially as the enemy. It is common for critics of our present system to portray it as one in which a relative minority—the owning class, the managerial caste, or the Establishment, for example—exploits and manipulates the rest of the citizenry for its own purposes. There is much justification for such a perspective. Certainly there are some who get much more out of present arrangements than others—who live longer and better, have nicer homes, more possessions, better health care, more varied opportunities for leisure and entertainment, and—perhaps most importantly—more power over their own lives and the lives of others. There is justification as well in the claim that those on top *use* that power to keep things as they are, to perpetuate inequalities and maintain themselves in positions of power and superiority. I am not sanguine about the motives of our corporate elite. The list of their overtly harmful and exploitative acts—dumping chemicals in a Love Canal, hiding safety defects in an automobile model, intimidating Southern textile workers attempting to unionize, fighting safety regulations on the job, or supporting the covert overthrow of legally elected foreign governments—is enormous and horrifying.

Yet despite all this—and despite my belief that corporate officials should be held personally responsible for their cynical and callous "business decisions"—I believe we can best understand our present situation as the result of a pattern of self-defeating choices and actions in which we *all* are caught. The system works better, to be sure, for the rich and powerful, but in the long run it works poorly for all. Even the winners are losers compared to what life could be like under different ground rules. Even executives are hurt by ozone depletion, toxic wastes, and unclean air. Their efforts on behalf of the system that "benefits" them require substantial self-deception, not just mystification of others.

Family therapists, applying a similar perspective to problems once thought to reside strictly within the individual, have shown how victim and villain alike, patient and "normal" family member, participate jointly in a repeated pattern from which none of them seem able to release either themselves or the others. All are ultimately deceived and cheated by the short-run gains or protections the system provides. Some fare better than others, but all have a tiger by the tail and fear letting go. The full ethical implications of this are still to be worked out. In one sense there clearly are still victims and there are still those whose acts are reprehensible. Yet hewing strictly and solely to such a view may prevent just the sort of change that ultimately will release the victim (and the perpetrator as well) from a way of life that is but a pale shadow of what should be our birthright.

Our continuation of a way of life that places accumulation of commodities ahead of enjoyment of living (and obscures the distinction between the two) is a result of our joint participation in a system that seems to have a life of its own. That system in one sense is the sum of our individual choices and actions, and yet it is also more than that: It presses us into action automatically and almost inexorably.

Such a perspective suggests that the potential exists for creating an empathic bond between social activists and many of those who initially are in opposition to them. It may be true that, as was said in the 1960s, "if you're not part of the solution, you're part of the problem," but membership in one or the other category is not fixed. Many of the opponents of the efforts of the Sixties were far more conflicted than either they or the activists recognized. They were decent people doing (or supporting) indecent things. What they were *doing* needed to be opposed, but *they* needed to be enlisted, not excoriated.

Attempts were certainly made in this direction in the 1960s. Many hoped to create a mass movement, and the cry "join us" was uttered frequently. But on the whole there was little empathy or sympathy shown for those who were conflicted and/or trapped in the kinds of roles in which the young protestors would themselves be enmeshed a decade later. On the issues, the protestors were right (I still believe), but one cannot recruit among the compromised majority by flouting one's moral superiority. That is gratifying but ineffective. It is also, if one has come by one's purity by not having yet to support a family or search for a job, unfair.

Parables and Utopias

There is a parable, popular among family therapists, that captures well much of what I have been pointing toward in this chapter. In this story, a sinner is being shown Heaven and Hell. He sees two large doors and is led through one of them, which he assumes at first is the door to Heaven because of the wonderful aroma of delectable foods that greets him. As he enters he sees a number of people sitting around a large round table. He notices that despite the wonderful feast in the middle, the peo-

ple look emaciated and groan with hunger. Each has a spoon
with a very long handle that can reach the food in the middle.
But because the handles are so much longer than their arms,
none can get the food into their mouths. They suffer terribly
from the unceasing hunger and frustration, and the man realizes he is in Hell. He is then led through the other door to see
Heaven. At first he sees what looks like the same situation — the
same delicious food, the same large table, people sitting around
it with long-handled spoons. But these people look cheerful and
well fed, and they are chatting and laughing. The man is puz-
zled and asks what the difference is here. The reply: They have
learned to feed each other.[8]

This parable and the analysis that preceded it are by no
means presented as a formula for assuring success. They are
rather a minimum for not assuring failure — a more modest but
nonetheless useful contribution. There are many features of
American life that make it difficult to persist for long, and even
more difficult to thrive, in an alternative to the consumer culture — the structure of our cities and suburbs; the nature of the
work available; the things our friends admire or envy us for; the
expectations and temptations our children encounter daily;
and so forth. Without a great deal of continuing support from
others, and without the creation of alternative structures that
can provide the feedback that sustains change, people who
have tried to change will begin to feel enormous pressure to go
back to the patterns that society at large calls forth. They will
begin to "feel" the needs they once spurned and will then conclude — as will those who watched them from the shopping center — that "human nature" was just too much to keep down.

The reader who is persuaded by the arguments in this book
may be assured that the changes in his or her perceptions will
be short-lived unless concrete steps are taken to create a structure of commitments. An individual decision to buy less, to
strive less for higher income, and to concentrate instead on
what really matters is likely to have all the impact and staying
power of a New Year's resolution.

What is required are concrete steps that are at least semi-
irrevocable: joining together, for example, with a few friends
who have similarly come to understand the contradictions and
self-deceptions of the consumer treadmill; making explicit and
public commitments to each other about changes you will make

in the next week or month; meeting regularly in consciousness-raising sessions to spur each other on to adhere to the mutually given promises; talking at those meetings about the difficulties of living differently when the rest of the society hasn't yet; and (crucially) considering how you might work to bring about the larger social changes that will make every step along the way easier.

Even if we avoid all the pitfalls discussed here, we may fail anyway. From the perspective of currently dominant assumptions, much of what I have been advocating can seem quite utopian. The forces aligned against change are formidable. But I believe that nothing is as naively utopian as continuing on our present course, using up nonrenewable resources, fouling our own air and water, stirring discontents we are increasingly unable to ease, and hoping for a *deus ex machina* under the name of "technology" to bail us out at the last minute. I do not know if we can make the changes we need to, but a hard-headed look at where we are now suggests we'd sure better try.

PART III

Against the Tide

NINE

The Dilemmas of
Psychological Man

THE ANALYSIS I HAVE PRESENTED thus far seems to be out of step with the times. We enter the 1980s in the spirit of cost-accounting, not of personal growth and psychological exploration. Inflation, not the search for meaning, dominates our national consciousness. The most influential social critics of recent years have decried not the soullessness of the search for profits but rather the soullessness of the search for self.

At the same time we are witnessing a recrudescence of the worship of the market as the "invisible hand" that benignly guides our destiny. Our problems, we are told, stem not from the values of the market place but from bureaucrats and do-gooders who tamper with this most extraordinary of worldly miracles. Indeed, to be quite frank, this is a time when selfishness is elevated and concern for others' welfare derided, when the cumulative intelligence of decades of insights into our interdependency is being submerged in a tide of the most unenlightened self-interest.

Tides ebb and flow, however, and in swimming against the tides that are currently fashionable I am not exhibiting courage so much as faith in our capacity to come to our senses before it is too late. This faith is a bit like Pascal's: I am well aware that it may be unfounded, but I dare not take the chance. It may not be possible to stem the tide before the worldwide consequences of exponential growth or of the worship of greed in a nuclear age overtake us. But we must proceed as if it is.

This last part of the book examines several themes that have recently been in the ascendancy in our culture, which present critical challenges to the ideas put forth here. Some of these challenges come from defenders of the status quo, some from those who regard themselves as critics of that status quo. But all are influential and must be confronted in advocating the position I do here.

In this chapter and the next I consider the implications of the increasingly critical stance toward psychology and psychologizing that the last few years have brought. In the last two I look at issues having to do with jobs and with the role of the market in governing human affairs.

Psychology Under Attack

Advocacy of a greater role for psychological concerns in our personal and cultural life is distinctly a minority position these days. We are far more likely to be told that we suffer from too much emphasis on the psychological than too little. Indeed, to many critics ours is a society in which psychology has run rampant. Philip Rieff, in several important works, has talked of the emergence of "psychological man" as the dominant character type of our time.[1] Martin Gross, in a far less substantial work[2] but one that has caught the attention of Congressional critics of the mental health movement,[3] has described us as a "psychological society." Michael Nelson, in the *Washington Monthly*, refers to our "insane . . . hunger for psychology" and tells us that psychology "has been Eve, Pandora, and the Sorcerer's Apprentice rolled into one, releasing selfish excesses in the human spirit that it cannot hope to control or contain."[4] Charles Krauthammer, in *The New Republic*, writes that the increasingly common picture of "the national body politic as some huge neurotic psyche with headlines for symptoms testifies to the ascendancy of psychological determinism as our favorite explanatory principle" and adds that "the psychologized view of the world carries with it a pernicious reductionism that debases and deforms moral discourse."[5] Christopher Lasch warns against the "inherently expansionist ambitions of modern psychiatry" and "the evil of psychologizing."[6]

Our overemphasis on psychology has also resulted, according to some critics, in a debilitating and misguided reliance on presumed psychological experts. Thomas Szasz's criticisms of psychological and psychiatric experts in the courts; Christopher Lasch's criticisms of our reliance on psychological professionals in family and school; Michel Foucault's questioning of the benign effects of our "enlightened" ideas about punishment, rehabilitation, and psychological illness—these and related criticisms have become increasingly influential in recent years.

We are told that we have become obsessed with our selves. I use here two words instead of the more common term "ourselves" in order to highlight what is at issue: The claim is that rather than experiencing ourselves in a natural, unself-conscious way, we are continuously, obsessively, and centrally aware of our "selves" almost as separate entities that we observe, evaluate, and try to improve. At the same time, in a fashion that at first seems paradoxical but on closer inspection seems perfectly straightforward, critics note that our self-obsessed populace seems to crave and strive for intimacy to an unprecedented degree. Our concern with achieving emotional immediacy, with assaying and refining the quality of our interpersonal relations, places an enormous burden on the institutions of marriage and family and makes even casual relationships a source of continual anxious and fetishistic evaluation rather than simple pleasure. According to Richard Sennett,[7] older ideals of sociability in terms of citizenship and cooperativeness have been replaced by ideals of closeness, with unfortunate consequences for both citizen cooperation and intimate relations. Others[8] have stressed how our concern with the psychological dimension of life has eroded commitment to social change. We have made, it is suggested, all aspects of our lives psychological, have subordinated every other category and ideal to that of individual experience and self-examination.

In their particulars the various critics I shall address in this and the next chapter are often in substantial disagreement. Some, for example, argue that we have been led astray by Freud,[9] others that we have retreated from the truth he wrested for us from the dark and menacing depths.[10] Some claim that we have overvalued psychotherapy and should emphasize instead psychoactive drugs,[11] others that the drugs are the major threat and that we should return to psychotherapy.[12] But there seems to be little disagreement that the role of psychology in our culture and the ways in which psychology is being used have become matters about which we should be seriously concerned.

I share this concern in certain respects. But I believe that most of the critics have failed to identify quite precisely enough the heart of the difficulty with the way in which psychology and psychologizing are being used in our culture. As a consequence they have not recognized how the same trends that now seem so regressive can, with some recasting, point toward precisely the kind of reorientation in basic values and in social relations that our situation requires.

Philip Rieff and the Critique of the "Therapeutic"

In many ways the most thoughtful and perceptive critique of the role in our society of psychology and the values associated with it has been that offered by Philip Rieff. Behind the more overt evidences of selfishness and withdrawal from social action that contemporary critics of narcissism and psychologizing have emphasized, Rieff sees a more profound difficulty. In both *Freud: The Mind of the Moralist* and *The Triumph of the Therapeutic*, Rieff is concerned with examining the implications of a trend in Western culture that pits the fulfillment of the individual against what are seen as the dead forms and empty traditions of the culture and seeks to "liberate" the individual from the deceptions and restrictions that culture imposes. Such an effort — in effect to live *without* a culture, to be free, separate, "autonomous" — involves a colossal hubris. Some fabric of symbols and social bonds is always necessary to control "the infinite variety of panic and emptiness to which [men] are exposed. It is to control their dis-ease as individuals that men have always acted culturally, in good faith. . . . Culture is another name for a design of motives directing the self outward, toward those communal purposes *in which alone the self can be realized and satisfied*."[13]

Yet, Rieff says, in modern times men have programmatically attempted to evade or oppose the network of meanings and obligations that constitute culture. This has occurred in a number of ways. First of all, he notes, "a culture survives principally . . . by the power of its institutions to bind and loose men in the conduct of their affairs with reasons which sink so deep into the self that they become commonly and implicitly understood."[14] But, says Rieff, ours is a culture "constantly probing its own unwitting part."[15] We "aspire to think without assent"; we desire "not to be deceived"; we engage in the "systematic hunting down of all settled convictions."[16] As a consequence we are continually undermining the basis for our shared cultural life and attempting to substitute the authority of our own urges—perceived with what is thought to be unprecedented clarity—for all previous authorities, whether parental, political, or moral.

The continual questioning of all cultural givens and all cultural demands has, Rieff suggests, its own programmatic ethic, but an ethic of a rather different sort. What is being created is essentially an anticultural culture, a culture in which good and evil are viewed simply as deceptions. We are to live "with a minimum of pretense to anything more grand than sweetening the time."[17] In the new culture, "men will have ceased to seek any salvation other than amplitude in living itself."[18]

Much of what Rieff has to say seems to me absolutely critical to any consideration of the change in values I am advocating in this book. Though I hope to distinguish my conception from that which Rieff labels as "psychological man," I view Rieff's critique of that creature as perhaps the single most important argument I must confront in articulating what I do or do not wish would happen in our collective evolution as a society and as a species. Rieff's most basic premise is mine as well: that only via an identification with some communal purpose, only through participation in a shared set of values and meaning-giving rules and assumptions can the search for fulfillment have any chance of real success. If a still greater turn toward psychology is to have the effect of further releasing us from ties of community and mutual responsibility, then it will indeed be a turn toward an emptier and even less satisfying way of life.

Rieff tells us he is aware that his speculations "may be thought to contain some parodies of an apocalypse. But what apocalypse," he asks, "has ever been so kindly? What culture has ever attempted to see to it that no ego is hurt?"[19] "To call corrupt a culture purchased at lower cost to our nerves, and at larger magnitudes of self-fulfillment, would show a lamentable lack of imagination."[20] Yet coming clearly through the layers of irony that characterize Rieff's prose is a vivid sense that imagination is precisely what is lacking in the *proponents* of that culture. Though he does recognize the value, and even the necessity, of the modern emphasis on the prerogatives of the self, the thrust of his argument clearly implies that a vain and foolish philistinism has led us to a wasteland, even if it be a wasteland in which not only milk and honey abound, but sex and "self-actualization" as well.

RELIGIOUS MAN, ECONOMIC MAN, AND PSYCHOLOGICAL MAN

The fulcrum of Rieff's critique lies in the shift in our culture from a religious to a psychological orientation to life. His concern is with the loss of the transcendant values and commitments that for centuries gave meaning to the lives of men and women in the (Judeo-) Christian West. In a sense, his work constitutes a form of mourning for something treasured that has been lost. Like most mourners, Rieff is in fact ambivalent about what has been lost. He does not idealize or romanticize life under the rule of Christian piety. But he is still deeply enough engaged in the mourning that he finds replacements inadequate.

Recognition of this elegiac air to Rieff's arguments provides us with one important key to constructing a meaningful alternative where Rieff would caution us there is none. To Rieff all potential replacements seem to be equally inadequate, and he brushes lightly over differences that for our purposes are critical. He notes, but does not emphasize, that between the era of "religious man" and that of "psychological man" an intermediate stage occurred: that of "economic man." The hold of religion on Western man was declining well before Freud made his own particular effort to analyze it away. Rieff himself notes "the general expansion of pleasure that had been in progress since the eighteenth century set Western culture on its course of revolt against Christian ascetic standards of conduct."[21] That revolt, however much its banner may now be carried by psychological man, originated in a pre-Freudian world. The first replacement for religious man was economic man.

The quest for material well-being and an intense concern with earning a livelihood have, of course, always been important parts of men's lives. But until relatively recently economic concerns, however much of the day they took up, were subordinated in important ways to other considerations viewed as "higher."[22] Probably part of the reason for this was that until relatively recently there was little prospect for improvement in the economic status of most people. Their framework of meaning, while influenced by the quest for material comfort, looked beyond it — indeed had to if life was not to seem intolerable.

For several centuries, however, the religious orientation has been declining, and we have been in an era of unprecedented economic growth and activity.* More and more, *economics*, concern with the accumulation and production of material goods, has become the measure of our lives. Transcendant values are not being undermined by the siren call of the psychologist; that job was accomplished long ago by the banker, the merchant, and the industrialist. And now, as this era of economic expansion is drawing to a close, it is the economic orientation to life that is being replaced by psychology, not the religious.

Many of the defects of the therapeutic or self-actualizing orientation are in fact vestiges of the values of "economic man," which are still quite influential in many aspects of our culture. What passes for self-actualization is all too often a model of self-enhancement based not on experiential but on economic metaphors. Our new psychological hucksters are hucksters first and psychologists decidedly second, whether they be formally trained in psychology or more nakedly revealed as public relations types. The est-chatology of the profiteering gurus reflects a vision part P. T. Barnum and part robber baron, not a cul-

---

*Most recently, of course, economic growth has been threatened. There seems too, in recent years, to have developed what looks like a resurgence of religious fundamentalism both here and abroad. In some ways both these trends bear on the concerns of this book and will be addressed at various points. But I believe that the reader will find that neither bears directly on my difference with Rieff as described here.

mination of our understanding of the experience of satisfaction, vitality, and relatedness.

Understanding the role of economic values in trends that at first appear more strictly psychological in nature tempers the view of these trends as primarily reflecting decadent decline. Such understanding suggests that the "therapeutic" orientation may be more aptly named than even Rieff intended, in that it may reflect not a continuation of the loss of transcendant values but a genuinely reparative effort to deal with that very loss — a loss largely the result of the rapacious individualism and crass materialism of "economic man."

Psychological Man and Freudian Man

How well the new turn to psychology can actually be reparative depends on a second consideration upon which I depart from Rieff's analysis. Put aphoristically, the problems Rieff attributes to *psychological* man I attribute largely to *Freudian* man. My disagreements with Rieff on this score are twofold. On the one hand, Rieff views many of the excesses of psychological man as a result of our having abandoned the profound insights of Freud and pursued instead ideas that are travesties and caricatures of Freudianism. At the same time Rieff does see Freud's own ideas as ultimately leading us to the same impasse, but he has such respect for Freud that he sees no way out of the cul-de-sac to which Freud has brought us. Freud has, it seems, analyzed the ground out from under our feet, and Rieff sees no way to achieve a genuinely solid new foundation, because he accepts Freud's analysis as correct. I wish to argue instead that many of the most problematic features of the contemporary "therapeutic" orientation are a consequence precisely of its tendency *to* follow Freud (even where its advocates think they depart), and that genuine alternatives to the Freudian vision, rooted in his most important observations but embodying them in a very different theoretical and philosophical context, do in fact exist and are far more powerful than Rieff is willing to acknowledge.

Central to what is problematic in the world view of Rieff's psychological man is the excessive individualism the latter manifests. It is in his belief that the narrow pursuit of his own pleasure is his only responsibility; that there is essentially no other reality than that of what feels good; that the public world need be of no concern to him—it is in his excessively private and inward focus that psychological man deserves the scorn and the pity he has received.

I concur with much of Rieff's rather dour assessment of these tendencies in our cultural life. Where I disagree is in his assessment of the alternatives offered us by the neo-Freudian revisions of Freud's formulations. Like other social critics of a Freudian bent (e.g., Christopher Lasch, Russell Jacoby, Herbert Marcuse), Rieff finds the neo-Freudians sunny, shallow, and insignificant. In fact, however, their formulations can account for all the observations of human behavior that Freud's did, and they do so in a way that has quite different implications for man's relation to the social order and for the possibilities of change and renewal. The potential soundness of a turn toward a greater psychological emphasis in our society depends a great deal on whether we must stick with the Freudian vision. Therefore the following discussion of the neo-Freudians and their differences from Freud is crucial to the concerns pursued in this book.

The neo-Freudians are not in intellectual favor these days. The ferment that they generated in the 1930s and 1940s has all but disappeared. It is not that Freudian psychoanalysis is without its serious critics today. Indeed, behavior therapists, family therapists, and students of pharmacologic and genetic approaches constitute a more considerable threat to Freudian hegemony than the neo-Freudians ever did. But among those who take at all seriously the discoveries of psychoanalysis, the orthodox Freudian version is clearly ascendant over the neo-Freudian. There are large numbers of therapists who describe themselves as "neo-Freudian" or "interpersonal" in orientation, but they have not sustained a vital intellectual tradition. Freudian groups seem more intellectually active, and Freudian journals more consistent sources of intellectual ferment. Why this should have happened—and especially why I think it happened despite what I believe to be the greater soundness of the neo-Freudian formulations—is a very large topic, one I hope to address in another book.[23]

As we saw earlier, the highly individualistic world view of nineteenth-century capitalism left its mark on psychoanalytic thought. By incorporating his new insights into a framework rooted in an atomistic vision, with society and culture just a backdrop to the main drama, Freud gave a particular cast to the role those insights would play in our culture. The implications of the neo-Freudian recasting of those insights are quite different.

For Freud, the basic unit of observation and analysis was the individual; for the neo-Freudians it was the individual in his context. The distinction is not just rhetorical. To be sure, Freud was frequently concerned with questions of the person's relation to his environment, and in psychoanalytic ego psychology such questions became of even greater concern. But at the heart of Freudian thought is an emphasis on intrapsychic considerations. The environment is seen to play some role in shaping the personality structure in the early years; and it is relevant later as a source of frustration or gratification (setting the limits within which the intrapsychic tendencies may manifest themselves) and as a trigger, releasing pre-set mechanisms and reactions at certain times and not others.[24] But the clear central emphasis in the Freudian tradition is on the influence of forces and structures within the individual personality. These are (at least by the time one is an adult) the givens, the prime movers. The person's daily world is the stage upon which these inner scripts are played out. The role of the conditions and events of daily life in rewriting the script—or a recognition that particular kinds of daily experiences are required to keep it the same—these are decidedly secondary in the Freudian view.

In contrast, the work of the neo-Freudians implied a more thoroughgoing incorporation of contextual influences. This was accomplished not by a theory of simple environmental determinism but rather by a transactional account, in which the needs, wishes, ideas, and characteristics of the person are as critical as the influence of the environment. What was offered was, in fact, a theory of how the two determine each other in a series of continuing transactions and equilibrations. I have elsewhere discussed this conception in terms of its implications for psychotherapy, for personality theory, and for psychological research.[25] Here I wish to concentrate on its relevance both to the social dilemmas of concern in this book and to the criticisms of psychologizing that have become so prevalent.

Both as an independent and continuing influence in its own right and as reworked by Freud, the conception of human behavior that underlay laissez-faire economic thinking continues to dominate our thinking about psychology. People are conceived of as separate and competitive units, each seeking his own satisfaction. If this individualistic seeking should produce some good for others, all well and good. But it is a widely shared core assumption that the aim of each individual is his or her own gratification or fulfillment and that other people are indeed *other*. Each person seeks to satisfy inner needs, to *get* something he doesn't have. Even self-esteem, for example, is spoken of by Freud in terms of narcissistic "supplies."

Consistent with the conceived "otherness" of other people, much psychological writing — and the social criticism that derives from it — talks of the person's "inner world" and often contrasts its depth and creative possibilities with the shallowness of "outward" or "external" adaptation. Freud's insights and observations, however, need not be construed in terms of such a sharp distinction between "inner" and "outer." Nor need they imply that the pursuit of personal pleasure is likely to be at the expense of, or even independent of, the well-being of others. They can be perfectly consistent with a conception of interdependency and with a view of "inner" experience that understands experience in terms of the real interactions in which the person is engaged. By examining Freud's way of observing and of formulating his ideas, we may see both how an alternative can be constructed and why exclusive reliance on the Freudian vision yields an unnecessarily negative estimate of the consequences of a greater societal emphasis on the psychological dimension.

Freud was struck by the lawfulness and the dynamic structure of what he observed. What seemed to "emerge" from the patient's free associations, what seemed to "unfold" in the transference, had an order and a structure and seemed to reveal something already "in" the patient. Terms like "unfold" or "emerge" — not particularly Freud's vocabulary, but quite consistent with his way of looking at things — are now common currency in psychological discourse.[26]

There is a certain validity in this way of looking at things. People do show certain consistencies. Blockages in expression do occur. And when they are diminished or resolved, what appears is at least to some degree predictable. This level of orderliness is what, for a number of interesting reasons, behaviorists tend to deny and to miss.[27]

But the picture Freud obtained, and the picture seen by many contemporary psychotherapists, is incomplete. Freud's free-associative method facilitated the therapist's discerning the connections between the ideas in the patient's mind and the nature of his prevailing wishes and fantasies, but it impeded the gathering of information about the context of the patient's behavior and the relation of his behavior and experience to that context. Moreover, the findings generated in this truncated way led to formulations that seemed to justify this way of gathering data. The limitations of the method were thus self-reinforcing; corrective ideas and observations were excluded by its very logic.

For example, Freud's focus on the unfolding of the inner characteristics of the individual led to an effort to reveal how the buried past distorted reactions in the present. Freud sought to demonstrate to his patients that their reactions were *not* realistic responses to the present but reflected instead disavowed wishes and ideas from within. Their reactions to him in particular were to be understood as having little to do with any real characteristics of his, but as stemming instead from parental images retained from early childhood. Consequently, Freud—and later analysts—strove for neutrality or anonymity, for a stance so unintrusive that the patient would have to recognize that the emotions he felt came from deep within, not from his perception of present "external" reality. Moreover, since the method of Freud's own research, as well as the path toward uncovering and unraveling the patient's secret wishes and conflicts, lay in finding the thread through the patient's free associations, relatively little stress was placed on discovering the details of the patient's daily exchanges with others.

Both these considerations led to a disinclination to question the patient actively, especially about his present interactions. But it is only through very careful, persistent questioning along these lines that the role of everyday reality in maintaining the seemingly out of touch, seemingly infantile fantasies and wishes can be discerned.[28] Since Freud and later analysts did not, with their methods, get the data that would make an explanation in terms of current input plausible, they continued to hold to a rather exclusively intrapsychic theory. And since they held such a theory, they continued to use a method consistent with it—a method that could not bring forth the kind of data needed to change the theory.

In the Freudian view, the infantile nature of the wishes, fantasies, and thought processes discovered in the course of psychoanalytic exploration is due to an intrapsychic, structural feature of the mind and to occurrences in early childhood: ideas and wishes that are repressed because they are too intolerable for the child to deal with are kept out of the growing organization of the ego, and thus are prevented from growing up and being brought into line with other ideas and with the hierarchy of values and aims that characterize the person's view of the world and of himself as he matures. The picture in this account of early psychic states and contents being preserved in their original form reminded me of the stories one hears of Arctic explorers who found woolly mammoths frozen in the ice, still fresh after thousands of years. Consequently, I have on several occasions described this aspect of the Fruedian model as the "woolly mammoth model."[29]

In contrast to what is implied by the woolly mammoth model, my reading of the neo-Freudians and my own clinical experience (in a psychodynamic approach that does include detailed questioning about the patient's daily interactions with others) suggest a different account of why such "infantile" features are found when one looks below the surface. This alternative view, a variety of interpersonal or transactional theorizing, is built on many of the same observations that undergird the Freudian view. But instead of seeing these seemingly infantile features as persisting *in spite of* the person's present reality, they are viewed as persisting precisely *because of* that reality. When one looks carefully enough at the person's daily interactions, one discovers that each person skews his environment in an idiosyncratic fashion.

Consider, for example, the person who despite an outwardly mild, cooperative manner—indeed a demeanor that is meek and unassuming to excess—reveals in his dreams, his slips, his associations, and perhaps occasionally in troubling conscious fantasies, a struggle with murderously destructive inclinations. Such individuals are usually characterized in psychoanalytic accounts as exhibiting a *reaction-formation*; that is, their exaggeratedly friendly and pleasant manner is seen as a way of defending against the hostile inclinations.

That much would be agreed to in the interpersonal framework as well. Where the two points of view differ is in their understanding of where the rage that is being defended against comes from. In the classical Freudian version, it is an impulse from the past, which exerts a continuing pressure upon the ego that has little to do with what is currently going on. The rageful impulse, a bit of preserved childhood irrationality, is viewed at all points of the analysis as the primary force; the defense is reactive to it.

In the alternative considered here the *origin* of this pattern is viewed somewhat similarly, but its *continuation* is seen differently. As the evolution of the personality continues, the rageful impulse is no longer so clearly the independent variable, with the defense clearly secondary and reactive. The manifestly gentle, kind, cooperative behavior that develops to defend against the hostile feeling not only serves to disguise the unacceptable feeling from the person himself; it has interpersonal consequences as well.

By being *exaggerately* nice, by bending over backward in order not to be hostile, the person sets up situations in which his own needs are ignored. He encourages others always to call on him without giving anything in return, or to treat him with disdain as harmless but insignificant, or to expect from him none of the contentious give and take they expect from others. In dozens of large and small ways — always going to the restaurant or movie others want instead of sometimes getting his own preference; helping someone out with school work when he himself has an exam the next day; reassuring a friend it is all right to ask out a girl he himself is interested in — this sort of person creates a social world that frustrates him. And, significantly, because of that frustration, it is almost inevitably a world that infuriates him.

The fury is mostly not experienced consciously; this is a person, after all, who cannot bear to be angry. Rather it is defended against in his characteristic way. He tries to push it down by being even more cooperative, nice, gentle, helpful, and so on. And in doing so he sets the stage for still more generation of rage, still more overly helpful and cooperative behavior to defend against it, and a continuing circular trap. Ironically, the impulse he defends against can be seen as itself the product of that very defense. Were he not trying so hard to be so much the opposite of angry, he would not generate the experiences that now make him so angry. Neither impulse nor defense is any longer meaningfully viewed as primary; each creates the other in a repetitive circular process. As I put it elsewhere, "Disavowed anger may be a continuing feature of his life from childhood, but the angry thoughts that disturb his dreams tonight can be understood by what he let happen to himself today."[30]

This alternative theoretical framework incorporates all the observations on which orthodox Freudian theory is based. Unconscious conflict; anxiety over impulses and defenses against it; destructive urges and sexual longings that are disavowed; self-defeating behavior based on unrealistic unconscious fantasies; consonances between the reaction to the therapist and earlier experiences with the parents—all this is encompassed in the alternative framework, though understood in a different structure of assumptions. But the implications of the interpersonal view for what the pursuit of individual satisfaction ought to entail differ significantly. Freud, says Philip Rieff,

> . . . speaks for the modern individual, elaborating his sense of separateness from the world and from even the most beloved objects in it. . . . The prevailing image of psychoanalysis as reintegrating the neurotic, making him again a constructive member of society, must be studied very closely, for this does not signify that the patient gives his assent to the demands society makes upon his instinctual life; on the contrary, the successful patient has learned to withdraw from the painful tension of assent and dissent in his relation to society by relating himself more affirmatively to his depths. His newly acquired health entails a self-concern that takes precedence over social concern and encourages an attitude of ironic insight on the part of the self toward all that is not self.[31]

Rieff is, I think, shrewdly accurate here about the implications of the Freudian view, though I think he does exaggerate them some. But I do not think such a description accurately depicts the implications of interpersonal psychoanalytic theories. The actual world of social relationships is much more critical from this latter perspective. One's "depths" and one's actual experiences with others are not such separate categories. From an interpersonal point of view, there is a very active two-way street between inner psychological structure and overt social relationships. Each creates the other, and in that process the larger societal context of values, beliefs, and opportunities plays a critical role.

Psychological well-being, it would then seem, is not an individual matter. It is very difficult to achieve in isolation. It depends on the feedback we receive from others (though, of
course, also on how we interpret it). The actual texture of our
daily interactions is of central importance and, though clearly
not related to the larger social context in one-to-one fashion, is
likely to reflect or transmit those larger forces. For many people
the social upheavals of the Sixties, with all of their ramifications
for how we acted with each other and what we thought was appropriate or to be expected, were a considerably more powerful
force than any psychotherapy could be. In a slightly different
vein, when Betty Friedan says of the feminist movement "it
changed my life," there is little reason to doubt her. Nor does
the fact that she herself played a major role in bringing the
movement about alter that conclusion. Our own creations
come back to create us. Sisterhood is powerful, not just sisters.

Self-expression and Its Excesses

Let us pursue these considerations further in examining two
closely related features of our contemporary culture that have
been frequent targets of the critics of the psychological thrust to
our culture. The phrases "do your own thing" and "let it all
hang out" capture both the style and the content of the trends
that will concern us here. Once again, part of the story is a misunderstanding and vulgarization of Freud and part is a failure
to capitalize on the alternative interpretations of psychoanalytic
observations provided by the neo-Freudians.

It does seem to be the case that in many quarters traditional ideas about right and wrong and social appropriateness
are being replaced by the view that there is little justification
for any kind of suppression or inhibition of individual desire.
Valuing sacrifice or bearing frustration is seen as based on
faulty, outmoded views of human nature. In this view, if we are
to be healthy and vital it is necessary to *express* all that is
within.

In practice this attitude has frequently led to a degree of
candor about seemingly intimate matters that, on the face of it
at least, is probably unprecedented. Americans today tell strangers things people once would have hesitated to tell their

spouses or confessors. The imperative to express has also encouraged in some an ethic of self-indulgence. Sexual exploitation, unhesitating venting of anger, or simple laziness are manifested not only without qualms but with an actual moralistic fervor: One must be true to oneself, to one's inner nature, and therefore this behavior is more honest and healthier than the Victorian hypocrisy that used to pass for morality.

The origins of these attitudes cannot be laid at Freud's doorstep. Historically, it is clear that both the compulsion to tell all and the ethic of doing whatever one feels have roots that predate Freud. The compulsion is express and reveal what is usually hidden can be traced at least as far back as Diderot's *Rameau's Nephew* and Dostoevsky's underground man. So too can the ethic that being "honest" is more important than being "good," that any outrage is acceptable if it is a sincere expression of what lies within, or at least that it is better to "express" it than to "hide" it. As Lionel Trilling has commented in an important work on this tendency in our cultural life, the "literature to which we give our admiration and gratitude fulfills its function exactly by rending the false veil of politeness, by refusing the compromises of urbanity."[32] Freud certainly contributed in his own right to rending the veil, but if some of us now think a bit more of politeness or urbane compromise might be refreshing, it cannot be Freud alone that we blame.

The compulsion to spill all is based on a misunderstanding of what modern psychological analysis has revealed. Freud did find that people could pay a very high price for not being honest with themselves. Moreover, he did require them to "tell all" to another—the analyst—in order to be cured. In the analytic situation nothing—no matter how trivial or offensive—was to be held back. But Freud never intended for the analytic situation to be a model of all human relationships. For everyday purposes there is still a great deal that ought to be recognized as trivial or offensive, and sometimes as both.

Freud did, however, alter our sense of just what is trivial or offensive. His discoveries provided us with a tool for finding meaning in much that had once seemed irrelevant. The excesses to which this has led are easy enough to point to. But the effect has not been entirely negative. Reducing the domain of the inappropriate can enable us to learn more about previously hidden aspects of others. It can also permit us to discover that habits and thoughts we had suffered in lonely shame are both more widely shared and more acceptable to others than we thought. Social conventions about what is fit for proper company can constrain the range and spontaneity of conversation, not only in placing explicit limits on what can be said but more subtly as well, by causing one's train of thought unwittingly and automatically to veer off into more familiar territory when even a quite approximate approach to an unacceptable topic occurs.

Richard Sennett has presented interesting arguments pointing to the salutary effects of formerly prevalent forms and rituals in social interchange and highlighting the banality of much modern, "liberated" discourse.[33] His point is well taken. Certainly I do not wish to claim that the conversations of Dr. Johnson or of Lord Chesterfield were inferior to those originating on New York analytic couches or in Marin County hot tubs. But for the average person the opening up of discourse to previously forbidden topics has been, all in all, enriching. It is important, to be sure, that we notice where we have abused the privilege, so to speak, of frank talk. When intimacy is cheapened by imitations and candor becomes indistinguishable from the patois of the soap opera, we have lost more than we have gained. But it is essential that we distinguish as clearly as possible between false intimacy or abuses of intimacy, on the one hand, and an increase in genuine frankness and emotional contact between people on the other. It is clearly not possible to be genuinely intimate with every stranger we encounter; but it certainly *is* possible to establish an atmosphere in which a wider range of one's thoughts and feelings can be revealed without fear of ridicule or rejection and in which, therefore, more of our daily interactions have the possibility of a sense of freshness, contact, and depth.

What is crucial is the attitude behind the words that seem to reveal one's emotion or to invite another to do so. Accompanying the recognition by psychotherapists that "self-expression" was not the sole hallmark of psychological healing was a developing understanding that cure occurs between people, not strictly within. A central contribution of the experience of revealing oneself to another is the increase in solidarity that it is likely to yield. One's security and sense of well-being are enormously increased when a shameful secret is revealed and the response is sympathetic. But the experience of revealing oneself to another does not come with a warranty. The optimal balance between revelation and prudence must be continually assayed, both by an individual and by the social order. The response of the other may be one of revulsion, boredom, moral judgment, or anxiety; empathic responsiveness and interest are not guaranteed. Moreover, the fault can lie not just with the listener. We are increasingly recognizing that revelations can be not only offensive but unrevealing. Self-disclosure has, to some degree, become a *form* in our culture, a ritual ultimately no more personal or intimate than those more obviously ritualized encounters of the eighteenth century championed by Sennett.

Indeed, the trappings of psychological-mindedness can at times serve to blur what is really coercive, rather than open and inviting. Consider the following interaction described by R. D. Rosen:

> While having drinks a couple of years ago with a young woman I had not seen for some time, I asked how things were going and received this reply: "I've really been getting in touch with myself lately. I've struck some really deep chords." I winced at the grandeur of her remarks, but she proceeded, undaunted, to reel out a string of broad psychological insights with an enthusiasm attributable less to the Tequila Sunrise sitting before her than to the confessional spirit sweeping America.
>
> I kept thinking I was disappointing her with my failure to introduce more lyricism and intensity into my own conversation. . . . I felt obligated to reciprocate her candor but couldn't bring myself to use the popular catchphrases of revelation. . . .
>
> "Whenever I see you," she said brightly, "it makes me feel so good inside. It's a real high-energy experience."
>
> So what was wrong with me that I couldn't feel the full voltage of our contact? Unable to match her incandescence, I muttered, "Yes, it's good to see you," then fell silent.
>
> Finally, she said, her beatific smile widening, "But I can really dig your silence. If you're bummed out, that's okay."[34]

It is actually the last two sentences that I find most disturbing. By commenting on her companion's silence in that way, the woman is the farthest thing from accepting; she is intruding into every bit of breathing room he might have. Not only does she imply, without questioning it at all, that if he is not emoting with equal voltage then he must be "bummed out"; she also, in making his *not* participating equally a focus of her attention, invades the private realm of nonverbal behavior in a way that cannot help but make her partner as self-conscious as a centipede who has just been asked the fateful question. To ask if anything is the matter when one's partner has hardly said a word through an extended conversation can be empathic and helpful; to do what this woman did is to bludgeon the psyche. Moreover, it has a chilling effect on the *content* of the conversation. Pregnant pauses while a topic is being thought about have no place here. The pause itself must become the topic in an endless solipsistic merry-go-round, a caricature of psychological-mindedness.

Nonetheless, the cheapening and the unintended self-caricature that have often characterized the modern striving after more open, honest, and emotionally full engagement with others should not blind us to the serious purpose behind the quest or to the basically correct intuitions about human needs that usually motivate such seeking. New forms of sham and new kinds of pomposity have certainly appeared in the era of "let it all hang out," and at times it does seem that Gresham's Law operates in the psychological realm as well as the monetary. But cheapened intimacy will not completely drive out the more valuable kind. Especially in our present rootless era, we are in great need of deeper and surer ties to others, and the danger of cheapened self-revelation seems to me less than that of retreat to an ethic of decorum.

Acting and Acting Out

The ethic of "do your own thing," like that of "let it all hang out," can be clearly shown to be a misuse of Freudian ideas, an instance of taking valid and useful notions to a point of absurd exaggeration. Again, it is useful to note that this is an ethic not really of psychological man but rather of economic man. Our everyday business ethic—in which laissez-faire is simply a French way of saying selfishness—has supported such an approach to life for quite some time. John D. Rockefeller hardly needed Sigmund Freud or Fritz Perls to tell him he could do his own thing.

To be sure, in its modern, quasipsychological garb the idea has been democratized and expanded. Now even the poor do their own thing—often as a substitute for recognizing how circumscribed the "thing" they are allowed really is. The ethic of laissez-faire has passed beyond economic matters. It is inscribed in our grafitti and followed by those who watch it get written but don't want to "get involved." It governs our behavior in bedrooms as well as board rooms. There are probably still complaints by chemical industry executives who do their own thing to the environment about young people who do their own thing with their bodies. But the former simply fail to recognize how successful they have been in promoting the idea of free enterprise.

In the psychological realm, the idea that it is essential that everyone be free to do what he or she wants is based on a widespread misunderstanding of Freud to the effect that one must give one's impulses active expression or neurosis will result. Freud did say several things that on superficial inspection resemble such a view, but the body of his work clearly suggests something quite different. Freud distinguished sharply between gaining *awareness* of one's impulses and *acting* on them. In the psychoanalytic situation Freud tried to bring about greater than usual awareness of previously repressed wishes, while at the same time pushing for even more severe abstinence than usual with regard to acting on or gratifying the wish. Indeed, for Freud the two were linked. The patient was discouraged from "acting out" his fantasies and the analyst from gratifying them, because it was assumed that this would increase the likelihood that they would then be consciously experienced. Release of the impulse was not the aim; awareness and conscious mastery were.

One exception to the claim that Freud did not view acting on one's impulses as necessary for mental health lies in Freud's discussions of what he called the "actual neuroses." Although Freud viewed most neurosis as resulting from the mental repression of impulses—those mental operations designed to keep the person from *awareness* of the forbidden desire—he did think for some time that certain disorders were a direct result of *frustration* of the impulse, and it was thought that providing for "discharge" of the impulse was required to restore a state of health. This view, however, was inconsistent with the rest of Freud's developing thought and was explicitly rejected in his later writings.

Erik Erikson described well the modern psychoanalytic view in this regard: "Ultimately, children become neurotic not from frustrations, but from the lack or loss of societal meaning in these frustrations."[35]

Many readers of Freud have confused his criticisms of our *hyprocrisy* regarding pleasure strivings, meanness, and selfishness with an *endorsement* of such trends. Freud is seen as an advocate of free love, the cathartic value of aggression and sadism, or the rejection of all traditional morality. In fact, Freud's effort to make the unconscious conscious had more the quality of a search and destroy mission than an effort to liberate. Freud was essentially a sophisticated conservative who knew that, like a village that flies the flag but harbors guerrillas, the civilized psyche could not be secure, and certainly could not prosper, until the enemy within was brought to light. Once out of hiding, it could be better controlled or perhaps reformed. "Where id was, let ego be" is clearly not a formula for expanding the territory of the id. It points rather to a repatriation program.

The ego, then, is ultimately Freud's real ally in the psyche, the agency with which he primarily identifies. The common recommendation to analysts that they maintain an evenhanded neutrality among ego, id, and superego must be understood as a tactical rather than a strategic recommendation. Only by enabling the id and the superego to reveal themselves, by not taking a stance that will drive them underground, can the conditions be established whereby the ego can be strengthened. But make no mistake: It is the ego that must come out the winner.

This does not mean narrow rationality or just aligning oneself with the defenses. Freud talks of "appropriating fresh portions of the id." Its vitality is essential, and its *exclusion* from the ego is precisely what impoverishes the latter—both because the ego's resources are depleted in maintaining the defenses and because it is deprived of the id's energies. The case with the superego is more complicated. Here too, I believe, the logic of psychoanalysis points to appropriation. The aim is not to live without morals but to make them part of the ego—that is, to integrate our morals with our conscious guiding intentions and our efforts to adapt to the world instead of keeping them as a separate walled-off system, opposed to and looking over the ego. I believe that analysts err most of the time when they talk of strengthening the superego. More accurately, what is sought is strengthening of controls over immoral behavior and strengthening of ideals, not strengthening such controls and ideals as a system apart from and even in opposition to the ego.*

Freud was not a hedonist or opposed to restraint. The discontents to which civilization gave rise seemed to him largely inevitable and, all in all, fair payment for the advantages civilization brought. He did feel that our rules and mores required us to keep *too* tight a rein on our impulses and that a better balance could be achieved. But the new balance implicit in his work was better at least as much because it permitted more intelligent and *effective* control over the impulses as for permitting *less* control. Not so much freer expression of impulse as rational and conscious decision as to which impulses must be suppressed was the social goal implicit in Freud's thinking.

Psychological Man and Social Change

Critics of the psychologizing trends in our culture have been particularly concerned about what attention to the self implies about our attention to the needs of others. In some ways we have already addressed ourselves to this question, but I would like here to approach it from a different angle. In Philip Rieff's writings, the loss of faith has been a particularly central concern. It is the displacement of "religious man," the inability to be reverent or to accept without questioning some moral affirmation, that he focuses upon most directly. But religion, of course, tends to serve not just man's spiritual needs but also as the basis for public morality, for the care of the poor and needy and the assurance of at least a modicum of justice in the distribution of wealth and privilege.

*The confusion here illustrates as well the problem with talking of these hypothetical constructs as if they were things. I largely agree with Roy Schafer's criticisms of such kind of theorizing, and am using it here, with some misgivings, as a literary device to illustrate certain points. As much as possible I try not to write in this way when engaged primarily in the task of formulating psychological theory. See Roy Schafer, *A New Language for Psychoanalysis* (New Haven: Yale University Press, 1976).

Rieff's concerns thus dovetail with those of critics like Edwin Schur, whose *The Awareness Trap* focused on a perceived antinomy between "self-absorption" and social change.[36] Schur, however, seems insensitive to the psychological dimension altogether, viewing the various self-improvement and self-awareness efforts of the affluent as simply an irresponsible abandonment of those in need by those who are privileged. Hewing to a narrowly economic conception of well-being, Schur views the middle class as little more than "haves" who want still more. Christopher Lasch, on the other hand, is closer to Rieff in his view of the emptiness and lack of real satisfaction in middle-class life.[37] Lasch too sees the prevalence of self-improvement and consciousness-expanding efforts as an impediment to any serious dedication to social change. But in a more complicated vision than Schur's he sees these activities as shoring up the capitalist structure even as it destroys those who support it.

Schur's analysis seems to me superficial and one-sided. His specific detailing of the foolishness of many human potential advocates is often apt, and he is correct that followers of such lines are unlikely to do much about — indeed, even to notice — concrete social injustices. His comment that human potential advocates talk only of psychic resources, never of economic resources, is well taken. But he escapes from caricaturing the movement only because it is sometimes so apt in self-caricature that the shoe fits.*

Schur and other economistically oriented radical critics would have us turn our backs on the psychological aspirations of the Sixties as simply an instance of the individualism that has been at the heart of our culture of inequality. But as discussed earlier, there is an important difference between competitive individualism and the individualism of self-expression. A long chain of socialist thinkers from Fourier to Fromm have seen the possibility — indeed the necessity — of combining the political effort to transform society with the effort to revitalize subjective experience and personal relations; and there are readings of Marx as well that differ radically from the brutal and insensitive version emanating from the Kremlin.

*See Chapter Six.

Only a false understanding of the nature of individual fulfillment pits concern with personal psychological development against a commitment to a better society. In fact inner harmony can be achieved only in concert with others. An enlightened pursuit of psychological well-being includes a recognition of how individual satisfaction, security, and vitality are themselves undermined by a competitive consumer society. It is not psychology that is our problem; it is the *wrong* psychology.

TEN

Misunderstanding Narcissism

Of all the criticisms of the supposed psychological ex-cesses in our culture, the one that has most captured pub-lic attention—and that is most confused and confusing—is the claim that we have become a culture of narcissists. In this chap-ter we will take a closer look at that claim and at the idea of "narcissism." Since much of what I am here endorsing or advo-cating seems precisely what it has become fashionable to criti-cize as narcissistic, it is essential that the idea of narcissism and the social analysis based on it be examined in detail.

To begin with, a distinction must be made between two different uses of the notion of narcissism by social critics. One, well represented by Peter Marin's influential essay "The New Narcissism,"[1] uses the term primarily as a moral category, a cri-tique of what is essentially selfishness. The second, finding its most influential expression in a slightly later work, Christopher Lasch's *The Culture of Narcissism,*[2] combines moralistic de-nunciation with psychoanalytic dissection. This second version of the critique of narcissism is more complex and in some ways richer, but it is also far more problematic. Both of these critiques can be seen as following from the earlier work of Philip Rieff.

Marin's use of the term "narcissism" is relatively straightforward. He uses this psychologically tinged term, rather than the more common moral category "selfishness," to indicate the linking of certain morally questionable behavior to a psychological rationale. Writing at a time when the movement for awareness and personal growth was still ascendant—indeed Marin's essay can be seen as one of the first rounds fired in the counterrevolution—Marin decried "the ways in which selfishness and moral blindness now assert themselves in the larger culture as enlightenment and psychic health" and "the trend in therapy toward a deification of the isolated self." Marin's concern was thus focused very sharply on the moral issue of selfishness versus concern for others. Framed in these terms, there is probably little new left to say about the topic. But Marin made a fresh contribution in pointing to how psychologists and psychotherapists, who one might hope would stand for more enlightened views of human relations, can actually contribute to a decrease in empathic concern for others by providing a justification and even a counter-communitarian moral imperative. The definitions of health and fulfillment being propagated by some therapists and leaders in the human potential movement made traditional moral concerns seem positively unhealthy.

Marin does, I think, focus one-sidedly—if acutely—on but part of the message implicit in the counterculture and human potential movements. What he said needed saying but should not obscure the fact that much of what now fosters amoral disregard for the needs of others started with a moral impulse, as part of the general questioning of societal demands and assumptions sparked by the Vietnam War and the civil rights struggle. But if incomplete, Marin's contribution is a useful one, and his use of the term "narcissism" presents little problem. He is clearly making a moral criticism *of* psychology, not using it as a technical term *from* psychology. His standpoint is unambiguously moral rather than psychological. He does not claim that those he writes about suffer from a personality disorder; it is their ethics, not their egos, that he is calling into question.

Christopher Lasch's conception of narcissism is more problematic. At times he sounds very much like Marin, Schur, and others who have criticized particular choices and trends in our society as politically regressive and morally questionable. His argument then is clearly stated and his focus sharp. Thus:

> After the political turmoil of the sixties, Americans have retreated to purely personal preoccupations. Having no hope of improving their lives in any of the ways that matter, people have convinced themselves that what matters is psychic self-improvement: getting in touch with their feelings, eating health food, taking lessons in ballet or belly-dancing, immersing themselves in the wisdom of the East, jogging, learning how to "relate," overcoming the "fear of pleasure." Harmless in themselves, these pursuits, elevated to a program and wrapped in the rhetoric of authenticity and awareness, signify a retreat from politics and a repudiation of the recent past.[3]

Clearly Lasch is here throwing down the gauntlet at the very trends that I have suggested are our best hope of resolving the dilemmas posed by the consumer society.

Lasch's judgment about these matters is based on a complicated and not always consistent set of arguments which it is essential we understand in order to evaluate its implications for the approach taken in this book. Particularly is this the case because Lasch sees these trends as a development perfectly consistent with the logic and the needs of industrial capitalism, whereas I see them as potentially offering an alternative to consumer capitalism's mores and values.

In some ways, Lasch's arguments echo those of Philip Rieff discussed earlier. In discussing present therapeutic trends, for example, he states:

> To liberate humanity from . . . outmoded ideas of love and duty has become the mission of the post-Freudian therapies and particularly of their converts and popularizers, for whom mental health means the overthrow of inhibitions and the immediate gratification of every impulse.[4]

Lasch, however, does not confine himself to an examination of the therapeutic ethic or to the retreat from social and political concerns to purely private ones. He sees these trends as but part of a far broader pattern of corruption and decay—one practically coterminous with our entire culture. Moreover, he addresses not just particular ideas and programs but the personalities of those who hold them, indeed the personalities of all of us. As his argument proceeds, it shades over from a moralizing one—a number of reviewers described his book as a jeremiad—to one couched in the language of psychopathology. In discussing, for example, Edwin Schur's contention that the self-preoccupation of middle-class Americans is "criminal" given the plight of their less affluent bretheren, Lasch suggests that this self-preoccupation "arises not from complacency but from desperation."[5] Elsewhere he asserts, "People today hunger . . . for the feeling, the momentary illusion of personal well-being, health, and psychic security."[6] If even the *illusion* of well-being is so hard to come by today, how can we blame those who simply don't have the wherewithal to attend to the needs of others? In Lasch's account they seem to have little choice.

Despite his warnings about the "evil of psychologizing," Lasch is a psychologizer par excellence. What confuses is that the moralizing and the psychologizing are so merged. Is he making a moral argument or a diagnostic one? It is often hard to tell and for that reason hard to hold on to the thread of his argument. One is left with a general sense that all is wrong, but neither cure nor reform is part of Lasch's agenda.

Part of why the moralizing and the psychologizing seem so merged in Lasch is that he writes from a particular corner of the psychoanalytic tradition—one that uses the tools of psychological analysis primarily to uncover hidden pathology, finds people sicker than they realize, and is basically contemptuous of, rather than sympathetic toward, the patient. In that sense he doesn't really absolve us at all. Pointing out the presumed desperation behind our self-preoccupation is not part of a plea for mercy but rather part of a more general condemnation of all of us as hopelessly ruined human debris. There is little compassion in his attempted dissection. Lasch despairs for us, but he does not sympathize.

This attitude in itself is something I find troubling about Lasch's work. But more important in the present context is that Lasch uses—really misuses—psychological analysis in a way that casts a pall on every effort to find an alternative to our dominant consumer way of life. Though his arguments are slippery and inconsistent, he uses effectively a number of rhetorical strategies, which have gained wide currency for his point of view.

The Narcissistic Personality of Our Time?

Let us begin by looking at how Lasch tries to link his criticism of supposedly narcissistic social trends to the psychoanalytic concept of narcissistic personality disorder. Lasch asserts that "pathology represents a heightened version of normality" and that therefore "the 'pathological narcissism' found in character disorders of this type should tell us something about narcissism as a social phenomenon. . . . Every age," he says, "develops its own peculiar forms of pathology, which express in exaggerated form its underlying character structure."[7] But what exactly does he mean when he says narcissism is the "peculiar form of pathology" of our age? In several places he alludes to the claims of various psychiatrists and psychoanalysts that narcissism and character disorders have become more frequent. That is a claim about which I shall raise some questions shortly, but it is at least a logical basis for describing narcissism as our peculiar form of mental disorder.* Elsewhere, however, Lasch seems to hedge his bet, saying that people with narcissistic personalities are "not necessarily more numerous than before."[8] Here he claims, however, that they are particularly well suited to rise to prominence in our society and as a consequence "set the tone" of our public and private lives. Moreover, Lasch says, besides providing opportunities for this kind of person to stand out, our society "elicits and reinforces narcissistic traits in everyone."[9]

Now just what are those narcissistic traits elicited in "everyone," and how do they compare to the properties of the clinical syndrome to which Lasch ties his argument? The character traits of pathological narcissism, Lasch tells us, appear "in less extreme form" throughout our culture. He includes here "dependence on the vicarious warmth provided by others combined with a fear of dependence, a sense of inner emptiness, boundless repressed rage, and unsatisfied oral cravings." Also

---

*Even here, however, it should be noted that those who claim that narcissism is on the increase do not so diagnose the *majority* of their patients. Even if one accepted the far from unassailable notion that the characteristics of a population as a whole should be inferred from those seeking psychiatric treatment, should not that majority of psychiatric patients with some other diagnosis have their democratic share in providing a name to the culture?

included are "the secondary characteristics of narcissism:
pseudo self-insight, calculating seductiveness, nervous self-dep-
recatory humor." Moreover, there are "connections between
the narcissistic personality type and certain characteristic patterns of contemporary culture, such as the intense fear of old
age and death, altered sense of time, fascination with celebrity,
fear of competition, decline of the play spirit, deteriorating relations between men and women."[10]

When reading this and other of Lasch's catalogs of our
woes, I am reminded of the almost universal experience of students taking an abnormal psychology course for the first time.
Chapter after chapter, students identify with the particular
kind of disorder described and worry in turn if they are obses-
sionals, schizophrenics, depressives, or — for those hip to the latest trends — borderline or narcissistic. Descriptions of psychological disorders are so general, and the human condition so far
from perfect, that it is easy for most people to find a match with
most descriptions. This is the basis for the so-called Barnum effect (a tribute to the man who said "There's a sucker born every
minute"). In studies of the Barnum effect, subjects are interviewed or given a battery of psychological tests and then presented with a report based on the results of the personality ap-
praisal. Unknown to them, however, the report they receive is
not really an individualized assessment at all. Rather, it is a description written even before the tests were given, designed to
be evocative for almost everyone. All subjects in fact receive the
same report (filled with such phrases as "You have a strong
need for other people to like you and for them to admire
you. . . . Your sexual adjustment has presented some problems
for you. . . . Disciplined and controlled on the outside, you
tend to be worrisome and insecure inside").[11] The great majority of people who were presented with such reports were im-
pressed with the perceptiveness of the report writer and his ability to capture the unique features of their personality.

I believe that such a phenomenon accounts for at least part
of the success of Lasch's book. The sense of resonance it evokes
in many readers is due less to any specific features of Lasch's
particular brand of *Weltschmerz* than to his skill as a writer
and rhetorician (about which more shortly). Had Lasch as skillfully described the character traits and "secondary characteris-

tics" of the obsessive, the depressive, or for that matter, to use categories that are not official diagnostic labels, the heart-attack-prone "type-A" personality or the "other-directed" character, he would have sounded equally perceptive. This is one of the crosses that a psychologically based analysis must bear. We build on very sandy foundations.

This is not to say that the characteristics Lasch describes cannot be found widely distributed among us. Rather, the question is whether they are any more characteristic of us than those of any other alleged syndrome, and whether they are more characteristic of us than they used to be. Moreover, are the traits on which Lasch builds his argument really the essence of our personalities or of our experience, as he seems to imply, or merely part of a larger picture from which he extracts them in a very selective way? No doubt many people do experience or manifest the things Lasch describes. But are there not also many people (and not just occasional paragons) who show at least some ability to love, who feel good about themselves a good proportion of the time, who can enjoy themselves, who can compete or assert themselves without being either needlessly deferent or ruthlessly dominating, or whose lives are not filled with "boundless rage"? I don't mean here perfection— love with no conflict or no anxiety about commitment: self-esteem that never fluctuates; a sense of fullness in living never tempered by doubts—but rather the complementary side of normal living that Lasch systematically leaves out.

Lasch plays on our fears like a bad analyst, convincing us that we are more damaged than we thought. Even the healthiest of personalities—in any age—has doubts and fears and can be convinced, at certain moments, that the good feelings are all a sham. Lasch's critique of the narcissist—who must strive for grandiose perfection in order to deal with an inability to accept life's inevitably mixed blessings without being crushed—is based on an outlook that strikingly manifests the very characteristics he attributes to others: Like the narcissists he describes, Lasch seems unable to tolerate everyday weakness and compromise. If he can sniff out any weakness, all strength is illusory. His antenna, tuned to unhappiness, picks up rage and despair, and to Lasch the despair is "deeper" and more real. Whatever positive feelings the rest of us can perceive are, for him, but a false patina. In a fashion strikingly like his description of the pathological narcissist, Lasch perceives the world in all-or-none terms. Any badness makes the goodness unreal.*

Lasch also presents it as a matter of course that the personality traits and modes of experiencing he describes are peculiar to our time and our society, that they have never been nearly as widespread or as severe. But is this really so, or is he describing (from a particular metaphysical vantage point) the human condition? As Lasch himself argues, little is gained by giving a psychiatric label such as narcissism to traits that are simply part of the human condition. But Lasch provides little evidence for his contention of "historical specificity" other than the Barnum reaction he evokes in the reader. Are there really more crime and violence today than there were a hundred years ago? Do people respect their elders less? Are they less considerate of others? My grandmother thought so. I suspect, though, that *her* grandmother told her that, too.

Some of Lasch's contentions may well be true. Sometimes when I read about muggings and knifings near my home I become very upset and feel convinced that things *are* deteriorating, that there *is* more violence today. At other times, though, I think of the old West, romantic from the safe vantage point of a seat in the movies, but terrifying when one thinks of the lawlessness actually being depicted. Or I think of the brigands lurking if one ventured along the beautiful eighteenth-century paths that Tom Jones trod in technicolor.[12] Lasch—and my grandmother—may well be right. But there is little hard evidence to justify Lasch's apparent certainty about the moral decline we are undergoing. Indeed, Yi-Fu Tuan's scholarly account of fear and violence through the ages suggests that, despite our romantic fantasies of a pastoral past, quite the opposite seems to be the case.[13]

Lasch tells us relations between men and women are "deteriorating." He could, I suppose, cite indisputably higher divorce rates as a kind of evidence for this assertion. But consider

*I am not here trying to psychoanalyze the private personality of Christopher Lasch, whom I have never met. Rather it is the structure of thought and perception that is evident in Lasch's published words that I am addressing—and in a straightforward descriptive way, not in an interpretive, psychoanalytic mode.

the following description by Abel Hugo in 1835 of Breton peasant life:

> The wives are the first servants in the household; they plow the soil, care for the house, and eat after their husbands, who address them only in harsh, curt tones, even with a sort of contempt. If the horse and the wife fall sick at the same time, the Lower Breton peasant rushes to the blacksmith to care for the animal and leaves the task of healing his wife to nature.

This description, cited by Edward Shorter,[14] is typical of numerous accounts collected by Shorter which suggest that for all the strains of modern marriage the conclusion of deterioration in male–female relations may require rather a selective eye.

The Rhetoric of Retreat

What makes these biases in Lasch's account so important in the present context is that Lasch's arguments are a particularly important set piece in a compaign to discredit the cultural themes that developed out of the social upheaval of the Sixties. If the 1970s were allegedly a "Me Decade," there are many who tell us the 1980s will be a decade of cost accounting. I don't think Lasch is particularly of that school, but he aids them considerably in his disparaging of almost every movement and thinker concerned with expansion of awareness, the quality of interpersonal relations, or the examination of the psychological dimension of life. Those who wish to retreat from the difficult questions about our basic aims and assumptions that were raised in the 1960s will find Lasch's book a useful weapon despite its putative radicalism.

The problem lies not so much in the specific points that Lasch makes as in its overall tone, thrust, and assumptions. Many of the specifics of Lasch's critique are perceptive and well taken. I would concur, for example, with much of what he says about advertising and the creation of needs; about the destructive effects of competitive individualism; about our failure to link ourselves with past and future generations and about ways in which psychological and psychiatric authorities have undermined the ability of parents to be firm with their children when that is required. Even in these specific contributions, his one-sidedness limits the value of his arguments—for example, in his insensitivity to how being centered in the experience of the here-and-now can be valuable in a society that plays down experience in favor of commodities and quantities, or in his almost total denial that we have learned anything about child-rearing from the observations of psychologists or psychiatrists or that professional advice can be helpful to parents. But it is in its overall Gestalt that his argument is most faulty and most misleading. Lasch disdains the difficult task of sorting out strengths and weaknesses, of analyzing at just what point useful insights and humanitarian impulses got sidetracked and in what ways currently erroneous practices contain any hints of something more useful. He opts instead for the considerably easier task of finding what is wrong and discarding the rest as a husk useless to his argument.

Much of the writing in *The Culture of Narcissism* is characterized by rhetorical excess and question-begging. Bold assertions often substitute for the details of evidence or logic that lead him to dismiss an opponent's ideas. A favorite rhetorical device of his is to dismiss any idea or trend of which he disapproves as a "cult." One finds reference in *The Culture of Narcissism*, for example, to the "cult of expanded consciousness," the "cult of consumption," the "cult of personal relations," the "cult of sensuality," the "cult of success," the "cult of authenticity," the "cult of intimacy," the "cult of the self," and the "cult of pragmatism." The unwary reader can readily be swept up in Lasch's summary judgments, swayed more by mood than by analysis.

The most important rhetorical tactic for present purposes is Lasch's linking of his judgments about contemporary concern with psychological self-development to recent developments in psychoanalytic theory. This is, of course, more than just rhetoric; one of Lasch's major explicit purposes is to join social criticism to the discoveries of depth-psychology. But his apparent success in this, I shall try to show, is due not to satisfactory analysis or development of an integrative conceptualization, but to his employment in shifting fashion of the ambiguous term "narcissism." Shorn of this specious link, Lasch's argument is likely to prove far less useful to those wishing to close the door once and for all on the cultural trends of the Sixties and to lead us into a counterreformation whose gaze is fixed on the "bottom line" and whose vision is limited to "getting the government off our backs."

It is easy to understand Lasch's interest in the psychoanalytic writings on narcissism. Social trends are elusive and ambiguous. The most significant often pass through the mesh of surveys and other formal and statistical approaches. The most important and useful social criticism often requires making intuitive leaps and sensing with disciplined subjectivity where we are heading and what we are feeling as a culture. But no matter how disciplined, such leaps are dangerous, and all but the foolhardy prefer a net under them to provide some security. For Lasch, the currently fashionable psychoanalytic writings on narcissism seem to provide such a net. Psychoanalysts tend to write with a ring of authority. They have an intimidating technical vocabulary, and the word "maybe" is rarely to be found. Moreover, they are heirs to one of the true giants in our intellectual life and one whose method was precisely that of disciplined subjectivity. When such a group seems to provide a scientific foundation for one's social perceptions, the temptation to cast one's lot with them may be well nigh irresistible.

As a psychologist I am pleased to see social critics turn to psychology, and I certainly believe there is an important place for psychological and psychoanalytic ideas in social criticism. But the recent psychoanalytic literature on narcissism may provide rather slender support for the enterprise of the social critic, for it is itself rather shaky, buttressed by a great deal of jargon and a naive faith in the veracity of reconstructions of the earliest years of life. Basing social criticism on such work is a bit like trying to hoist oneself by one's own bootstraps while suspended from a sky hook.

To describe current social trends as "narcissistic," and particularly to invoke the clinical psychoanalytic literature on this topic, is to prejudge the meaning of these phenomena and to lose an important distinction. Both the clinical and the social phenomena do seem to involve a kind of self-absorption, a heightened concern with self. But whereas the former is based largely on self-loathing and an underlying *lack* of self-esteem, the latter include some potentially quite healthy and even socially necessary developments. It is precisely these valuable features of the search for personal fulfillment that are obscured by

tarring them with the same brush used to describe severe psychopathology.

Narcissism or Individualism?

At one point early in his book Lasch describes its focus as "the
culture of competitive individualism." Had he kept that focus,
his contribution might have been more valuable. That is precisely what is wrong with so many of the efforts at psychological
self-improvement that the last decade has spawned. Based on
the assumption that "looking out for number one" is both natural and ethical, that we bear no responsibility for each other's
welfare, that we can thrive just by freeing ourselves from within
without regard to the world around us and the relationships in
which we participate, much of what has been passed off as socially progressive and psychologically liberating has been foolish and selfish. The links between these ideas and movements
and the pervasive influence of competitive individualism in our
culture are important to spell out.

But Lasch does not do this. Such an effort would separate
the chaff from the wheat. Lasch sees all chaff. Rather than analyze these movements, he dismisses them as psychopathology.
He treats them not as ideas requiring examination but as symptoms. This is by now a familiar — and rather generally discred-
ited — kind of reductionism. But Lasch has added some wrin-
kles to it that have thus far largely enabled him to get away
with it.

First of all he relies on the ambiguity of the term "narcissism" itself. "Narcissistic" is a label that has gained common
currency as a nontechnical ethical judgment roughly equivalent
to selfish, vain, or interested only in oneself. Whereas calling
someone paranoid or obsessional automatically evokes in the
reader the recognition that clinical terms are being bandied
about, we are not so alerted with regard to "narcissistic." It is a
judgment we are readier to accept as appropriate to ordinary
discourse. Indeed, it is a term that had already been applied to
the same set of trends by others, with no intention of invoking a
psychiatric bludgeon.

Having gotten his foot in the door, as it were, Lasch then
attempts to use our assent to the term "narcissism" to take us

farther along the path to a view of society through the lens of psychopathology. This is a fascinating journey: Starting with a term from psychoanalysis that has entered common discourse — a term by now more common to the realm of ethics and values — we end up with a view of social trends not only built entirely upon a model of psychopathology, but a model of psychopathology of the most invidious sort, the kind of use of diagnosis as epithet to which we would be instantly alerted were we to be described as a "schizophrenic" or an "anal" culture.

Even in the realm of clinical discourse, "narcissism" is an exceedingly confused and ambiguous concept. Narcissus looked into the pool out of genuine admiration for and enchantment with the image he saw. The clinical narcissist looks into the mirror out of anxious concern and is as likely to express perfectionistic criticism of what he sees as smug self-satisfaction. It is as likely to be the gray hair, the wrinkle, the crooked nose, or the subtly discolored tooth that he sees as the noble brow or the winning smile.

Freud originally had in mind something very close to the Narcissus myth. Narcissism was an investment of the self with libido, the energy of love and sensual desire. Later the term also came to imply *interest* in the self, which precluded interest in the world. The poor reality-testing of the schizophrenic was seen as resulting from diversion onto the self of the energy ordinarily responsible for clear apprehension of the world.[15]

Narcissism is still frequently used by analysts to designate something like self-love. A modicum of narcissism is regarded by most analysts as essential for mental health. But increasingly the term has come to stand for something quite different — for a defensive grandiosity or self-inflation intended to ward off self-*hatred* or *low* self-esteem. Though some individuals exhibiting "narcissistic" personality disorders in this latter sense do at least overtly appear to be in love with themselves, others who merit the same diagnosis are characterized primarily by self-doubt and feelings of failure. These doubts and self-denigrations are, to be sure, related to failure to match up to another, less conscious, image of the self that is indeed grandiose; but that image is itself in turn a defensive structure developed to ward off feelings of helplessness and insignificance. This latter focus — on helplessness and insignificance — is still another facet of the use of this extraordinarily chameleon-like word. Narcissism often is used to refer not to self-*love* in any erotic or romantic sense but self-regard or self-esteem along some such dimension as competence or the ability to cope with life, the sense of being in charge, in control, able to deal with life's contingencies. It is in this sense that the death of a loved one, for example, is frequently referred to by analysts as a "narcissistic injury." Feeling more vulnerable, not less attractive, is at issue here.

"Narcissism" has been used to refer to self-love; self-hatred; self-esteem; vulnerability and invulnerability; a genuine and healthy regard for oneself; an inflated and pathological self-regard; a lack of interest in others; an interest in others only insofar as they confirm one's sense of self; a pathological defense against feelings of rage and disappointment at the mother; a normal phenomenon of grandiosity through which most people pass unscathed; and even, in Lasch, the psychological dimension of our dependence on bureaucratic organizations. From another realm, it has meant as well selfishness, insensitivity to the needs of others, and vanity. Such a protean term hardly seems like a sound basis for a careful and precise analysis of social trends. When, like Lasch, one further includes in the package of purportedly narcissistic phenomena such things as wishing to eat foods less contaminated with toxic chemicals, getting more exercise than our rather sedentary civilization usually permits, or wanting to communicate with others more honestly and effectively, the stew gets complex indeed. But it is an ideally vague notion if one wants to play on the vague anxieties that have always been men's lot in order to persuade them that everything they are doing is part of a "syndrome" and thereby to raise doubts about the efficacy and validity of any efforts to make things better.

A New Personality Structure?

Central to Lasch's argument—and seeming to bolster his contention that what look like efforts to lead a healthier, psychologically richer life are really just the products of psychological deterioration—is the claim that "narcissistic personality disorders" are the epitome of what is happening to all of us and represent the "underlying character structure" of our age. A corollary claim is that such disorders have greatly increased in recent years.

Lasch cites a number of psychoanalystic authorities who report such an increase, and it is certainly true that this perception is widespread in psychoanalytic circles. There are, however, reasons to be skeptical about such reports. One major reason is that analysts have not really taken into account the effect on their practices of competition from other therapeutic approaches.

In the last quarter-century important alternative therapies to psychoanalysis have developed that have challenged its role as the most effective and theoretically sound therapeutic modality. Behavior therapy and family therapy approaches, though they have antecedents, are essentially new developments of these years, and the efficacy of pharmacologic approaches — however unwise a predominant emphasis on drugs may be — has clearly increased drastically from that of several decades ago. Thus, whereas it was once the case that almost any patient who could afford it would choose psychoanalysis or psychoanalytic therapy, increasing numbers of patients instead consult behavior therapists, family therapists, or pharmacologically oriented therapists. Moreover, the decline in the percentage of patients whose preference is for analysis does not represent just a random redistribution of cases. There is a systematic skewing in a number of ways. For example, of the patients opting out of psychoanalysis, a disproportionate number are likely to be those with rather specific complaints — isolated phobias, impotence or frigidity, assertiveness difficulties — where behavior therapists in particular have reported considerable success. This means that a higher percentage of the patients seen by analysts are likely to be those who do *not* present specific complaints but rather suffer from vague and diffuse dissatisfactions. Even if their numbers haven't changed in society at large, the shifting landscape of psychotherapy and the sorting and distribution of patients that results would be likely to increase the "density" of such patients in any particular analyst's practice.

A second systematic factor in the sorting out of patients among the various modalities is the patient's degree of dependency. Patients who would like a good deal of structure, who like to be given advice and direction, are likely to be far more comfortable with a psychiatrist who prescribes medication or a behavior therapist who makes quite specific recommendations than with the far more nondirective stance of the psychoanalyst. Analysts may thus be getting a higher percentage of the people who are not really particularly interested in what the therapist has to say, who are self-contained and isolated from others, or who are so preoccupied with their own psyches they have little use for others except as an audience. Far fewer of *those* types of patients would be drained away to behavior therapists or drug therapists, and consequently they too would increase as a percentage of the analyst's practice.

A third type of skewing may be occurring as a result of the kind of patients who end up going to see family therapists. It may be that the patients who do end up in that modality are, as a group, more likely to be people who acknowledge the importance of their relatedness to others, who recognize their dependency and belongingness; hence, again, analysts would be seeing a skewed sample, denser in those more unable to acknowledge such feelings and/or more isolated and unrelated to others. A number of complexities, however, make this particular source of potential bias more difficult to evaluate.[16]

One final source of artifact in the changing patient picture reported by analysts is introduced by the analyst's own perceptual and conceptual processes. A central theme in the evolution of psychoanalysis in the 1930s and 1940s was the recognition of the characterological basis of neurosis. Two of Lasch's *bêtes noires*, Wilhelm Reich and Karen Horney, were particularly influential in this conceptual shift in psychoanalysis. Horney, for example, taught that *all* neuroses were character neuroses and that no matter how narrow the patient's presenting complaint, his entire way of life and pattern of relationships needed to be examined. As this perspective began to be assimilated into everyday practice, the number of patients who were seen as suffering only from isolated symptoms was bound to decline. Increasingly, patients' problems were seen as pervasively characterological.

More recently the characterization of patients as "borderline" or "narcissistic" has become very fashionable. Therapists have become increasingly attuned to those characteristics that can be assimilated to such a diagnosis and also more inclined, when they do see such characteristics, to view them as implying such a diagnosis. This again makes it likely that the reported increase in such cases is exaggerated and that at least part of the increased number are people receiving different labels rather than people with different personalities.

Lasch himself acknowledges this latter likelihood: "The attention given to character disorders in recent clinical literature probably makes psychiatrists more alert to their presence."[17] But in what seems like a *non sequitur*, he then adds that this "by no means diminishes the importance of psychiatric testimony about the prevalence of narcissism, especially when this testimony appears at the same time that journalists begin to speculate about the new narcissism and the unhealthy trend toward self absorption.[18] Lasch overlooks the fact that the journalistic commentators make no reference to "primitive internalized object relations," to "splitting," to "projective identification," to "archaic elements in the superego" or to any of the other speculative psychoanalytic concepts that Lasch employs. The underlying identity between what in large measure are two different uses of the term "narcissism" (see, for example, the opening section of this chapter) is precisely what Lasch is trying to demonstrate. It can hardly be used as a starting premise.

Thus far I have discussed possible artifacts that may distort and exaggerate the reports of psychoanalysts regarding the kinds of patients they see. But if shifting fashions and bandwagon effects have made claims about narcissism somewhat suspect, this does not mean that there is not *some* change to which the reports may be responsive. I believe there have in fact been important shifts in the kinds of psychological problems experienced by people in our society, and these changes both reflect and tell us about changes in social mores and institutions. I do not, however, consider it either accurate or useful to describe these changes as changes in "personality structure." Such a way of looking at it obscures the links between these psychological changes and broader social changes and impairs the contribution of psychology to social criticism.

It is a clinical commonplace that patients who are unable to function in the everyday world can look quite healthy in the structured environment of the hospital. In a sense, all of society has always been a kind of hospital, providing structure and order that prevents us from falling apart or becoming paralyzed with conflict and decisions. In recent years that structure has been substantially diminished. Social and moral guidelines have become much more ambiguous, and we have been thrown back upon our own resources. As a consequence patterns and directions of psychological adaptation have changed, and at times, confronting a different set of circumstances, we can appear "sicker." Were the "classical neurotics" of Freud's Vienna or the "good analytic patients" whom American analysts say they *used* to see to be immersed in the present open-ended situation, they too would seem to have a different "personality structure." What has changed, I suggest, is not the structure of personality but the structuring of social guidelines. If one understands personality structure *in context*, then the same "structure" will lead to different behavior and different modes of relating and experiencing when the social guidelines are different.

We live today with many more choices than any previous generation. It is true, as many critics point out, that not all our choices are "meaningful." The sense of option is often illusory; we choose what the system can safely let us choose, but choices that could really make a difference are frequently foreclosed. The increasing dissatisfaction with the "choices" offered us in major elections is a clear example. Nonetheless, there are many ways in which, for better or worse, we have to choose where previous generations felt things were largely laid out. Staying married, for example, was something that until relatively recently people did pretty much as a matter of course. The option of divorce has long been available, of course, but it felt like an exception, an exit pass if things got really desperate. Now divorce is for many a constant possibility. To a far greater extent than previously, people who do stay married are aware of *choosing* to do so. Divorce as an alternative is in many people's consciousness not just a response to a desperate situation but a possibility when a marriage is good but not quite good "enough." The search for greater "fulfillment" has become almost as standard a reason for divorce as the escape from a situation of unambiguous unhappiness.

Indeed, the two experiences tend to merge today. A marriage that is not totally "fulfilling" begins to be *experienced* as unhappy. People who once would have described themselves as happily married now feel uncertainty, feel the press of the question of why they are together requiring a constant answer.

Choice similarly intrudes in new ways around the decision to have children. Since it has become respectable not to, with substantial social support available for either choice, many people are discovering a depth of ambivalence people didn't have to face when having children seemed automatic.

The possibility of staying single and of being childless—and of receiving social support for this, being regarded as "normal," not being universally told there's something wrong or you're missing something—probably accounts for a very substantial portion of the practice of most psychotherapists. People who would once have "settled" for someone as a mate when it came to a societally recognized time to "settle down" (is the use of the same word here just a coincidence?) now seem unable to "find" anyone or to "commit" themselves. Troubled by it, but finding substantial societal support for their search for the perfect mate, they experience a degree of conflict substantially greater than those for whom such matters were settled (that word again).

Even sex roles, once one of the central guiding structures for our behavior, are now up for grabs. What once seemed God-given and engraved on tablets must now be chosen. Faced with so few clear and settled directions, people today *must* turn inward to a far greater degree. There *are* no answers "out there," it seems, and only the exploration of what one "really" wants seems to hold any promise of resolution.

This is certainly not to argue that lack of structure is the only determinant of changes in psychological complaints or in the experience of large numbers of people. Many of the causative factors, for example, are well understood in terms of traditional social and economic categories, and the lack of structure itself is largely attributable to the sequelae of our economic system discussed in Chapters Four, Five, and Six. The main point of the present discussion, rather, is that phenomena discussed by Lasch in terms of a new "personality structure" can be understood as a response to current pressing realities. The kind of psychological analysis employed by Lasch actually drives a wedge between psychological and social analysis. Emphasis on the internalized, structural continuation of very early experience obscures the responsiveness of people to the social circumstances in which they live.* Social realities, if one tries to carry out such an analysis consistently, can have an impact only

*For a discussion of why an emphasis on such responsiveness need not discard our understanding of unconscious motivation, self-deception, and human irrationality, see Paul L. Wachtel, *Psychoanalysis and Behavior Therapy: Toward an Integration* (New York: Basic Books, 1977), and "Vicious Circles: The Self and the Rhetoric of Emerging and Unfolding," *Contemporary Psychoanalysis*, 18 (1982): 259–73.

indirectly, at best, by gradually altering childrearing patterns over generations. Any given generation—already "structured"—must be written off. Indeed, in Lasch's case, that seems to be the purpose of his choice of models to borrow. Social change efforts that are too "meliorist" for his tastes (and/or too optimistic in their assumptions) appear, through the filter of Lasch's analysis, to be just the foolish or desperate symptomatic acts of ruined narcissists.

For all his criticisms of other writers for ignoring broader social and historical influences, Lasch pays little attention to the environmental limits that constitute perhaps our most important historical watershed. Though his book is subtitled *American Life in an Age of Diminishing Expectations*, one gets hardly any sense in his book that these diminishing expectations have anything at all to do with the environment. By emphasizing psychopathology and notions of "personality structure" that stress "feelings of oral deprivation" that originate in "the pre-Oedipal stage of psychic development," Lasch shifts attention away from the real situations people are responding to.

World population growth has accelerated to a rate of a million people every five days. The equivalent of the entire population of the United States is added every three years.[19] Yet Lasch sees couples who postpone or decide against parenthood, or social reformers working for zero population growth, as manifesting symptoms of our "shattered faith in the regeneration of life"[20] rather than as responding rationally and usefully to the situation we face—indeed, as the ones with a real concern for the future.

Every day we read of a new toxin that has leached into our soil or seeped into our ground water; increasingly we are learning of the adverse health effects of the "convenience foods" that advertising promotes; scientific reports accumulate about the harmful effects of fats and cholesterol, and the egg, meat, and dairy industries pressure the Department of Agriculture not to release a nutrition book suggesting reduced intake of fats.[21] But to Christopher Lasch, concern with health foods is narcissistic.

The newspapers report study after study showing that a sedentary way of life (the life of a nation with drive-in banks and drive-in churches) increases the risk of heart attacks. But Christopher Lasch tells us jogging is narcissistic.

Trapped in the vicious circles that our commercial civilization promotes, our population increasingly turns to products and money to assuage the psychological costs of competition and the loss of community—and thereby exacerbates these problems further. Christopher Lasch, however, tells us that the effort to get closer to others and more in touch with one's feelings is narcissistic.

According to Lasch, the reason people are concerned with being more in touch with what they really want or feel, with improving their relations with others, with learning to understand the conflicts that prevent them from enjoying life—even with preserving their health—is that they have lost hope in improving their lives "in any of the ways that matter." To Lasch, people have apparently "convinced themselves" that such things matter when they do not. The best he can say for them is that they are "harmless."[22]

Lasch is correct that these aims have been pursued at times in foolish and socially regressive ways, and that often they have implied a retreat from politics and social concern. But his own position is at least as dangerous. The efforts he so readily and contemptuously dismisses are not simply "harmless"; they represent a potential alternative to a way of life that is environmentally disastrous and increasingly unlikely to provide a secure and satisfying existence. To modify an old saw, with enemies like this capitalism doesn't need friends.

ELEVEN

Jobs and Work

THE CONSEQUENCES of what I am advocating are not just subjective. There are numerous social and economic consequences of a more psychologically and ecologically attuned way of life. The question I would like to address in this chapter is the one that is likely seriously to concern the largest number of readers: What will happen to people's jobs if large numbers of consumers begin to buy less? Many of the policies and directions I have criticized in this book have been defended on the grounds that they provide jobs, and people will not easily countenance policies likely to have the opposite effect.*

In addressing the question of what would happen to jobs if the point of view advocated here gained wide currency, it is necessary first to examine more closely just what jobs mean to us. Work serves many functions for society besides producing goods and many functions for the individual besides providing a livelihood. It is important to be clear about the aspects of

---

*The Reagan Administration has, of course, brought us our highest unemployment rate in decades at the same time that it shows almost total disregard for the environment in a dogged pursuit of economic growth. The tolerance thus far of such policies testifies to the power of wishful expectations to override perceptions — at least for a time.

work that are not primarily economic in order to see just what alternatives to the present distribution of jobs might prove feasible.

Work, Identity, and Self-Esteem

One important function of work in our society is to help provide a sense of identity. In the preindustrial world the first question one was likely to ask a stranger in order to get a bead on him was, "Where are you from?" Now we are more likely to ask, "What do you do?" Place no longer gives us the same sense of a person, nor is it for many people the core of their sense of who they are. One's work, rather, is one's badge of identity, indicating the kind of person you are likely to be and your position in the social order as well.

To some degree this has always been a function of work; work was part of your role, part of the basis of your belonging to the community, part of how you organized your sense of what your life was about. But though people spend less of their time working than in years past, work has become much more central in a society like ours. In earlier eras, when almost everyone was a farmer, the occupations of the vast majority in no way set them off from everyone else they knew. Today, with the enormous variety of occupations and of levels within each occupation, one's work conveys a much more specific and distinctive message about who one is. Moreover, people today move around far more than they once did, and their personal horizons are much less determined by the family into which they were born.[1] This means that work is not only a better *indicator* of one's characteristics and position but also the vehicle for *creating* an identity. And since our position in the social order is no longer guaranteed by place, family, or station, and our connections to a particular community are more tenuous and transient, work must serve to provide our identity and sense of belonging. Thus the personal meaning of work is greatly increased in a society such as ours, and the loss of a job means far more than just the loss of the income it entails. Consequently a great deal of anxiety is stirred not only by the prospect of a decrease in income but by the threatened loss of a place in the social order. The preservation of existing jobs has become for many *the* overriding social goal. Initiatives and changes that might be of substantial benefit, even to the person whose job is in question, are dismissed out of hand if they threaten the existing job structure.

The point is not that we should take lightly people's loss of jobs. That attitude has already been reserved by those on quite the other end of the political spectrum from me. Rather, it is that we need to rethink just *why* jobs are so important and how best to arrange for people to have them (or to derive in some other way the satisfaction jobs now provide). It is important, in considering this, to be very clear about the identity and social membership functions jobs serve. For many people it is not enough to be provided with a job *per se* or even a job that pays the same salary. What feels subjectively essential is to have a job that maintains their particular role in the community and/or the relationships, surroundings, and expectations they have become accustomed to.

To be sure, striving for a better job is an important feature of our way of life, and I have noted how readily many people seem to discard ties to a community or to workmates in the search to "move up." But there are millions of others who feel it is imperative not just to have a job but the job they hold right now. In many instances the efforts of unions are directed at this goal even when retraining might be financially beneficial to both worker and employer.

Jobs and the Social Order

Jobs serve functions not only for the individual but for the social order as a whole. If large numbers of people are thrown out of work, this constitutes not only a deprivation for them but a threat to the social order as well. Work both channels energies that might otherwise be disruptive and provides a structure that keeps people busy rather than having too much time on their hands for mischief. And of course the large-scale disappearance of expected job opportunities creates resentments that can smolder or even explode.

Attribution theory, an increasingly influential theory in social psychology, suggests another important social function of work as well. Individuals who have participated in the social order and have exerted effort and organized their lives around its required disciplines would—just by virtue of that—experience an increment in commitment and assent to that order. Seeing themselves at work on its behalf and according to its rules, they conclude, in effect, that, however much they may grumble, they must be feeling it is legitimate.[2]

A related effect derives from the actual compromises people must make in order to participate in the system. As one enters the job market and does what is necessary to get ahead, one accepts new responsibilities and commitments that bind one to the system and change one's point of view. The idealistic lawyer who enters a firm with large corporate clients when work with more broadly social goals is not available is likely to find himself changed by the experience and perhaps to feel too compromised to pursue seriously the critical stance he once held. The binding effects of such participation in the economic system were recognized by many of the activists of the Sixties who tried to find a way to function outside the system in order to be able to maintain the inner freedom to sustain dissent. And in at least some instances, their earlier predictions were confirmed by their own experiences when changed circumstances and economic pressures drove them back into the regular job market. Few became the rather total converts the media are so fond of portraying, but the cutting edge of their critical attitude was frequently blunted.

Jobs and the Distribution of Goods

Keeping people working serves still another function for the system as a whole, one that is particularly problematic in the present context. I have suggested that much of our economic activity does us more harm than good; that much of what we produce we don't really need, and that the social and ecological consequences of mobilizing for maximum production often more than offset the gains. It is very difficult for us to change our orientation, however, because under our present system it seems to be necessary to produce a great many things we don't need in order to produce those that we do.* As a corollary, of course, we must also persuade ourselves that we really do need

---

*Ironically, we also do *not* produce a great many things we do need, such as better housing. We seem not to be able to "afford" this because our resources are so tied up in compulsively keeping busy and keeping people employed.

the things we produce (and we employ a substantial work force in addressing this task as well; the total outlay for advertising in the last decade was over 350 billion dollars).[3]

Put aphoristically, we have to keep people working in order to keep people working. When a substantial number of workers stop and then buy less of what others produce because their buying power is reduced, still other workers must stop too. There is a "multiplier" effect, with ripples that extend beyond the initial area of impact. In order to keep the wheels turning, a certain amount of work—or make-work—is required. As things now stand, if everyone suddenly stopped buying everything except necessities, the necessities too would begin to disappear, as the buying power to purchase them dried up. The system would grind to a halt.

At the heart of this difficulty, and of the broader fear of any change that might eliminate jobs, is the role jobs play in distributing wealth. As Galbraith noted some time ago,[4] jobs today are often more important for their function of providing a means of *distributing* goods than for their role in *producing* them. This is even truer today when (despite the current mood of belt-tightening and deprivation) we have even more than we did when *The Affluent Society* was published and when, as well, the drawbacks of high levels of production—in terms of pollution and resource depletion—are so starkly evident. It is difficult for us to respond appropriately to the situation we face because our system requires people to keep busy in some economic activity in order to have a rationale for distributing to them those things which really are valuable. Welfare payments and unemployment insurance provide some stopgaps, but they are deeply flawed and stigmatizing. Thus, even if what is being produced by a given worker is not needed—indeed even if, on balance, its production is harmful—we need to keep him working in order to have a rationale—an excuse—for providing him with a share of that portion of the economic product that really is valuable. Every society requires a means of distributing its product that is experienced as legitimate and that does not undermine the incentive system or the guiding mythology of the culture. For us that is achieved primarily by pay for work performed.

This system, reasonable (though not necessarily equitable) when it first evolved, has now become acutely problematic. The tail now wags the dog. What we produce is now very largely determined not by what we need but by the requirements of the distribution system for legitimization. Producing what we need is now easy. What is hard is getting it to people. The solution has been to produce a great deal we don't need as well. Then everybody is working and has a right to a share—of much that we don't need but also of much that we do.*

In one sense getting the goods out by producing still other goods has "worked"; it has kept us going as an affluent society without thus far producing cataclysmic upheaval. But it has worked at a very high, and growing, cost: a cost to our health, to our relations with each other, to our sense of contentment and well-being. It has led to a state of affairs in which the richest nation in the history of the world is now feeling poor and deprived and in which enormous inequities create ghettos, despair, crime, and the danger of ugly reaction by the confused majority.

Our present mode of economic organization developed at a time when producing enough for everyone—and certainly for everyone to live amply—*was* the problem. Until relatively recently, only if almost everyone worked as hard as possible would there be any chance of developing a surplus. The distributive function of work was secondary; the main issue was to get things done. There is still, of course, a need to get things done. We could not survive for very long if *everyone* stopped working. But our problem today is really how to keep the requisite number of people working to produce the optimal (rather than the maximum) product and still retain a sense of fairness; how to live in a society where less work is needed than what can be provided by the labor force. This is a new problem in human history, and we have yet to face it, have yet even to acknowledge its existence.†

---

*Not everyone works, of course. Substantial unemployment has in fact been a frequent accompaniment of our present way of doing things. But we make life unpleasant enough for those who don't work that the basic rationale for the distribution system remains intact (the one exception to this being those who are heirs to a large fortune, who are treated with rather more deference than those who have to work for their daily bread).

†This is a different problem from that faced in poor countries, where it is often the case that less work is *available* than the labor force requires. There, a great deal really does need to be done, but shortages of capital and structural problems prevent it.

In less economically advanced societies it was reasonable to strive for growth in material product and even to sacrifice a good deal in the pursuit. Though it was some time before the common man felt the benefits, the prospect of economic growth—once it became a possibility—did provide a path out of the life of subsistence and privation that has tended to be the lot of most men. Concern with productivity, efficiency, and expanded output, however self-serving the aims of those who organized it, was progressive and was in the long-range interest of the citizenry at large.

But the structure within which the pursuit took place had flaws. Some flaws were evident in the beginning, when the imperfect foundation was visible to the naked eye: Inequality was a foundation stone, and many suffered while a few reaped the benefits. Later, with prodigious effort and talent—and counter to all expectations*—a magnificent edifice was constructed on this unlikely foundation. General affluence was achieved, not for an aristocratic few, but spread widely among millions. Free enterprise seemed to have liberated mankind. Perhaps, had the grandeur of the structure been recognized, it could have been stabilized. Had it been recognized that the economy had reached a size large enough to provide commodious shelter for all, the various buttresses added through the years could have permitted renovation of the foundation and the achievement of a lasting monument. But flushed with success, we continued to build, expanding the economy to a point at which further flaws in the foundation began to become evident as well. Today, we continue to insist on "more, more," while, like a child's tower of blocks to which too much has been added, the entire edifice sways menacingly.

The newly evident flaws, which cause us to overtax the structure,† are, ironically, precisely what enabled us to achieve

---

*Even the great founding geniuses of the economics of capitalism— Smith, Malthus, Ricardo—never expected it would yield affluence to the majority of the populace. What they saw as immutable laws seemed to require that the bulk of the work force live at a subsistence level no matter how much growth occurred. It was the outcome that economics predicted—not the fact that it had so few Galbraiths among its stylists—that led economics to be called "the dismal science."

†Not, I hasten to add, in Milton Friedman's or Arthur Laffer's sense of overtax.

what we have thus far. Central to our economic system is the constant generation of desire, envy, and discontent. So long as that desire is what keeps the economy moving, we cannot rest content or we will rest entirely. Our system is not set up to run as a steady-state economy. According to the common economic wisdom, the economy must expand or it will collapse.* We have achieved a level of affluence beyond the wildest dreams of the founders of the capitalist system. But we cannot enjoy it. We are not even able to see that we *have* succeeded so. For the very way of thinking that enables us to do so also prevents us from appreciating it.

But it is more than just a matter of going farther than we need, more even than the environmental threats that going farther has called forth. We have also, in achieving our level of material productivity, paid a price in *other* sources of security and satisfaction, such as our sense of being rooted in a community. Up to a point that price was reasonable; increasing levels of affluence compensated for what was lost. But as we saw in Chapter 4, we are now caught in a vicious circle in which we keep sacrificing those things which could really make a difference in our lives for those which no longer do.

Our problem, then, is not, as we have been told so often recently by those mired in our old grounding assumptions, that we are insufficiently productive. It is close to the opposite. We have organized our lives and our society around maximizing production at any cost. And the cost has mounted steadily. We are drowning in our own effluents and in our discontents. What we need now is not still "more." What we need is a way off the treadmill. What we need is a way to come down from our reckless high without crashing, a way to maintain an affluent way of life without a compulsive commitment to growth. We need to learn to enjoy and savor instead of "moving up," to learn how to reestablish roots, how to conserve instead of wasting, and, most difficult of all, how to give a new place to work and jobs in our lives, one that does not compel us to put people to work first and consider the damage they are doing second.

---

*Important alternative conceptions, more suited to a society of satisfaction rather than of growth, have been offered by some economists, such as Herman Daly and Nicholas Georgescu-Roegen.

What Is Our Task?

The key to addressing the unemployment issues raised by the value changes sought here is to keep firmly in mind just what kind of potential unemployment we are discussing. Our old assumptions are so deeply rooted in our thinking that they are likely to continue to influence our thinking about these matters *even when what we are exploring is precisely the question of what would happen if those assumptions changed.* It is essential to be clear about this if the real implications of such a change are to be grasped. One cannot assume that people will continue to experience the same desires they now do, for if that were the case then there would be no unemployment problem to discuss (or at least there would not be one due to what I am advocating—there would still be the unemployment problems due to Reaganomics and the like). If I am to be confronted with the economic consequences if people should think as I am suggesting, it seems only fair that for the duration of the discussion I be granted the assumption that they do so think.

Perhaps it will be easier for the reader to grant me this if what follows is thought of as a kind of fantasy, but a fantasy of a very particular sort—a *logical* fantasy, as it were. I wish to play out the logic of the values and assumptions I am advocating in order to clarify their potential consequences. I ask the reader at this point not to evaluate whether large numbers of people are likely to think in the way discussed here but to consider what would happen if they did, to see if what I am saying makes sense in its own terms.

To grant me this much assent is not to agree that people will in fact change in this way. I myself am not sanguine about the prospects. But I believe that we are in a great deal of trouble if we do not change along these lines in some fashion, and that it is necessary to assume that such change is at least a possibility and to examine its consequences. Moreover, I believe that one of the greatest impediments to such change is precisely our lack of understanding of what would result from it. The fear that adopting the point of view discussed here will produce hardships results, I suggest, from failing really to assume that the point of view is actually adopted. Or more accurately (and more problematically), a change in the reader's viewpoint is likely to occur silently and in midstream: The premise is granted sufficiently to blame the new outlook for costing people jobs but not sufficiently to see how—given such an outlook—this could be dealt with in a satisfactory way.

The possible job loss we are discussing here would result from a decrease in "demand." But it would be a very different kind of situation from the usual decrease in demand that leads to loss of jobs. In the more familiar situation, people still want more but don't have the purchasing power. If you will, demand is low but desire is high. In contrast we are asking here what happens when *desire* is low. Job loss then presents rather different issues.

Most essentially, the problem then is not one of lost production. Production in this case has declined because people don't feel they need as much. This is a matter not just of making do or of belt tightening, but of a positive sense that there is much more to be gained by concentrating instead on the quality of our experiences and our personal relations and on developing the kind of community that makes that possible. We are talking about a population that has concluded that further gains in "efficiency" and "productivity" are not worth it at the cost of compulsive attitudes toward work and a competitive organization of society, a population that would rather enjoy the health and longevity that come from cleaner air and water and uncontaminated food than to have a few more toys and gadgets.

I have suggested that such a population might conclude that we would be better off, all things considered, if many people did *not* do the work they currently do. It is important to be clear that it is not just the workers directly involved in the production process whose work we might be better off without. Even more perhaps is this so for many of those in positions of greater prestige and influence. Society would have much to gain if instead of being paid to keep doing what they have been doing, we could find a way to pay a great many people simply to *stop* what they have been doing—the advertising person who persuades us to be anxious about the smell of our bodies or our genitals; the corporate lobbyist who persuades a senator to vote against a tough pollution control bill; the chemical executive who directs dumping of toxic wastes; the auto executive who contributes to people's deaths in the way described by Ralph

Nader in *Unsafe at Any Speed*; the oil company president who does everything fair or foul to prevent the development of cheaper fuels not in his control.[5] There are literally millions of people in this country whose daily work detracts from rather than adds to the common good.

This is not to suggest that all of those millions are as morally reprehensible as the examples in the preceding paragraph. Most are simply decent people trying to earn their daily bread (and, of course, a little cake). But in many instances the only socially useful thing they do all workweek is to collect their salaries. At least *that* contributes to feeding their families. And it helps to legitimatize and keep going the entire system, without which (under present arrangements) what we do need would not get made either.

What we require is a mechanism to enable this harmful work to stop while still distributing to these individuals a share of that part of the social product which really is of value. The first step in developing that mechanism is understanding that the problem *is* one of mechanism and not of there not being enough to go around. That is, if many jobs disappeared because we decided that, on balance, their performance did more harm than good, we would not have lost anything by their nonperformance.* In terms of total net social welfare, there would in fact be a gain. It is true, "less" would be produced, but the compensations would more than make up for it. Fewer cars would be made each year, and fewer people would have a new car, but for most people transportation would be more comfortable and convenient (see Chapter Seven). Attending to the consequences of toxic wastes might increase the "cost" of certain products. One fewer polyester suit or carrying a string bag to the supermarket instead of automatically getting a paper bag might be the result. So too would be fresh water fish that don't contain PCBs when we eat them and backyards without a toxic time bomb underneath. Our plastic bills would go up; our hospital bills would go down.

If we eliminated what was unnecessary or harmful there would still be as much of the rest to "go around." Since the

---

*Such questions as just who it is that decides what is meant by adding or subtracting from the common good, and how to assure that such decisions are made democratically and with full respect for human rights, are likely to occur to the reader. They will be addressed in the next chapter.

workers put out of work would not be those producing the things still desired,* the amount of the latter would remain undiminished and the newly unemployed could continue to receive as much of those goods as before without anyone else having to reduce their share. The problem would be in how to get it to them without creating a sense of unfairness or sapping the motivation of those who would still be working to produce the goods and services still viewed as desirable and worthwhile.

To begin with, it would be important to promote a program of public education aimed at assuring that those whose jobs are a casualty of our new set of values be able to maintain self-respect and the respect of the community. Such a program would encounter great difficulties in our present social context, but again it must be recalled that the job displacement we are talking about here would occur only if a substantial change in outlook had already taken place. What would be required is recognition that these displaced workers have not ceased to be productive but are in fact just beginning to be in a position to *be* productive. It requires as well a recognition that they are not freeloaders or people getting off easy but really quite the opposite; they deserve to continue to receive a generous share of the remaining social product, because they are in the more difficult position of having to disrupt a familiar routine in order to learn a new set of skills. They would be the front-line troops who bear the brunt of the struggle to live by a more sensible set of values; their shift from holding down useless jobs that keep us all hostage to the productive machinery to becoming trainees for the future is a gain rather than a loss for the rest of us.

The money to pay these men and women would have to come from the public treasury, and hence from taxes, but these people would not be on the dole. The aim is not charity but the creation of a way of life that works better for all of us. They would not be wards of the state but individuals actively training for a role in society that serves all our needs better than their previous role. The problems posed by a suggestion of higher taxes are difficult and will be addressed (partially) in Chapter 12. Here I wish to consider simply the question of what kind of work these new trainees would do.

*Under present arrangements, of course, this would not be the case. Unemployment has a ripple effect, throwing other workers out of work too because of reduced purchasing power. The strategy described below is one designed to prevent that from happening.

Essentially, there would be two main directions toward which they would move: sharing jobs with those already working at producing things that would continue to be valued, and entering new fields that would be created by the shift in social values and life-styles. It is tempting to emphasize the latter, and indeed, as I shall discuss shortly, there will be a good deal of it. But it is important to resist such a temptation initially, because our preference for it reflects in large measure the assumptions and values I am trying to question. Doubtless there would in fact be new "growth industries" if consumer preferences were to change.* But it would defeat the whole purpose of what I am advocating if we continue to work just as hard and to organize our lives just as much around work and around purchasing power, simply with different objects being sought after. A magnification of the already strong shift to services, as discussed below, would certainly have an important benefit in reducing pollution and toxic wastes. But I am trying to address the possibility of a world where buying and selling altogether had a diminished role, a world in which emotional and aesthetic experiences and relations between people were more at the center, a world in which the need for income and the demand for work did not keep growing.

Thus job-sharing needs to be considered, both because in practical terms it will probably be needed and because examining our attitudes toward it reveals to us how difficult the value change I am describing is to maintain or even to keep clearly in mind, how readily the old assumptions, which have pervaded our thinking in the past, slip back in again like a bad habit one thought had been exorcised. In principle, there is always enough work to go around. All you have to do is divide the required work by the number of available people, and everyone is working. There is, however, a widespread assumption that people are entitled to not just a job but a "full-time" job, and that settling for something less is an unsatisfactory compromise. This is an understandable attitude, but on reflection it seems less sound than it does at first. After all, what we now call full time would have seemed part time a hundred years ago. If our vision of an appropriate number of working hours could shift from 80 to 40, why not from 40 to 20?

*Perhaps the term consumer itself would begin to seem anachronistic as our sense of identity and of our social roles began to change.

A decent society should certainly provide opportunities for meaningful work, for all to share in the tasks that must be performed and to have room to develop and demonstrate skills and to assume responsibilities. Both unemployment and demeaning, unfulfilling work are social blights that critics of our society have deplored for good reason. But work, I believe, has frequently been too central a feature of social critics' visions. Many of our best social critics are as rooted in the assumptions of scarcity as are those who run our corporations and government bureaucracies. The creative and rewarding use of leisure should be at least as central a concern as the need for meaningful work. It is true that as things are now, leisure is often an extension of our dependence on the corporation. Expensive stereo components, snowmobiles, video games, and even some how-to-do-it sex manuals (which really imply how to do it better than your neighbor) do represent an intrusion of the "heartless world" into the "haven," an imposition of values of buying, achieving, competing, and status hierarchy into the realm of the private and personal. But criticisms of these intrusions often seem designed less to protect leisure than to put it in its place and to reflect a Puritan (or a scarcity society) view of work that views it as what "real life" is about.

Work has played such a central organizing role in the lives of almost all of us, and in the ordering of society, that we are made anxious by considering an order in which work plays less of a role. We manifest a fetishism of labor every bit as much as a fetishism of commodities. It is important for us to recognize the many and varied needs work serves beyond those of producing and providing income. But the expectation that these needs will continue to be served primarily by work, and especially by *paid* work — that is, work that economists can easily track — limits the possibilities we can consider.

It is certainly the case that, other needs notwithstanding, people work in large measure to receive income. An obvious objection to job-sharing is that if three people now do what previously only two did, then the original two will earn only two-thirds of what they did before. Actually, this need not be strictly the case. We might decide as a matter of social policy to upgrade the salaries in jobs that have been designated for job-sharing. It is true that if the changes I would like to see adopted did come about, "Gross National Product," and hence total "income," would be less than they otherwise might be; but we could decide to spread that difference around rather than let the burden fall disproportionately on those involved in job-sharing.*

The notion of job-sharing, however, does in principle imply a reduction of income, either for those sharing the job or for all of us. It means accepting and even regarding as desirable a state of affairs in which many are producing less than they did previously and hence in which there is less product to go around. Here it is necessary to remind ourselves again that the necessity of job-sharing—at least of the sort discussed here—would arise only if people had concluded that their previous higher incomes or "standard of living" were in fact misleading. The job loss that would require the redistribution of work would be a consequence of large numbers of people having already decided they were better off without the package of more products, more pollution, and more psychological unease. Thus one could not posit the same sense of deprivation that would hold if the population as it *currently* sees the world were to find its "income" reduced.

New Jobs for Old

Having looked into the abyss of job-sharing and reduced "income," we can now afford the luxury of noting mitigating factors that don't require us so thoroughly to keep our present habits of mind at bay. To begin with, it is useful to be clear that a decline in purchasing power does not necessarily imply an equivalent decline in standard of living, even as traditionally measured. The reason is that only some of the things we need must be bought each year. Food, of course, must be purchased continuously, and money spent on travel or entertainment must be spent anew each year to maintain a contant standard. But if one has bought a color TV in 1983, then (one hopes) TV purchase money will not be needed in 1984. So too for many other purchases. Since most of us have been continuously *increasing*

---

*Clearly this would require some other means of determining income than "the market." I shall discuss in Chapter Twelve why I do not share the widespread American reverence for market mechanisms as the ultimate determiner of who should get what.

our material stocks over the years, we have needed considerably more income than just replacement income. To maintain our *present* standard of living, a considerably smaller income than we have now would suffice.*

We may also note that the entire problem of lost jobs under the new set of values would not be quite as large as at first it seems. For one thing, the alteration in our habits and our values would make certain things more desirable even as others became less so. Jobs would be lost manufacturing private automobiles or building highways. But some would be gained in building mass transit vehicles or laying tracks. There would be fewer jobs in industries that depend on consumers becoming discontent with serviceable items and buying the latest model or fashion change; but there would be much work to do in renovating housing in our decaying central cities and perhaps in converting parking lots into attractive community parks. In all, the "new" work would be less than the "old" — if *total* steel production, energy consumption, or other measures of resource use and environmental strain did not decline, the change would not really be working — but the largest number of new jobs would be concentrated in the period of transition. Once the tracks were in place and the requisite number of vehicles produced, say, it would take far less continuing work to keep things maintained than in our present system of rapid turnover and of manufacturing with planned obsolescence in mind. It is also in the transition period that the need for jobs would be greatest. Thus there would be a cushion provided while people learned how to organize their lives around other centers than work.†

Still another mitigating factor in the transition to a less growth-obsessed society derives from the distinction between a manufacturing economy and a service economy. We have already made a substantial shift away from an economy centered on the production of goods to one centered on the provision of

---

*I am here referring to income in constant dollars. If inflation were high, one would of course need more money for the same purposes. But the changes advocated here would reduce production through reducing demand and thus should not exacerbate inflation.

†Considerable work will be generated for some time in addressing the deterioration of our infrastructure — bridges, roadways, water pipes, sewers, and soon — which resulted from our pursuit of the new, shiny, obvious, and profitable. See, for example, "The Decaying of America," *Newsweek*, August 2, 1982, pp. 12-18.

services.[6] The changes that would follow from the ideas advocated here would have their greatest and most immediate impact on the commodity sector of the economy (which is already contracting) rather than on the service sector (where jobs are increasingly concentrated).

As I have indicated, I am not automatically opposed to any and all kinds of economic growth. Although I question what I believe to be a compulsive and unthinking allegiance to growth, there is still clearly room for growth that can be shown to have genuine net benefits for people. This does not mean that I am simply advocating growth in the service sector and retrenchment in commodities. It is true that growth in production of goods is much more likely to have a deleterious effect on the environment and thus seems to me to require a greater burden of proof to demonstrate its net benefits. But the "service sector" is an exceedingly complex and variegated enterprise.

Much of what it provides is simply a part of the consumer society, and its benefits are likely to be as ephemeral as those discussed in Part I. The financial planning and credit arrangements that permit us to buy more, for example, are limited in their value by the value of what they let us buy. The legal services each corporation must increasingly employ in order to deal with the lawyers of the other corporations only increase the costs of goods for all of us. These are "services," but of little net value.

Even the services—very loosely, "human services"—that are most likely to provide genuine benefit are not without their problems. I do not agree with the most extreme critics of the human services professions, those who see them as rather thoroughly self-serving, manipulating others in order to make them dependent on organized professionals;[7] but I do think that professionalization of human contact has at times been excessive and has led to mystification of simple matters or the false impression that complex matters become less so when viewed from a technical vantage point. All things considered, such services as medical care, psychological counseling, or teaching (not just in schools, but of tennis, flute, or pottery) clearly seem to me to enhance our lives—and to do so considerably more than do the commodities for which so many strive—but a "service society" still dominated by economic considerations, albeit with different contents of striving and competition, would be only a minor improvement.

As I see it, there is bound to be a deep gulf between what can be achieved via the private striving after profit and what can follow from societal actions expressing compassion and a sense of shared fate and shared humanity. So too is there a difference between a society where "services" are important because that is the way to "get ahead" and one in which the pole of community is stronger than that of competition. In the society I envisage, neither the market nor the profit motive would be likely to disappear altogether, but both would be vastly reduced in influence compared to what we have now.

Such a change is not only desirable on abstract humanitarian grounds but absolutely essential if the kind of transition I have described in this chapter were to be accomplished. Even with a very different attitude on the part of large numbers of people, the changes I am discussing could not occur without a modification of our existing economic structures; and the psychological conceptions I have stressed point strongly to the conclusion that a different attitude could not at any rate occur independently of changes in our social arrangements and in the realities of our everyday lives. It is also difficult to imagine people agreeing to job-sharing or to a reduction in nominal income without a good deal more equality than we have today and without institutions that facilitated a cooperative rather than a competitive orientation.

Reducing the role of the market is to some people a daunting prospect, raising specters of maddening inefficiency and diminished freedom. In the next chapter I shall try to show why such fears are unfounded.

TWELVE

The Myth of the Market

T HE CHANGES IN VALUES that this book advocates would no doubt bring corresponding changes in basic social institutions. The broad strategies regarding jobs outlined in the last chapter, for example, would require a good deal of social planning and collective determination of goals for production and distribution. Such a prospect makes many people uneasy. The market has served us as a model not only for our economic system but for our thinking about democracy as well. Phrases such as "the market place of ideas" reflect the way in which our identities as citizens and thinkers lean upon our identity as consumers.

The system we have at present in fact represents a rather substantial departure from a hypothetical pure market system. In a world of giant corporations and complex technology, economists have had to construct more and more imaginative Ptolemaic epicycles to demonstrate that society revolves around the free market. Managing the economy on the basis of such a model is not easy, and attempts to do so have not been particularly impressive in recent years. But the market has remained a vital force in our society, less as an economic reality than as a central feature of our reigning mythology. Suggestions that we modify the workings of the market still further, that we concern ourselves more explicitly with the results we wish to obtain rather than letting the chips fall where they may, elicit in some quarters powerful subcortical anxieties about "creeping socialism" or "collectivism."

There are also, to be sure, more thoughtful concerns raised about social planning and further deemphasis of market forces—concerns I take seriously enough to call attention to them myself in order to address them. In order to compare the potential risks and benefits of alternative approaches with those of continuing on our present course, it is necessary to look more closely at how we actually make decisions now. Over the years we have introduced many features into our economic set-up designed to provide a little guidance to the "invisible hand." It would be nice to think that the reasons for those interventions have lain in considerations of social justice and of human relations, that it was recognized that it was demeaning and ultimately destructive of the social fabric to organize our daily activities so centrally around the idea of trying to get the best of others. But in fact it was largely the economic misfunctioning of the market system that has led to its modification through the years.

The unfettered market, if it ever existed, is a thing of the past. The corporate leaders who publicly mourn its passing clearly prefer eulogizing to resurrection. They complain about government interference in the market mechanism but are disingenuously modest about their ability to make that interference profitable.

Our business leaders, in fact, have always been skillful in conveying one picture of their effectiveness to the public and a different picture to the stockholders. To the latter they must be powerful, effective generators of large profits. To the public they present themselves as straws in the wind, powerless to influence events, the mere servants of market forces and consumer preferences. The parable of the "invisible hand" was a wonderful device for this latter purpose.

The "invisible hand" moved much like the hand on a ouija board. It depended for its credibility on the illusion that it moved quite apart from the will of men. But those who understood what went on under the table could make it spell out what they wished. If the distribution that resulted was due to an "invisible hand," it was invisible only because most people never got into the boardrooms where they might actually see the hands that fed them (though, of course, only to the degree the market would bear).

The illusion of the "invisible hand" enabled all to feel that they had no responsibility for the way goods were distributed. We must, after all, bow before the objective laws of economics. It is sad that some have so little while others have so much, but little can be done about that. To "interfere" with the distribution that results from market forces is to tamper with nature. That, we are assured by our high priests, is an exceedingly dangerous thing to do. The wrath of the "invisible hand" is great. Bite the hand that feeds you — worse, call into question its existence, or accuse it of being a puppet hand controlled by people who know just how they want it to move — and it will take revenge. Pestilence and boils are nothing compared to the "leveling down" it will wreak. Try to help the poor gain some of what the rich have and we will *all* be poor, we are told. Men don't create unequal distribution of wealth; the "invisible hand" does. And men dare not run an economy, because only the "invisible hand" knows how. If the results seem harsh, we can at least be sure they are just, for they are meted out by the invisible hand in its infinite wisdom and ultimate, if inscrutable, love of mankind.

Any faith, of course, must change and evolve if it is to stay vital in a changing world. The genius of a successful faith is to accommodate to changing circumstances while retaining uncompromised its essential foundations. Such has been the case in our thinking about economic matters. Despite much revision, the basic cosmology and basic morality remain intact. Changes there have been aplenty, enough so that a breed of new evangelists has flourished recently, calling us back to the old-time religion of free enterprise and unfettered markets they fear we have abandoned. But they fear for our souls needlessly. We have not lost faith in selfishness or the narrow calculation of individual advantage; we have only modernized. We have shown our faith in many ways, not the least of which is making their sermons bestsellers (for in what better way than in making them commercial successes can we show our fidelity to these prophets' teachings?).[1]

There is certainly an important difference between the capitalism of the welfare state and that of the robber barons (however much the present Administration is trying to build a bridge from the one to the other). I share none of the nostalgia of some on the left for the more stark and primitive capitalism, red in tooth and claw, of days gone by. Even at the risk of being less clear as to just who or what the enemy is, or the risk of seeing those who work for change co-opted, I would choose without hesitation the present welfare state as a major step in the direction of a more humane and rational social order.

But the problems addressed throughout this book are problems that have become most acute under the social arrangements of the last few decades. There are those, I suppose, who take this as a lesson about what happens when the market is interfered with. That is clearly not my own view. As I see it, the problem is that we have not interfered enough. Despite important and valuable constraints upon the unfettered play of amoral market forces, ours is still basically an economy that relies on the profit motive and the pursuit of individual self-interest.

Whether what is required to address the problems discussed in this book is a full-scale conversion to a socialist economy or instead some mix of capitalist and socialist modes of organization of the sort striven for, but not yet fully attained,[2] by some Western European Social Democratic governments, is not a matter that can be answered at this point. It is difficult to see how the suggestions put forth in Chapter Eleven and elsewhere in this book could be implemented in an economy anything like our present one, but just what are the minimum changes that would make it feasible, and what precise kinds of changes would be most desirable, are questions whose answers will best emerge from gradual experimentation and ongoing debate.

I do wish, however, to address a number of more general concerns about any strategy that implies greater social planning and a reduced role for the market. Especially in America, there is a common assumption that such a trend implies both reduced efficiency (and hence diminished prosperity) and a real threat of a loss of freedom. I believe these fears to be unfounded. In presenting my own arguments and perceptions in this regard and contrasting them with those of market advocates, I am obviously also implicitly drawing on a long tradition of debate about these matters. Rather than review this enormous literature, however, or examine in detail where I do or do not depart from what various others have said, I shall simply indicate what I regard as some of the more compelling and important considerations. It is my hope that in the present context the reader will find brevity, freshness, and a focus on the arguments themselves more useful than a detailed history of what others have said on these matters.

The Absence of Comparisons

When considering both the issue of efficiency and that of freedom, it is important to recognize that the implementation of a socially planned economy in a democratic society has not really been tested. The societies that call themselves socialist — viewed by many on the left as actually "state capitalist" — have all been the result of either violent political revolution (as in Russia or China) or of outright military conquest (as in Eastern Europe). Though there are substantial variations among these societies — not all of them are as oppressive as the Soviet Union — all bear the stigmata of their origins, and none are in any way appropriate tests of whether democracy and socialism can coexist. The potentially most appropriate test of this idea was aborted by the guardians of freedom and free enterprise: the CIA, in making the world safe for ITT, did not seem to make it safe for democracy, at least in Chile, where the Pinochet regime seems a poor testament to the belief in the link between capitalism and freedom.

The Chilean experiment having been forcibly terminated, we have in the world today no democratically elected government that has achieved widespread social ownership and a planned economy. Among the variants that do exist today, the economies of the Scandinavian countries seem closer than most to what free-market capitalists object to; they also offer precious little support for the notion, preferred by Hayek, Friedman, and others, that planning and democracy are incompatible. These are among the freest societies in the world — as well as among the economically most successful — and I wonder if even Milton Friedman would feel less free there from the threat of arbitrary government intrusion into his life and liberty than in Pinochet's Chile, which has found his advice so congenial.

The Sovereign Consumer?

Proponents of the market system tell us that in such a system decisions about what is produced and how it is distributed are the product of uncoerced choices by autonomous individuals. Each person is free to buy or not to buy what he pleases. On the basis of these individual choices, a certain aggregate demand is manifested, and on the basis of that demand other individuals conclude that it will be profitable to try to meet that demand. The glue that binds together and coordinates all these millions of individual choices is the price system, and it functions to signal to millions of individuals what is the most profitable activity in which to engage. The sovereign consumer, by buying or not buying as he sees fit, sets into motion an economic machine that is custom-tailored to his desires. No dictator or bureaucrat tells the manufacturer what to make. Autonomous individuals do that, and woe betide the businessman who does not listen to the voice of the people.

There is certainly a measure of truth in such a picture. At times consumers do say no to what is offered, and manufacturers who have improperly gauged the public mood bear the burden of their error. The Edsel is probably the classic example of this, with the more general difficulty in peddling gas-guzzlers a more widespread recent instance. This classic portrait of the market economy also has some phenomenological validity. People often do *feel* they are freely choosing, even where their desires are manipulated and their options foreclosed.

Nonetheless, there is a great deal in this vision of the sovereign consumer and of the thoroughly voluntary nature of market exchanges that is misleading, and this must be made clear in order to compare the risks and benefits of our present system with those of a potential alternative.

For one thing, some consumers are more sovereign than others. Vast differences in wealth and income create vast differences both in the degree of influence any individual or group of individuals exerts on what is produced and in the leverage that any participant can bring to bear in an exchange. Parallels are frequently drawn between the votes individuals cast in an election and the votes they cast in the market place by what they buy or don't buy. The implication seems to be that just as political democracy protects us against tyranny in the political sphere, so too does the market, as a kind of permanent, floating voting booth, assure us of freedom in the economic realm. Indeed, some worshipers of the market go so far as to argue that it is a far better guarantor of personal freedom than are democratic elections.

We are told by William F. Buckley, Jr., for example:

> Let the individual keep his dollar—however few he is able to save—and he can indulge his taste (and never mind who had a role in shaping it) in houses, in doctors, in education, in groceries, in entertainment, in culture, in religion; give him the right of free speech or the right to go to the polling booth, and at best he contributes to a collective determination, contributes as a rule an exiguous voice. Give me the right to spend my dollars as I see fit—to devote them, as I see fit, to travel, to food, to learning, to taking pleasure, to polemicizing, and, if I must make the choice, I will surrender you my political franchise in trade, confident that by the transaction, assuming the terms of the contract are that no political decision affecting my sovereignty over my dollar can be made, I shall have augmented my dominance over my own affairs.[3]

Now of course Mr. Buckley, the son of a millionaire, may be just a mite self-serving in this argument. His poignant defense of the right of the ghetto dweller to choose to spend his dollars "indulging his taste" in houses, travel, education, culture, and so forth, just as freely as Mr. Buckley can with his seems but a prelude to a defense of the equal right of the rich and poor to sleep under bridges. Buckley's rather cavalier attitude toward the political franchise sets him off here from many other believers in the virtues of the market as society's principal means of regulation.

Or perhaps it would be more accurate to say it sets him off from other *public* statements. David Vogel and Leonard Silk reported on a rather extraordinary meeting held by The Conference Board, a forum for big business leaders to exchange views in a candid and off-the-record manner. "Many businessmen," they report, "have begun to fear that capitalism and democracy may be incompatible in the long run."[4] This is not, however, an attitude they express publicly. "Executives," Vogel and Silk observe, "like all serious participants in the political process, are at least publicly bound by the norms of the political culture, and those norms presently include an unquestioned acceptance of the principle of democracy."[5] Nonetheless, in summarizing the actual attitudes expressed at the meeting, Vogel and Silk conclude that "[w]hile the critics of business worry about the atrophy of American democracy, the concern in the nation's boardrooms is precisely the opposite. For an executive, democracy in America is working all too well—*that is the problem.*"[6] (Italics in original.) This rather disturbing picture is made all the more remarkable when one realizes that it was presented not by radical critics of big business but by two men trusted enough by these business leaders to be invited to observe and report (though with guarantees of anonymity for those whose opinions were described) and whose report was praised by The Conference Board's president.

There are others, no doubt, whose public pronouncements about the democratic virtues of the market deserve to be taken as a straightforward expression of their beliefs. Whether correct or not, the view of the market as a paradigm for democratic decision-making is widespread, as is the idea that a market system extends democracy into the deepest recesses of everyday life, enabling the choices of individuals, rather than the formulas of bureaucrats, to determine what is desirable.

Thus Milton Friedman, while granting us that "[m]ajority rule is a necessary and desirable expedient," nonetheless wants us to know that it is

> . . . very different from the kind of freedom you have when you shop at a supermarket. When you enter the voting booth once a year, you almost always vote for a package rather than for specific items. If you are in the majority, you will at best get both the items you favored and the ones you opposed but regarded as on balance less important. Generally, you end up with something different from what you thought you voted for. If you are in the minority, you must conform to the majority vote and wait for your turn to come. When you vote daily in the supermarket, you get precisely what you voted for, and so does everyone else. The ballot box produces conformity without unanimity; the market place, unanimity without conformity. That is why it is desirable to use the ballot box, so far as possible, only for those decisions where conformity is essential.[7]

There is, however, another crucial difference between the operation of the market and that of a democratic election—a difference less convenient for market advocates to cite. Elections operate essentially on the principle of one person–one vote.[8] The market doesn't even begin to approximate this principle. In the market place, a Rockefeller has thousands of times as many votes as the average citizen. Both in the money he spends for personal consumption and the money whose investment he controls, such an individual has incalculably more to say about how the society's resources will be deployed. The market works on the principle of one dollar–one vote, and those on the top have garnered far more extra votes for themselves than Mayor Daley or Boss Tweed could ever have dreamed of.*

This means that in a market economy the products and services produced and offered are not those needed or desired by the largest number of people but those desired by those who control the most dollars. This is relevant not only to the questions of fairness and control over one's life that we are considering here. It bears as well on the ecological concerns addressed earlier. While urban housing and mass transit, relevant to large numbers of people with relatively few dollars to vote with, go wanting, environmentally damaging luxury items are voted for in the market place by those with dollars to spare.

The realities of the market economy differ substantially from the picture offered by its apologists. As they present it, it is a wondrous thing indeed. Milton Friedman, for example, following a line of argument traceable at least back to Adam Smith, tells us that two parties will not engage in an exchange unless each sees some gain in it. Thus, no one loses; everyone comes out with more than he would otherwise have had. According to Friedman, "Most economic fallacies derive from the neglect of this simple insight, from the tendency to assume that there is a fixed pie, that one party can gain only at the expense of the other."[9]

The real fallacy comes in elevating this pious tautology into a defense of the unmodified market. Yes, given any particular

---

*We may also remind ourselves that most market exchanges in which individual consumers engage are not with other individuals but with large corporations. Great as are the disparities in wealth and power between individuals at the top and bottom of the economic ladder, they pale to insignificance next to the disparity between the average consumer and General Motors.

distribution of wealth and power, and any particular set of rules, two parties will not voluntarily agree to an exchange unless each expects to benefit from doing so.* But that does not mean that the results of such an exchange will benefit him more than those of a different exchange which might be possible under a different set of rules and with a different distribution of power and wealth. The poor man who takes a job at minimum wage (or below the present legal minimum under Friedman's "freer" arrangements) is, we may assume, better off than he would be not taking the job if the alternative — under the "discipline of the market" — is to starve. But the market system, which has provided him with this job and thereby staved off for the day the growls of an empty stomach, has also been responsible for the distribution of wealth and the system of reward that makes such a low-paying job his only alternative to starvation. Under a different system — one that placed limits on the sovereignty of the market — he might be guaranteed a larger share of the social pie in return for his work (and, most likely, his boss would end up with a smaller share than he would have in the first case; I am not minting my own hypothetical coin).

Under present arrangements it is true that all are free to take or leave what the market offers. But not all are offered the same deal. Indeed, it is not even solely a matter of more or less. With regard to employment, for example, some can refuse *any* deal, while others are desperate and must accept essentially whatever comes their way. There is indeed a sense of freedom associated with a millionaire's choice of whether to accept a particular offer for his services as chairman of the board. Upon reflection, he might decide he would rather not work at all. Such is hardly the case for the unskilled day laborer, especially if the "restrictions" on the market which Friedman so decries are removed. Indeed, even Adam Smith notes this clearly:

> It is not difficult to foresee which of the two parties [masters or workmen] must, upon all ordinary occasions, have the advan-

*Even here, it must be noted, expectation of gain and actually ending up better off are not the same thing. People can be fooled, and they can fool themselves, and we are not nearly as rational or prescient as the market model implies. And what of the man (or woman) with an unconscious desire to fail (and importantly, a conscious — and also real — desire to succeed)? What is *he* up to when he engages in an exchange, and when has he fulfilled his aims?

tage in the dispute, and force the other into a compliance with their terms. . . . A landlord, a farmer, a manufacturer, or merchant, though they did not employ a single workman, could generally live a year or two upon the stocks which they have already acquired. Many workmen could not subsist a week.[10]

The Panglossian picture of the market's benefits offered by Friedman and others is based on assuming that no alternative means of determining wages other than a relatively unregulated market economy are available to the person. The choice the working man makes *within* the market system is his "best" choice only if one rules out certain other possibilities, such as *changing* the market system. By expanding our view of the person's options, it may appear that he has *less* by virtue of engaging in unmodified market exchanges than he would if he instead wished to change the rules and mechanisms that determine who gets what. Under a system in which considerations of equity in the outcome of distribution tempered market mechanisms to a greater degree, he might have quite a different set of choices. Even with a model of market exchanges, if redistributive mechanisms resulted in his having more in the bank than he now has, and in his boss's having less, the wage he could hold out for would be different.

I am not concerned here, however, only with possibilities of distributing wealth more equitably or with the impact of unregulated market exchanges on the poor alone. There is a largely unacknowledged impact on the rest of us that also is obscured by what might be called the fundamental error of individualistic calculation—focusing on each transaction separately without examining the larger context of alternatives. Again, it is (tautologically) true that an individual will not voluntarily participate in an exchange unless he or she sees some gain in doing so. But again, by narrowing their vision, analysts like Friedman exclude what they wish not to see. It is not just the poorer party to an exchange who might benefit more from a substantial modification of market supremacy. In many instances, *both* parties to the exchange might be better off if they had available certain choices that the market system just doesn't provide.

This is so because unless there are specific external restrictions, a deal between two parties does not take into account the effect of their exchange upon a third party. But we are all third parties to enormously more exchanges than we are first or second parties to. My purchase of an automobile may seem to both me and the dealer a gain. I prefer the car to the money, and he prefers the money to the car. We are both better off than before the exchange. Moreover, I may be even more pleased — in a system where the government has gotten even further "off our backs" — to pay less for a car without emission controls; knowing that my own addition to the total pollution I must breathe is negligible, my individualistic calculation is that I am better off not having to pay for what — viewed in isolation — won't benefit me very much.

But whereas I am the purchaser in this one transaction, I am a bystander in the millions of other auto sales that are made in the year. If all of these purchasers also decide to save money because the contribution of their own exhaust pollutants (viewed individually) is minimal, then the total impact on my lungs of all these transactions is very powerful indeed and is likely to greatly outweigh what I gain by saving money in my one purchase. The same is true for each of the others.

Each of us, however, who are third parties to millions of other people's transactions, are, in an unfettered market, powerless to affect their transactions. So the best we can do is make the best of a bad situation by not paying for our own emission controls, which will not after all affect what millions of others put into the air.*

That is what the unrestricted market so often promotes: making the best of a bad situation, and a bad situation that is, ironically but inevitably, precisely the result of scrambling by all of us to make the best of it. Far from maximizing our freedom, the market tends to trivialize it, to leave us free to choose within a set of constraints created by the inevitable workings of the market system itself. In many instances, it is only when we

---

*In the economist's lexicon there is, to be sure, a term to address all of this: externalities, or external diseconomies. But as E. J. Mishan of the London School of Economics puts it, "all too many [economists] tend to look at such effects merely as one of the chief obstacles to facile theorizing — as the sort of possibility that detracts from the optimal properties of the popular theoretical construct, a perfectly competitive economy — rather than as an existing social menace. Familiarity with so simple a concept, and ritual footnote references to it, seem to have imparted a feeling that the matter is well under control." E. J. Mishan, *The Costs of Economic Growth* (New York: Praeger, 1967), p. 56.

restrict the forces of the market that we begin to have any meaningful and valuable degree of freedom. The freedom to face a different set of choices altogether is, for many of our social and environmental problems, the only freedom really worth having. For this opportunity — often obtainable only through laws that restrict market exchanges in certain ways — the price of such restriction is well worth paying.

The Question of Efficiency

When market enthusiasts address at all the issues just raised, their response is essentially that deals obtainable under other systems need not be considered because they are inevitably less desirable. The efficiency of market determination of production and distribution is presented as so far superior to any alternative that even those at the bottom have far more then they would with a more equal slice of what we are told must be a much smaller pie. In this view, the complexities of determining an overall plan for the economy are so great that no central agency can hope to do the job at all efficiently. Only by utilizing the decision-making abilities of millions of individuals — more in touch with the limited segment of the economic enterprise relevant to their particular business than any bureaucrat can possibly be with regard to the system as a whole — can the efficient deployment of resources be achieved. By relying on the profit motive, it is contended, and on the signals provided by prices as to supply and demand, abundance can be achieved as in no other way. Strive instead for greater equality or greater attention to the needs of the poor or of the majority, and you will achieve instead economic chaos. Not only the rich but the poor as well will be worse off. In effect, these arguments suggest that we need not consider the deal the individual might get in a less market-dominated society because that deal will inevitably be worse.

There are several ways of dealing with this contention. Let us first rid ourselves of the most tiresome red herring. The poor performance of the Soviet economy and of many of the economies of Eastern Europe is frequently cited as a demonstration that reliance on social planning is less efficient than reliance on market forces. It is certainly true that the quality and variety of consumer goods provided by the Soviet economy have not compared favorably with our own.

There is, however, some controversy among economic historians about the growth rates that have been achieved by the Soviets over the years. Whether in 1917 Russia was a feudal backwater, awakened only by the collective efforts and planning that followed the revolution, or whether it was a budding industrial power just about to take off and hampered by foolish efforts at collectivization, is a matter of some debate. What seems much less controversial is that whatever gains were achieved in the Soviet Union were on the backs of tens of millions of people and that widespread misery, coercion, and even murder were a central feature of the process.

As a consequence (and perhaps as a consequence as well of traditions dating back to the autocracy of the Czars) attitudes of cynicism and alienation, unwillingness to stick one's neck out, and a combination of corruption and resignation all seem to be common. Planning is undertaken not in a spirit of consultation and cooperation but in a dictatorial fashion under circumstances well designed to minimize honest feedback. It is not surprising that in such circumstances efficiency should suffer. Indeed, what is surprising is that in certain limited areas, such as weaponry and space exploration, the achievements are so substantial and the stimulation of innovative thought by its scientists so effective.

The relevance of the failures of "planning" in the Soviet Union to the prospects for planning in our own society is minimal. They are failures of dictatorship, not of planning. And dictatorship would be an unpalatable alternative to me, and I hope to most Americans, even if every Soviet citizen had a digital watch, a snowmobile, a two-car garage, and ten pairs of designer jeans.

A planned economy that was the result of democratic choices by the people would be a very different kind of animal. In a system where the people felt they had a stake in how things ran and had some say in important decisions, there would be no reason to expect the same cynicism and corruption as in an imposed system. Information flow is seriously hampered in totalitarian systems by the fear and apathy of those below. The possibilities for effective planning are substantially underestimated when there is not effective two-way communication, when the people who are in touch with what is really going on send back only the messages that will protect them from the wrath of those above them, or when they have no interest in sending back any messages at all that are not explicitly required. Given a genuine spirit of cooperation and engagement, there is reason to expect that planning would be much more effective.

There is a tendency to equate central planning with decision-making being made only at the top. This is never the case. Those at the top of the decision-making pyramid are responsible for setting broad guidelines, but operational decisions are made at every level. Moreover, those decisions that are made at the top are dependent on input accumulated through every level of the hierarchy. The highest-level planners couldn't begin to make decisions without the data provided by experts in a vast range of operational activities. Moreover, the data they receive are not only *provided* by many others, they are also *selected* and *analyzed* by them. The raw data are far too vast for any central decision-maker to cope with. At every level, the input of those below is digested and passed along to the next level in altered form for the assimilative and reductive process to occur again. And, it must be added, at every level what is passed along is not just input that *leads to* decisions (from above) but input *about* decisions already made below. This is absolutely inevitable, or no economic activity could occur at all, efficient or inefficient. No central guidelines are *ever* clear enough to eliminate the necessity for decisions below.

Galbraith has described in detail how this process works in large corporations and has shown how the decision-makers at the top are dependent on the technocrats below them.[11] In principle, this is no less true for the Soviet economy. Its leaders are no less dependent on those below. The difference is that the leaders in the Soviet Union, as a consequence of their own doing, are far less well served by those below. The input they get is not as accurate because the system is built on fear and oppression or toadying and cynical seeking of privilege. Stalin established firmly the tradition that the bearer of unpleasant news will not survive to disturb those above him again. His successors — at all levels of the bureaucracy — have learned the lesson well, with regard both to those above them and to those below. Under such circumstances, how could any planner hope to make sensible decisions or, as importantly, to expect sensible decisions from those below (who even in the most centralized of systems account for the vast bulk of actual judgments)?

A second critical difference between the planning in most corporations and that in the Soviet Union is the considerably lower degree of autonomy and initiative that is explicitly permitted to those at lower levels. This is not unrelated to the first difference, but it compounds it. The complexities of the real problems any middle-level manager encounters are such that it is not really possible to follow very faithfully the line from above. Some degree of initiative will be necessary whether desired or not. But the effectiveness of those initiatives is not likely to be enhanced by the effort to disguise that it is occurring. As much effort is likely to go into making the decision invisible as to making it a sound decision.

There are many varieties of central planning. What should interest us is not the question of central planning *per se* but whether it is good planning or bad planning. Large corporations are directed from above, and at least some of them are fairly efficient, if not as generally superior to government enterprises as prevailing myth would have it. Management of a corporation the size of General Motors or as diverse as some of our newer multinational conglomerates is as substantial a task as would be the central direction of the entire economy of a country like Sweden or Holland. In such corporations the chairman of the board is a powerful man.* But one of his most important skills, we must note, is likely to be the ability to delegate authority and to encourage such delegation in turn all through the hierarchy. There is in principle no reason a similar attitude could not characterize the structure of responsibility for directing a planned national economy. Those elected, or chosen by those we elect, to occupy the highest administrative posts would set broad guidelines and review decisions as they filtered back. But — as in those other bureaucracies we call corporations — initiative (and the responsibility for good or bad decisions) would be dispersed widely through the system.

What the foregoing discussion really points to is that "planning" is not a very useful or meaningful term. There are a great many ways to administer an enterprise, whether it be a corporation, a university, or an entire national economy. In almost

---

*It is unfortunately the case that the male referent here is just about universally the applicable one.

all instances, what those at the "center" can effectively do is set broad guidelines and oversee how well those guidelines are being fulfilled. Sometimes this includes reviewing whether particular activities and decisions made elsewhere in the system are consistent with those guidelines, and it ought to include as well a continuing reexamination of the guidelines themselves to clarify the meaning and definition of the seemingly agreed upon first principles. *Heavy-handed* application of central planning—at the extreme, *paranoid* application of central planning—is certainly inefficient. Delegation of authority and encouragement of initiative seem essential, as does alongside it a structure of discipline and responsibility. But this is not a matter of central planning or none. It is a matter of enlightened planning or needlessly autocratic planning.

The facts simply do not support the contention that government intervention into the "free" market place impairs economic performance. The MIT economist Lester Thurow notes that

> . . . it is well to remember that none of our competitors became successful by following [the route of "liberating free enterprise"]. Government absorbs slightly over 30 percent of the GNP in the United States, but over 50 percent in West Germany. . . .
>
> Other governments are not only larger; they are more pervasive. In West Germany, union leaders must by law sit on corporate boards. Sweden is famous for its comprehensive welfare state. Japan is marked by a degree of central investment planning and government control that would make any good capitalist cry.[12]

Interestingly, even the defenses of unfettered capitalism by its strongest proponents cast doubt on its supposed efficiency. Perhaps no one has waxed more rhapsodic about this system than George Gilder, whose bestseller *Wealth and Poverty* has the endorsement of the President and of his budget director. One of the chief virtues Gilder finds in capitalism is its encouragement of people to take risks. Among the facts about capitalism he finds most heartening are the following:

> [S]ome 4,700 small manufacturers are spawned in this country each week, while 4,500 others fail. More than two-thirds of all ventures collapse within five years, and the median small businessman earns less than a New York City garbage collector. Of

the thousands of plausible inventions, only scores are tested by business, and only a handful of these are an economic success.[13]

Not only do these figures point to a great deal of frustration and disappointment on the part of hundreds of thousands of failed businessmen and their employees, but they suggest as well that under our system an enormous number of incorrect investment decisions, representing faulty deployment of personnel and resources, occur each year. As Paul Samuelson has noted, ours is "a vast system of trial and error."[14] Probably all economic systems must involve a great deal of trial and error, but the record Gilder cites with evident satisfaction (to him it signifies the bold "defiance of the odds" that makes businessmen a creative force) suggests that there are a lot of wrong moves a planner could make before he approached the inefficiency of our more random approach to deployment of resources.

Our presumptions to the contrary reflect a deeply held prejudice in American life. In our popular mythology organizations run for profit are creative, productive, and efficient whereas government enterprises are bureaucratic, slothful, and productive of little but waste. Large corporations, however, are bureaucracies every bit as much as government, and precisely how Oriental rugs in the chairman's office or lunches at four-star restaurants help us to purchase our goods at a lower price has never really been adequately explained; we have been trained to accept a very narrow definition of waste. As the matter is put in a highly influential book on the American business creed, "Government is powerless to create anything in the sense in which business produces wealth and individuals produce ideas [and] inventions."[15]Galbraith deals with this nonsense in his typical pithy manner: "The case involves some rather strained argument—it makes education unproductive and the manufacturer of the school toilet seats productive—but, nonetheless, it has a position of considerable prominence in the business liturgy."[16]

The Problem of Incentive

When the possible efficiency of alternatives to the relatively unregulated market is under consideration, doubts about how well planners can anticipate the needed flows of materials and labor represent only one pole of the skeptical position. A second centers on the question of motivation and incentive: If the opportunities open to those who work hard and use their wits are diminished, if the same rewards are available whether one's work is outstanding or mediocre, why would anyone try? The genius of the market system, we are told, is that it permits anyone to rise, or at least to try to rise, as far as his talents and persistence will take him.

Now in principle there is nothing about diminishing the influence of market forces that requires a greater equalization of income. In the Soviet Union, for example, there seems to be actually a greater disparity of income than in the United States.[17] This is, from my point of view, one more failing of the Soviet system, but it does show that a planned economy and an egalitarian distribution of income are by no means equivalent.

Nonetheless, the reader would certainly be correct in concluding that I am presenting arguments that point toward a greater equalization of wealth and income and in requiring me to discuss the consequences of such a shift. Not only my view of fairness and justice but the particulars of my arguments about the meaning of wealth and the determinants of well-being point in this direction. Greater equality is needed to lessen the invidious nature of social comparisons and to still the engines of envy that have powered our economy to the verge of environmental collapse. Widespread contentment is difficult to achieve when inequality is great, especially in a society that has a myth of upward mobility and classlessness. In addition, the strategies discussed in Chapter Eleven for dealing with the impact on jobs of changing attitudes toward the consumer way of life would require a considerable redistribution of wealth as part of their implementation.

The view that such a policy would "kill incentive" is widespread in our society. Not surprisingly, it is encouraged particularly by those at the top of the income scale. Interestingly, this is pursued in large measure by their shrewdly engaging in implicit and selective bad-mouthing of themselves. In a variety of ways they try to convince us they are so venal, lazy, and irresponsible that unless their current incomes are maintained, or even increased, they will deprive us of a substantial measure of their skills and services and/or will perform in a subpar, perfunctory way. (The message sounds more polite, of course, in the sanitized language of "incentive.")*

I do not believe that such people are as shiftless as they would have us think. Even as hard-headed a pillar of the economic establishment as Paul Samuelson acknowledges that the desire for achievement and pleasure in their work can motivate successful leaders in business and the professions just as monetary incentives can, and he cites studies that point to this conclusion.[18] In a slightly different realm, few observers have suggested that professional athletes hustle more in these days of mega-salaries than they did in the old days. The complaint, in fact, is often quite the opposite.

The point is not that the opportunity to earn more money cannot motivate people to work harder. Clearly that is not true. The differential yield when peasants work both on a collective farm and on their own private plots demonstrates the power of incentive very plainly.[19] But those peasants are poor, their task is of relatively low complexity, and the effects of working harder on their plots are immediate and concrete. Problems arise in generalizing from such observations to the behavior of wealthy Westerners performing complex administrative and technical tasks. Such tasks have a number of properties that make such generalization extremely hazardous: They require the participation of large numbers of other people, making the relation between any one person's behavior and the desired outcome extremely tenuous and hard to evaluate; the results of any effort may not be evident for several years, and the degree of success may be rather ambiguous, thus further diminishing the experienced link between increased effort and improved outcome; the nature of the task is often such that "trying harder" doesn't help and may even be counterproductive (in complex performance, excessive motivation can actually impair performance by increasing stereotypy, narrowing attention, and

*To the degree that the rather unflattering picture of themselves proffered by our leading money-earners is true, there is a clear solution. If indeed the heads of our corporations and other well-placed individuals have become so bloated with their present accumulations that it takes hundreds of thousands of dollars to make them even notice they are getting paid for their work, we could tax their present wealth to bring it closer to the level of everyone else. They could then experience the same needs as the rest of the population and be relieved of the ennui that today robs them of the ability to respond to ordinary incentives.

diminishing the capacity for creative solutions);[20] finally — and perhaps most important of all — such activity is often inherently stimulating and enjoyable, and motivation deriving from the challenges of the task itself, or from the possibilities of increased prestige that success brings, may considerably outweigh the importance of the money itself for someone already relatively well-to-do.*

Much of the cant and confusion about "incentive" that permeate debates on national policy is based on naive overgeneralization from simple situations where more money brings more effort and more effort has fairly immediate and unambiguous results. Businessmen talk about themselves as if they were peasants or piece workers, and the fallacy is hidden in abstract words like "incentive" or "productivity." The consequence is that we persist in policies that create enormous income differentials in fear of killing the geese that supposedly lay us golden eggs.

One rationale sometimes offered for the extraordinarily high salaries of those who run our major corporations is that they deserve it because they have created jobs and created wealth. But the "creation of jobs" or "creation of wealth" is not a result of special gifts of these particular people such that without them the jobs and wealth would not exist. What would be more accurate is that they have *been put in a position* to create jobs and wealth. The need for work, the existence of a potential market, and — very importantly — the existence of an infrastructure that permits manufacturing, transporting, and purchasing of products all are the result of large social forces that our high-salaried executives simply ride. To be sure, some ride them more skillfully than others; but even presidents and board chairmen of companies that are doing poorly receive annual incomes most Americans would be pleased to earn in a decade. As John Kenneth Galbraith has put it, "The salary of the chief executive of the large corporation is not a market reward for achievement. It is much more in the nature of a thoughtful personal gesture by the individual to himself."

---

*This is complicated and distorted in a system such as ours in which money serves not only as a means to meet material needs but also as the primary medium for symbolically bestowing prestige. The changes I am suggesting are in part designed to diminish that artifactual connection.

Also frequently cited as a rationale for extremely high executive salaries is that whoever pays such a salary is trying to offer more than any competitive bidders are offering, in order not to lose the desired person's services. The large salary is in this sense "necessary."

It is necessary, however, only because the rules are set up in a particular way. Were there, say, a maximum legal salary, they would *not* have to offer an astronomical amount to attract the desired individual. Perhaps they would instead have to lure him or her by demonstrating that they have set things up in such a way that he could really accomplish the tasks he is trying to achieve. Such a framework for attracting desired individuals would seem to be not only likely to promote a more egalitarian distribution of income but to be more efficient as well, for it would motivate those within the organization to remove internal obstacles to the achieving of tasks.

We are not used to thinking of competition as something that reflects a particular decision to set up the rules in a chosen way. We are so used to the present system that much of it seems "natural," and only variations from it seem "artificial." To set a maximum legal salary seems to us restrictive; to let people get what the traffic will bear seems libertarian, seems like simply permitting natural forces to have their free play.

But how does a corporation get to have the resources that enable it to offer its board chairman a million dollars a year in salary and other compensation? Indeed how does it get to exist at all? Without the elaborate, deliberately planned—may we say artificial?—set of rules creating this artificial entity and limiting the liability of those who own it, there would be little likelihood that the real individual human beings who own the shares would get together and offer a million dollars to anybody to run their business. And without the government-built roads and the enormous complex of government-created rules and regulations, there would be no business to run.* For better or worse, our economic system is a social invention, a complex and

---

*Some—indeed, a great many—of the government regulations are highly controversial and opposed by market proponents. Regardless of whether that opposition is in fact short-sighted and if achieved would work to their detriment, there is also an enormous web of relatively noncontroversial rules designed to facilitate commerce, without which modern complex industry could not exist.

elaborate deviation from the state of nature. It operates by a man-made set of rules that are no more natural than any other set of rules. They may be better or they may be worse, but either way they are our responsibility and not God's. They must be defended by the consequences they bring (including certainly, not just the degree of economic well-being but of freedom, justice, and enjoyment of living) and not in terms of whether they introduce artificial constraints; that much all systems do.

Our present system of incentives is in fact quite inefficient and wasteful. Our income differentials are considerably greater than are necessary to accomplish the dual task of motivating people while retaining our justly valued freedom to choose the work and workplace we want from those available to us. At present the *average* total take (salary, bonus, dividend income, and pension income) of the chief executives at the 50 largest industrial corporations is over a million dollars a year.[21] Indeed, as Paul Samuelson notes, "If we made an income pyramid out of a child's blocks, with each layer portraying $1,000 of income, the peak would be far higher than the Eiffel Tower, but almost all of us would be within a yard of the ground."[22] Clearly much smaller differentials would do the job of luring people into the jobs that require harder work or more preparation.

"Imagine," asks Lester Thurow

> what those who believe that all work is dependent upon large income differences would predict about an economy where large firms give lifetime jobs, where relative wages are almost completely dependent upon seniority rather than personal skills and merit, and where income differentials are 50 percent smaller than in the United States. Yet the Japanese have the world's highest rate of productivity growth.[23]

FOREIGN COMPETITION?

Foreign competition is another factor that would make some people leery of interfering with the market place: If competition were prevented from bidding up salaries here, what would prevent foreign concerns from hiring away our top executives and other important individuals? It is possible that some "brain drain" might result from such a situation, but several considerations should temper our concern. First of all, it is not that easy to leave one's country permanently, and many who initially intended to go abroad would decide to stay. Even within the United States in recent years there has been a growing tendency for executives to refuse to move from one city to another, to forgo promotions and even risk their jobs.[24] Apparently the disruption of family life has begun to be recognized by some as at least as important as an increase in salary.

Some, no doubt, would move anyway, but their going might not be such a loss. For one thing, very few of us are really irreplaceable. In a country as large as ours there is plenty of talent waiting to be used. Those most likely to leave under such circumstances would be the most self-seeking and self-serving, who cared more about making money than about accomplishing the task *per se*. They would be the individuals, however hotshot, who lacked any real loyalties or commitment. The myth of the irreplaceable executive is in large measure a projection of our own narcissism. The unique talents of our business leaders was a matter about which John Maynard Keynes was particularly skeptical. When asked, in light of his low estimation of their special skills, why they succeeded in making money, Lord Keynes is reported to have replied, "by competing against other businessmen."[25]

The Mixed Blessings of Competition

I have argued that many of the problems facing us cannot be solved via individualistic, competitive market approaches and that only through cooperation, through a recognition of our shared stake in certain solutions that cannot be achieved by any of us alone, can we deal effectively with the issues we face. This suggestion runs counter to a deep strain in American life. Competition is almost our official state religion. Like all religions it is often honored in the breach, but also like other religions it nonetheless plays a pervasive role in ordering our relationships with others and our sense of ourselves. Part of the rationale for promoting competition is libertarian. In the "market place of ideas" we expect the truth to win out and those who seek it to be most free to pursue whatever clues appear to them. In the interplay of competing power centers, we expect the circumstances to be created for maximum free expression of individual tastes and values. In economic competition itself, we expect the conditions for freedom to be most firmly established.

But by far the most powerful source of the passion for competition in the popular mind is the belief that it will provide — and has provided — the greatest amount of material abundance. In one sense this is probably true. I have, after all, suggested that our competitive, market-oriented system leads us to produce a good deal more than we need. At the same time, however, it has left us seriously deficient in things we need very much — housing, public parks, public transportation, not to mention clean air, water, or soil.

Moreover, contrary to a common popular myth, competition does not always provide us with the best-quality goods or the best opportunity to make sound and meaningful choices. Consider the case of the DC-10, which illustrates both. It has been suggested by the author of an important study of air transport policy that the rush to beat the competition may have led to design defects that played a role in one or more fatal crashes. As Frederick C. Thayer puts it,

> Serious observers ask if the DC-10 was designed too hastily, a necessity in the race to capture a share of the market for wide-body jets. While no manufacturer would build an unsafe aircraft intentionally, competitive pressures can affect judgments. [26]

Then to compound the felony of competition, as it were, National Airlines, which had been displaying the words "DC-10" on the body of its planes, painted over the words after a crash that killed 272 people.[27] So much for the competitive system's laying out the options for people and letting them choose! (It remained *possible*, of course, to obtain the information necessary for an informed choice — I assume that National did not actually lie if people took the initiative to ask what kind of plane would be used — but clearly they were doing their best to minimize the passenger's knowing what he was choosing.)

Nor, unfortunately, are these isolated examples. It is in the very nature of a system in which one must constantly look over one's shoulder at the competition that corners will be cut — in design, in information to the public, and in morals. Heilbroner and colleagues' book *In the Name of Profit* documents a variety of serious offenses by respected corporate executives in the ordinary course of doing business: faking lab reports, bribing city officials, knowingly selling dangerous drugs—and getting promoted after their acts are exposed. Anyone who doubts that our competitive system is corrupting should read it.

Paternalism, Democracy, and Useless Goods

There is still another dimension to the defense of the market system and to the unease that the present arguments may stir. At numerous points in this book I have referred to useless goods or goods that bring only illusory satisfactions. I have argued that we would all be better off if such goods were not produced, and I have even discussed strategies for finding work for those who previously had been involved in the production or distribution of such goods. Yet the goods to which I am referring are things that up to now people have been quite willing, and sometimes even eager, to purchase. People have quite voluntarily decided to give up substantial amounts of their own money for what they have judged to be the benefits of these goods. Who, then, am I to say that such goods are useless? Who am I to judge what is best for someone else and what that person should have? Does not such an attitude lead to paternalism—even, some might say, to dictatorship?

To understand why it does not, it is necessary to look at the assumptions that have tended to underlie our thinking about both economic and political matters. Despite the enormous influence of Freud in our culture, our thinking about economic matters often retains a quaint rationalism. The model of economic man typically implies an individual rationally calculating gains and losses, secure in his knowledge of what he wants, and making the best deal possible given the (inevitable) scarcity of resources. The model underlying the present argument, derived from psychological rather than economic theories, is quite different. It implies that what we want is not so simple and straightforward; that often we want conflicting and incompatible things; that we frequently deceive ourselves about the nature and range of our aims; and that as a consequence the choices we have made and actions we have taken are a quite imperfect index of what our actual preferences really are. It implies as well that we are often poor judges of what is in our own best interests and finally—a departure in some ways as much from Freud as from the economists—that the desires we express are as much the product of our immersion in a particular social milieu as the expression of a spontaneous upwelling from within.

The reader concerned about the authoritarian implications of an argument that people deceive themselves about what is in their best interests might note, to begin with, that I have not attempted to *impose* my values on others. I have not taken up a gun or fired someone from a job (as have, in fact, many defenders of "free enterprise"). I've written a book. My aim is to persuade, to point out what is usually overlooked or brushed aside, not to bring about change by force or coercion.

My skepticism about how deeply or reliably consumer purchases reveal people's real interests or desires derives, to a substantial degree, from my training as a psychologist. Shortly, in fact, I shall argue that the compatibility between such a view and the democratic ethic can be clarified by a consideration of the process of psychotherapy. But it is important to note that this skepticism is hardly unique to psychologists or to this book. John Kenneth Galbraith, for example, has consistently and persuasively pointed to the ways in which our needs are shaped by the system of production and by the ads that are so pervasive a part of it.[28] By the time the average person reaches the age of 20 he will have been exposed to approximately 350,000 television commercials.[29] Whatever mainstream economists may say, clearly those who head our large corporations believe that people's desires can be influenced by ads and are willing to spend a rather large fortune in the attempt.

The social historian Stuart Ewen has further illuminated the role of advertising in shaping our consciousness, emphasizing how ads serve to deflect discontent with the system into discontent with the self, and then to bolster the system by implying that this discontent can be remedied by buying the appropriate products.[30] The creation of the discontent that leads to buying is generated by making people anxious about what they formerly took for granted. Ewen cites a number of interesting statements by members of the advertising industry addressing their colleagues in their trade journals. In their own words, these individuals reveal the conscious attempt to direct people's critical faculties against themselves. One writer remarks that advertising can serve "to make [people] self-conscious about matter of course things such as enlarged nose pores, bad breath." Another notes that it "helps to keep the masses dissatisfied with their mode of life," and (correctly) adds, "Satisfied customers are not as profitable as discontented ones."[31]

My conviction that assuming that people deceive themselves need not make one disrespectful or authoritarian derives from my experience as a psychotherapist. Psychotherapy presents us with a rather different model for how change can occur in human affairs from those which inform more traditional political efforts to bring about change. In particular, the model that guides the psychotherapist includes very centrally the idea that people are often not clear about what will really make them happy or about what the consequences are of various patterns that are central in their lives. To the psychotherapist, however, this is not an occasion for him to assert his superiority or clearer vision, or to attempt to coerce the patient into adopting the therapist's values or beliefs. Rather, the therapist, if he is a good one, attempts to help the patient see more clearly and make his own choices, and the therapist respects those choices as the decisions of an independent moral agent. Good psychotherapy is a democratic, not an authoritarian, process.

Admittedly, this is an idealized picture. Not all therapists even come close to it, and the best approach it in only approximate fashion. We still have a great deal to learn about how psychotherapy works and particularly about the role of the therapist's values. There is evidence that patients who derive benefit from psychotherapy tend to shift their values in the direction of those of the therapist, and the implications of this finding remain to be fully understood.[32]

I am not arguing here that psychotherapy is a value-free enterprise, nor do I believe that it can or should be completely nondirective. I have in fact written critically of such notions in other places.[33] Clearly the present volume—in some ways an application of a psychotherapeutic perspective to social issues— is neither value-free nor nondirective. I do believe, however, that therapy at its best is profoundly respectful of the other person and illustrates well how a belief that someone is fooling himself can be combined with a commitment to taking him seriously and accepting that he is the final arbiter of his own experience and direction.

Some, no doubt, would shudder at the suggestion that we should in any way model our politics after psychotherapy. It is currently fashionable to view therapists as either shallow or dangerous—and frequently both. I have dealt in previous chapters with some of the antipsychotherapeutic currents in our present intellectual life. One line of criticism that needs to be taken more seriously asks us who is to be the patient and who the therapist. Whose motives are to be interpreted and whose assumptions examined? And who is to do the interpreting and examining? In psychotherapy proper the answer is clear. The patient has come to the therapist for help and has more or less explicitly *asked* him to raise questions about his (the patient's) life.

Some patients, of course, are involuntary patients. They are committed to mental hospitals; required by a judge to see a therapist as an alternative to prison; or (without the aid of the legal system) coerced into therapy by a spouse as a condition for the continuation of a marriage. These are much more problematic situations, where the critics of the therapist's power, his wolf-in-sheep's-clothing stance, are on much more solid ground. Such a structure of the therapeutic process is not what I am pointing to here. While even in such structures genuinely helpful interactions can sometimes occur, there is a real danger of abuse. The parallel to the thought reform confessionals practiced by totalitarian regimes is not entirely far-fetched. The Hungarian film *Angi Vera* and Arthur Koestler's *Darkness at Noon* provide chilling examples of such authoritarian probing into the psyche.

One feature of these abusive variants on psychic self-exploration is their asymmetrical power relations. In my own therapeutic practice I have no external power or authority to yield. There is, to be sure, a kind of power that frequently devolves to the therapist, of the sort that is usually designated by therapists as transference and is due to the tendency for the very structure of the situation to evoke feelings deriving from parent–child interactions (where there *is* an objective power relation). Part of the aim of the therapist in many instances is precisely to dissolve this irrational influence, to help the patient become more fully aware of his equal status and of how he reacts to the therapist as a powerful parent when he is in fact just one adult talking to another.

Importantly, this latter aim need not undercut the therapist's ability to help the patient see where he has deceived himself, nor need it prevent the patient from being receptive to whatever is valid in the therapist's message. The fate of the therapist's statements, like that of the arguments in this book, depends ultimately not on the authority of the interpreter but on whether the reframing of experience that is offered resonates with the experience of the listener or reader. Who is to be the therapist with regard to social values? Whoever offers himself in that role and is able to be persuasive. In a democracy anyone can offer an interpretation. And anyone, if he so chooses, can ignore it.

That is the difference between a psychological model deriving from the psychodynamic tradition and one built along lines suggested by B. F. Skinner. Skinner's is a rhetoric of control, not of persuasion. Those who have attempted to apply Skinner's ideas have often tended to do so within the context of institutions that authoritatively and artificially limit the alternatives available to the individuals whose behavior is to be changed. Moreover, the effort is often undertaken without the consent of the person who is to be its object. The question of who is to control the controllers in such a context is a disturbing one. The notion of counter-control offered by Skinnerians is of value in an abstract, philosophical sense but not very reassuring when some have rather exclusive control over the most basic reinforcements. Stripped of the element of control—which derives not from any essential determinism in psychological matters *per se* but from the structure of the institutions (including the laboratory) in which Skinnerian efforts are undertaken[34] —Skinner's ideas can be useful. Indeed, I have, in the course of a broader study of psychotherapy, suggested ways in which the empirical findings of Skinnerian psychologists can usefully complement more traditional psychodynamic approaches.[35] But in the present context I think it useful to distinguish quite sharply between the two psychological models.

Psychotherapy, then, as I am using the term here, refers to a process in which one person listens to and observes another and offers his comments as to what he thinks is going on. The psychotherapist has been trained to be aware of the pervasive importance of conflict in psychic life and of the requisite tendency for most people to blur, blunt, distort, and bury aspects of their experience in order to achieve some sense of peace and unity. In pointing this out to the patient, the therapist, if he is to be effective, must clearly communicate respect for the person. If he is condescending or supercilious, if he lacks empathy or sympathy, if he speaks from a stance that implies that he is not prey to the same kinds of anxieties and the same pressure to distort his own experience, then however brilliant a diagnostician, he is not likely to be therapeutic.

In the view of most therapists, the patient holds the ultimate responsibility for his life and the choices he makes. Some of those choices may seem foolish or tragic to the therapist. That he not try to influence such choices, as is the claim and the ideal put forth by some therapists, seems to me both more and less than human. I part company with those of my colleagues who advocate such an ideal. But I fully endorse, in all but the most extreme instances of psychosis or suicidal despair,* the canon that after one has had one's say, when all is said and done it is for the person whose life it is to make the final decisions.

So too with my unsolicited interpretations of our social patterns. In suggesting that what we buy does not necessarily represent what we really want or what is best for us, I am unabashedly trying to influence. There are those who argue, in defense of present patterns of consumption, that since people would not buy things if they did not want them, who am I to say they don't or shouldn't want those things? Perhaps their more behavioristic (and, it seems to me, tautological) position is correct. If so, arguments like the present one should present little threat. People will continue to buy and perhaps in addition will gain a measure of amusement from the cranks who question the wisdom of their choices. And if, perchance, there is some validity in the present point of view, that too will present no threat — at least to those whose interest is in human happiness and freedom. The present economic system may be threatened, but not democracy. If institutional changes are required to unbind us from the wheel of wanting and buying and wanting some more, those can come from the will of the people, with votes and ar-

*I am not implying here that in such instances coercive intervention is always justified, only that the issue is then more complicated — much more complicated than critics like Szasz imply — and that in such circumstances it *may sometimes* be the most ethical course.

guments the mechanism, not guns and dictates. Like the psychotherapist of the sort I am describing, the believer in democracy must be patient. He must persistently strive to change the
consciousness of those he addresses, but he must accept the necessity of waiting until change appears attractive to those he
hopes will choose it. He must resist the temptation to seek an
imposed change, in the faith that, when chosen rather than imposed, change is likely to be both more secure and more benign.

Notes

Chapter Two: The Illusions of Growth: Economic Abundance and Personal Dissatisfaction

1. *The New York Times*, November 29, 1979, p. A26.
2. Lester Thurow, *The Zero Sum Society* (New York: Basic Books, 1980).
3. *The Wall Street Journal*, December 2, 1980, p. 56.
4. Shlomo Maital, *Minds, Markets, and Money* (New York: Basic Books, 1982), pp. 254-56.
5. *The New York Times*, October 16, 1981, p. A16.
6. *Statistical Abstracts of the United States* (Washington, D.C.: U.S. Department of Commerce, 1981).
7. *Ibid*.
8. See, for example, W. S. Lowinski, "The Squeeze on the Middle Class," *The New York Times Magazine*, July 13, 1980, pp. 27 ff.; J. Adams, "Conversation with a Successful Man," *across the board*, April 1982, pp. 47 ff.; Paul Blumberg, "White-collar Status Panic," *The New Republic*, December 1, 1979. pp. 21 ff.; "The Middle Class Poor," *Newsweek*, September 12, 1977, pp. 30-34; and A. Tobias, "Getting By on $100,000 a Year," *Esquire*, May 23, 1978, pp. 21-24.
9. See, for example, Thurow, *Zero Sum Society*, p. 50.
10. *Statistical Abstracts of the United States*, 1981.
11. Thurow, *Zero Sum Society*, p. 49.

12. David Potter, *People of Plenty: Economic Abundance and the American Character* (Chicago: University of Chicago Press, 1954), p. 48.

13. M. Rosenberg, "The American Dream: Is the Pie Still in the Sky?" *Columbia*, Winter 1980, p. 48.

14. John O. Wilson, *After Affluence: Economics to Meet Human Needs* (New York: Harper & Row, 1980), pp. 47–48.

15. H. Husock, "The High Cost of Starting Out," *The New York Times Magazine*, June 7, 1981 pp. 42 ff.

16. Paul Blumberg, *Inequality in an Age of Decline* (New York: Oxford University Press, 1980), p. 93.

17. *Ibid.*, e.g. pp. xii, 66, 77.

18. Wilson, *After Affluence*, pp. 72 and 113.

19. Harry Helson, *Adaptation Level Theory* (New York: Harper & Row, 1964).

20. See, for example, Daniel Yankelovich, *New Rules: Searching for Self-Fulfillment in a World Turned Upside Down* (New York: Random House, 1981).

21. W. S. Kowinski, "A Mall Covers the Waterfront," *The New York Times Magazine*, December 13, 1981, p. 112.

22. Fred Hirsch, *Social Limits to Growth* (Cambridge, Mass: Harvard University Press, 1976.)

23. *Ibid.*, p. 20.

24. *Ibid.*, p. 7.

25. Elliot Liebow, *Tally's Corner: A Study of Negro Streetcorner Men* (Boston: Little, Brown, 1967).

26. Richard Easterlin, "Does Money Buy Happiness?" *The Public Interest*, Winter 1973, p. 4.

Chapter Three: The Unperceived Realities of the Consumer Life

1. Herbert A. Simon, *Models of Man* (New York: John Wiley & Sons, 1957), p. xxiii.

2. Roland Barthes, *Mythologies* (New York: Hill & Wang, 1972) p. 88.

3. *The New York Times*, June 14, 1979, p. A1.

4. Quoted in W. Serrin, "Detroit Strikes Back," *The New York Times Magazine*, September 14, 1980, p. 30.

5. J. Rifkin, *Entropy: A New World View* (New York: Viking, 1980), p. 143.

6. *Ibid*, p. 142

7. See, for example, A. Q. Mowbray, *Road to Ruin* (Philadelphia: Lippincott, 1969); Emma Rothschild, *Paradise Lost: The Decline of the Auto-Industrial Age* (New York: Random House, 1973); Philip Slater, *Wealth Addiction* (New York: Dutton, 1980).

8. *Statistical Abstracts of the United States* (Washington, D.C. Department of Commerce, 1981).

9. Cited in radio advertisement for Honda Motors, 1982.

10. *The New York Times*, August 15, 1980, p. 22.

11. Rifkin, *Entropy*, p. 179.

12. A. Campbell, *The Sense of Well-being in America* (New York: McGraw-Hill, 1981), pp. 28–29.

13. Jonathan Freedman, *Happy People* (New York: Harcourt Brace Jovanovich, 1978), p. 136.

14. Lester Thurow, *The Zero Sum Society* (New York: Basic Books, 1980), p. 120.

15. Kimon Valaskakis, P. Sindell, J. G. Smith, and Martin I. Fitzpatrick, *The Conserver Society* (New York: Harper & Row, 1978), p. 181.

16. Freedman, *Happy People*, p. 140.

17. Stuart Ewen, *Captains of Consciousness: Advertising and the Social Roots of the Consumer Culture* (New York: McGraw-Hill, 1976).

18. Tibor Scitovsky, *The Joyless Economy: An Inquiry into Human Satisfaction and Consumer Dissatisfaction* (New York: Oxford, 1976), pp. 195–96.

19. Bertrand Russell, "In Praise of Idleness," cited in Fred Hirsch, *Social Limits to Growth* (Cambridge Mass: Harvard University Press, 1976), p. 44.

20. Scitovsky, *Joyless Economy*, p. 94.

21. Fred Powledge, "Water, Water, Running Out," *The Nation*, June 12, 1982, p. 714.

22. P. Ognibene, "Vanishing Farmlands: Selling Out the Soil," *Saturday Review*, May 1980, pp. 29 ff.

23. Natural Resources Defense Council Memorandum, 1981.

24. T. Monte, "Antibiotics in Feed Becoming Useless in Human Therapy," *Nutrition Action*, February 1980 (Washington, D.C.: Center for Science in the Public Interest), pp. 3–6.

25. E. J. Sternglass, "Cancer Mortality Changes Around Nuclear Facilities in Connecticut." Testimony presented at Congressional Seminar on Low-Level Radiation, February 10, 1978, Washington, D.C.

26. *The New York Times*, April 10, 1979, p. A16.

27. Barry Commoner, *The Closing Circle* (New York: Bantam Books, 1972).

28. Robert L. Heilbroner, *An Inquiry into the Human Prospect* (New York: Norton, 1975).

29. Dennis Gabor, *The Mature Society* (New York: Praeger, 1972), p. 3.

30. A particularly revealing interchange occurred in a televised news analysis following a major address by President Carter on energy policy. Robert Strauss, representing the President's position, referred to comments by Barry Commoner as those of an "environmentalist," and hence as representing a "special interest." Apparently, in this semiofficial view, concern about the air we all breathe, the water we all drink, or the radiation we all absorb is narrow and sectarian, whereas the energy to produce more and more is what America as a whole is all about.

31. G. Bunin and M. Jacobson, "Does Everything Cause Cancer?" Washington, D.C.: Center for Science in the Public Interest, 1979.

32. Gabor, *Mature Society*, p. 25.

Chapter Four: Vicious Circles

1. George Katona, *The Mass Consumption Society* (New York: McGraw-Hill, 1964), p. 65.

2. The recent revision of the American Psychiatric Association's official diagnostic manual has essentially eliminated the term. To a large degree, this change simply reflects psychiatric politics: It is part of the continuing battle between the psychoanalysts (who use the term regularly) and the biological psychiatrists (who seek to extirpate psychoanalytic terminology). It reflects as well the effort of the psychiatric profession to give as "medical" an aura as possible to mental and psychological disorders in order to prosper with the advent of national health insurance. Nonetheless, it is well to note that the term, if not necessarily the concept, is problematic. *Neurosis* has nothing to do with *neurones*, except that those who do not have the latter have never been known to have the former.

3. See, for example, Jacob Burckhardt, *The Civilization of the Renaissance in Italy* (New York: Harper & Row, 1958).

4. See, for example, T. Massey, "The American Class System and How to End It," *Washington Monthly*, February 1978, pp. 6 ff., and Paul Blumberg, *Inequality in an Age of Decline* (New York: Oxford University Press, 1980).

5. Jeremy Seabrook, *What Went Wrong?*: Why Hasn't Having More Made People Happier? (New York: Pantheon, 1978), p. 151.

6. George Santayana, "Materialism and Idealism in American Life," in A. Theodore Johnson and Allen Tate, eds., *America Through the Essay* (New York: Oxford University Press, 1940), p. 139.

7. United States Census Bureau report, cited in *Behavior Today*, October 1, 1979, p. 8.

8. Karl Polanyi, *The Great Transformation* (Boston: Beacon, 1944), p. 33.

9. Max Weber *The Protestant Ethic and the Spirit of Capitalism* (1904) (New York: Scribner's, 1958).

10. Polanyi, *Great Transformation*, p. 39.

11. See Anna Freud, *The Ego and the Mechanisms of Defense* (New York: International Universities Press, 1946).

12. Fred Hirsch, *Social Limits to Growth* (Cambridge, Mass.: Harvard University Press, 1976), p. 77.

13. The "authoritarian personality" would seem to be an exception to this general picture. He is compulsively driven to be dominant with regard to those below him and submissive to those above. Both stances, however, can be seen as consistent with a general "moving against" trend: His submissiveness is in the service of identification with those who seem to possess absolute power. The commitment to brute dominance as the route to quelling feelings of anxiety and vulnerability unites the two seemingly disparate stances.

14. M. Pines, "Good Samaritans at Age Two?" *Psychology Today*, June 1979, p. 73.

15. Karen Horney, *The Neurotic Personality of Our Time* (New York: Norton, 1937).

Chapter Five: The Cultural Context of the Growth Ideology

1. In this context, see M. Orvell, "Digital Watches Tell More than Time," *Philadelphia Inquirer*, December 7, 1978, p. 23A.

2. George Santayana, "Materialism and Idealism in American Life," In A. Theodore Johnson and Allen Tate, eds., *America*

Through the Essay (New York: Oxford University Press, 1940), p. 146.

3. Robert L. Heilbroner, *The Quest for Wealth* (New York: Simon & Schuster, 1956), p. 39.

4. *Ibid.*

5. *Ibid.*

6. Ruth Benedict, *Patterns of Culture* (Boston: Houghton Mifflin, 1934).

7. René Guenon, *The Reign of Quantity* (Baltimore: Penguin Books, 1972).

8. See, for example, M. Moss, ed., *The Measurement of Economic and Social Performance* (New York: Columbia University Press, 1973).

9. Paul Samuelson, in his classic text, *Economics*, Tenth Ed. (New York: McGraw Hill, 1976), argues (p. 196) that when GNP is "correctly measured" it will not be enhanced by pollution or other "regrettable costs." His assumption is that the availability of clean sources of power would free resources for things like books and paintings. Now, I'm all for clean sources of power, as I am for books and paintings, but surely Samuelson realizes that our present system is designed to make things dirty and *then* clean them up—and to make money out of both. The GNP (as opposed to net welfare measures) is blind to whether money is spent on books and paintings or on cleaning up the mess we have just made (and the social dynamics of a GNP-obsessed society make the latter more likely than the former). As things stand now, Ralph Nader is certainly correct when he says, "Every time there is an automobile accident, the GNP goes up."

10. See, for example, W. Nordhaus and J. Tobin, "Is growth obsolete?" in M. Moss, ed., *The Measurement of Economic and Social Performance* (New York: National Bureau of Economic Research, 1973), pp. 509–32.

11. Within the profession of economics these indices have gotten somewhat mixed reviews. On the one hand it has been pointed out that one leading measure of this sort made economic well-being seem to increase during the Depression. J. R. Mayer, "Comment on Nordhaus and Tobin," in *ibid.*, p. 550. See also diagram in Samuelson, *Economics*, p. 4. It has also been noted that if people did for themselves what they now hire others to do, the "Measure of Economic Welfare" (one of the "corrected" indices) would appear to go down, though actually the same activities went on. O. C. Herfindahl and A. V. Kneese, "Measuring Social and Economic Change: Benefits and Costs of Environmental Pollution," in Moss, *Measurement*, p. 447. Samu-

elson, on the other hand, gives the Nordhaus and Tobin MEW high grades as an effective measure of real economic well-being. Samuelson, *Economics*, pp. 195–96.

12. Samuelson, *Economics*, p. 201.

13. Maital, *Minds, Markets, and Money*, p. 147.

14. Albert Hirschman, *Shifting Involvements: Private Interest and Public Action*, Princeton: Princeton University Press, 1982, p. 21.

15. Thurow, *The Zero Sum Society*, p. 108.

16. J. W. Smeed, *Faust in Literature* (London: Oxford University Press, 1975), p. 3.

17. *Ibid.*, p. 9.

18. John Kenneth Galbraith, *The New Industrial State* (Boston: Houghton Mifflin, 1971).

19. Philip Roth, *Portnoy's Complaint* (New York: Random House, 1969).

20. W. Lloyd Warner, *The Corporation in the Emergent American Society* (New York: Harper & Row, 1962), p. 51.

21. W. Lloyd Warner and J. Abegglen, *Big Business Leaders in America* (New York: Atheneum, 1963), p. 62.

22. Arthur Miller, *The Price* (New York: Bantam, 1969).

23. Paul Roazen, *Erik H. Erikson: The Power and Limits of a Vision* (New York: Free Press, 1976).

24. R. W. B. Lewis, *The American Adam* (Chicago: University of Chicago Press, 1955).

25. Lionel Trilling, quoted in Morris Dickstein, *Gates of Eden: American Culture in the Sixties* (New York: Basic Books, 1977), p. 253.

26. For an excellent discussion of Aristotle's view of the proper role of economic and commercial matters, see Joel Whitebook "Economics and Ethical Life: A Study of Aristotle and Hegel," doctoral dissertation, New School for Social Research, 1978.

27. *The New York Times*, June 5, 1978, p. D4.

28. John Stuart Mill, cited in Kimon Valaskakis et al., *The Conserver Society* (New York: Harper & Row, 1978), p. xiii.

Chapter Six: Economic Growth and Personal Growth

1. Charles Reich, *The Greening of America* (New York: Random House, 1970), p. 2

2. *Ibid.*, pp. 241–42, italics added.

3. *Ibid.*, p. 242.

4. *Ibid.*, p. 307.

5. *Ibid.*, p. 247–48.

6. *Ibid.*, pp. 328–29.

7. *Ibid.*, p. 342.

8. *Ibid.*

9. *Ibid.*, p. 394.

10. *Ibid.*, p. 398.

11. Philip Nobile, ed., *The Con III Controversy: The Critics Look at the Greening of America* (New York: Pocket Books, 1971), pp. 39–44.

12. See P. Amacher, "Freud's Neurological Education and Its Influence on Psychoanalytic Theory," *Psychological Issues*, Vol. 4, No. 4, 1965; R. R. Holt, "A Review of Some of Freud's Biological Assumptions and Their Influence on His Theories," in N. S. Greenfield and W. C. Lewis, eds., *Psychoanalysis and Current Biological Thought* (Madison: University of Wisconsin Press, 1965); *idem*, "Beyond Vitalism and Mechanism: Freud's Concept of Psychic Energy," in J. Masserman, ed., *Science and Psychoanalysis*, Vol. II (New York: Grune & Stratton, 1967), pp. 1–41; and F. Sulloway, *Freud: Biologist of the Mind* (New York: Basic Books, 1979).

13. Karl Polanyi, *The Great Transformation* (Boston: Beacon Press, 1944), p. 57.

14. *Ibid.* p. 30.

15. See, for example, B. F. Skinner, *Science and Human Behavior* (New York: Macmillan, 1953); E. L. Thorndike, *The Psychology of Learning* (New York: Teachers College, 1913); and C. L. Hull, *Principles of Behavior* (New York: Appleton-Century-Crofts, 1943).

16. See, for example, R. Carson, *Interaction Concepts of Personality* (Chicago: Aldine, 1969); J. W. Thibaut and H. H. Kelly, *The Social Psychology of Groups* (New York: Wiley, 1959); and G. C. Homans, *Social Behavior: Its Elementary Form* (New York: Harcourt, Brace, 1961).

17. Behavioristic theories and the social exchange theories differ very basically on a number of important issues, particularly with regard to the role of cognition. My concern here is with a level of analysis for which it is their commonalities that is relevant.

18. Abraham H. Maslow, *Toward a Psychology of Being* (Princeton; N.J.: Van Nostrand, 1962), p. iii.

19. *Ibid.*, p. 11.

20. Erik H. Erikson, *Life History and the Historical Moment* (New York: Norton, 1975).

21. Maslow, *Toward a Psychology of Being*, p. 11.

22. *Ibid.*, p. 33.

23. *Ibid.*, p. 37.

24. *Ibid.*

25. *Ibid.*, p. 35.

26. *Ibid.*, p. 32.

27. *Ibid.*, p. 38.

28. *Ibid.*, p. 32.

29. See, for example, Paul L. Wachtel, "Psychodynamics, Behavior Therapy, and the Implacable Experimenter: An Inquiry into the Consistency of Personality," *Journal of Abnormal Psychology*, 82 (1973): 324–34, and K. S. Bowers, "Situationism in Psychology: An Analysis and a Critique," *Psychological Review*, 80 (1973): 307–36.

30. Maslow, *Toward a Psychology of Being*, p. 32.

31. Stephen A. Appelbaum, *Out in Inner Space: A Psychoanalyst Explores the New Therapies* (New York: Anchor, 1979), p. 83.

32. Michael Rossman, *New Age Blues: On the Politics of Consciousness* (New York: Dutton, 1979), pp. 141–42. Italics in original.

33. Peter Marin, "The New Narcissism," *Harper's*, October 1975.

34. David Riesman, *The Lonely Crowd* (New Haven: Yale University Press), 1961.

35. See, for example, Erich Fromm, *The Sane Society* (New York: Holt, Rinehart & Winston, 1955).

36. Riesman, *Lonely Crowd*, p. 65.

37. W. O. Webb, quoted in M. Millgate, *American Social Fiction* (Edinburgh: Oliver & Boyd, 1964), p. 206.

38. See, for example, Dennis Gabor, *The Mature Society* (New York: Praeger, 1972), p. 10.

39. Max Weber, *The Protestant Ethic and the Spirit of Capitalism* (1908) (New York: Scribner's, 1958), p. 222.

40. Steven Lukes, *Individualism* (New York: Harper & Row, 1973).

41. See C. B. Macpherson, *The Political Theory of Possessive Individualism* (Oxford: Oxford University Press, 1962).

42. Alisdair MacIntyre, "Durkheim's Call to Order," *The New York Review of Books*, March 7, 1974, p. 26.

Chapter Seven: New Alternatives

1. Milton Friedman and R. Friedman, *Free to Choose* (New York: Harcourt Brace Jovanovich, 1980), p. 285.

2. John Maynard Keynes, cited in Paul Samuelson, *Economics*, Tenth Edition (New York: McGraw-Hill, 1976), p. 14.

3. Philip Rieff, *The Triumph of the Therapeutic* (New York: Harper & Row, 1966), p. 65.

4. Seymour Sarason, *Psychology Misdirected* (New York: Free Press, 1981).

5. Daniel Yankelovich, *New Rules: Searching for Self-Fulfillment in a World Turned Upside Down* (New York: Random House, 1981), pp. xix and 4.

6. *Ibid.*, p. 69.

7. This figure is based on an earlier analysis in Julian Simon, *Issues in the Economics of Advertising* (Urbana: University of Illinois Press, 1970), which yielded a figure of $60 billion in the late Sixties. Given the inflation and increase in the GNP that has subsequently occurred, the figure of 100 billion is quite conservative.

8. Tibor Scitovsky, *The Joyless Economy: An Inquiry into Human Satisfaction and Consumer Dissatisfaction* (New York: Oxford, 1976), p. 255.

9. *Statistical Abstracts of the United States* (Washington, D.C.: Department of Commerce, 1981).

10. Yankelovich, *New Rules*, p. 42.

11. *Statistical Abstracts of the United States*, 1981.

12. See, for example, S. Melman, *Pentagon Capitalism* (New York: McGraw-Hill, 1970), and J. Fallows, *National Defense* (New York: Random House, 1981).

13. *Statistical Abstracts of the United States*, 1981.

14. S. Epstein, *The Politics of Cancer* (San Francisco: Sierra Club Books, 1978), p. 23. See also R. Doll and R. Peto, "The Causes of Cancer: Quantitative Estimates of Avoidable Risks of Cancer in the United States Today," *Journal of the National Cancer Institute*, 66 (1981): 1191-1308.

15. Scitovsky, *Joyless Economy*, p. 159.

16. *The New York Times*, April 30, 1980, p. A2.

17. Philip Slater, *Wealth Addiction* (New York: Dutton, 1980), pp. 23-25.

18. Samuelson, *Economics*, p. 638-39.

19. "America's New Immobile Society," *Business Week*, July 27, 1981, pp. 58-62.

20. See, e.g., M. Bousqet, "The Poison Factory," *Working Papers*, Spring 1973, pp. 20-27; M. Maccoby, "Changing Work," *Working Papers*, Summer 1975, pp. 43-55; and D. Jenkins, "Beyond Job Enrichment," *Working Papers*, Winter 1975, pp. 51-57.

21. Dennis Gabor, *The Mature Society* (New York: Praeger, 1972).

22. Yankelovich, *New Rules*, p. xv.

23. Karl Marx, quoted in Marshall Berman, "All That Is Solid Melts into Air," *Dissent*, Winter 1978, p. 57.

24. Staffan Linder, *The Harried Leisure Class* (New York: Columbia University Press, 1970), p. 79.

25. Scitovsky, *Joyless Economy*.

26. Herbert Marcuse, *Eros and Civilization* (Boston: Beacon, 1954), and Norman O. Brown, *Life Against Death* (Middletown, Conn: Wesleyan University Press, 1959).

27. Wilhelm Reich, *Character Analysis* (New York: Noonday, 1945).

28. N. E. Miller, "Biofeedback and Visceral Learning," *Annual Review of Psychology*, 29 (1978): 373-404.

29. M. Lieberman, I. Yalom, and M. Miles, *Encounter Groups: First Facts* (New York: Basic Books, 1973).

30. See, for example, F. Sander, *Individual and Family Therapy* (New York: Jason Aronson, 1979).

31. Jeremy Seabrook, *What Went Wrong? Why Hasn't Having More Made People Happier?* (New York: Pantheon, 1978).

32. *Ibid.*, p. 5.

33. *Ibid,*, p. 14.

34. *Ibid.*, p. 95-96.

35. Cited in L. Bernikow, "Alone: Yearning for Companionship in America," *The New York Times Magazine*, August 15, 1982, p. 29.

36. *Ibid.*, p. 26-27.

37. *Ibid.*, p. 27.

Chapter Eight: Strategies and Pitfalls

1. Paul L. Wachtel, *Psychoanalysis and Behavior Therapy* (New York: Basic Books, 1977).

2. Marshall Berman, *The Politics of Authenticity* (New York: Atheneum, 1970) p. ix.

3. *Ibid.*, p. x.

4. Eli Zaretsky, *Capitalism, the Family, and Personal Life* (New York: Harper & Row, 1976), p. 118.

5. Christopher Lasch, "The Narcissist Society," *New York Review of Books*, September 30, 1976, p. 8.

6. See, for example, Kenneth Kenniston, *Young Radicals* (New York: Harcourt Brace & World, 1968).

7. M. Pickett, "A Story of 3 Promises — or, The Deflation of Ideals in Everyday Life," *The New York Times*, November 15, 1980, p. 23.

8. A version of this story appeared in an article by C. Fellner, "The Use of Teaching Stories in Conjoint Family Therapy," *Family Process*, 15(1976): 427-31.

Chapter Nine: The Dilemmas of Psychological Man

1. Philip Rieff, *Freud, The Mind of the Moralist* (Chicago: University of Chicago Press, 1979) and *The Triumph of the Therapeutic* (New York: Harper & Row, 1966).

2. Martin Gross, *The Psychological Society* (New York: Random House, 1978).

3. *Behavior Today*, August 14, 1978.

4. Michael Nelson, "What's Wrong with Psychology," *Washington Monthly*, December 1978.

5. Charles Krauthammer, "The Expanding Shrink," *The New Republic*, September 22, 1979, pp. 10-12.

6. Christopher Lasch, *The Culture of Narcissism* (New York: Norton, 1979), p. 164-65.

7. Richard Sennett, *The Fall of Public Man* (New York: Knopf, 1977).

8. See, for example, E. Schur, *The Awareness Trap* (New York: McGraw-Hill, 1976).

9. E.g., Gross, *Psychological Society*.

10. E.g., Lasch, *Culture of Narcissism*.

11. E.g., Gross, *Psychological Society*.

12. E.g., P. Schrag, *Mind Control* (New York: Pantheon, 1978).

13. Rieff, *Triumph of the Therapeutic*, pp. 3-4 (italics added).

14. *Ibid.*, p. 2.

15. *Ibid.*, p. 19.

16. *Ibid.*, p. 13.

17. *Ibid.*, p. 22.

18. *Ibid.*

19. *Ibid.*, p. 27.

20. *Ibid.*, p. 12.

21. Rieff, *Freud: The Mind of the Moralist*, p. 337.

22. See, for example, Robert L. Heilbroner, *An Inquiry into the Human Prospect* (New York: Norton, 1975); Karl Polanyi, *The Great Transformation* (Boston: Beacon, 1944); and J. D. Whitebook, "Economics and Ethical Life: A Study of Aristotle and Hegel," doctoral dissertation, New School for Social Research. 1978.

23. See, in this regard, Paul L. Wachtel, "Karen Horney's Ironic Vision," *The New Republic*, January 6, 1979, pp. 22–25, and *idem*, "Vicious Circles: The Self and the Rhetoric of Emerging and Unfolding," *Contemporary Psychoanalysis*, 18(1982): 259–73.

24. See, in this regard, Paul L. Wachtel, *Psychoanalysis and Behavior Therapy: Toward an Integration* (New York: Basic Books, 1977), Chapters 2 through 4, especially pp. 42–43.

25. See, for example, *ibid.* Also Paul L. Wachtel, "Psychodynamics, Behavior Therapy and the Implacable Experimenter." *Journal of Abnormal Psychology*, 92(1973): 324–34, and *idem*, "Interaction Cycles Unconscious Processes, and the Person-Situation Issue," in D. Magnusson and N. Endler, eds., *Personality at the Crossroads: Issues in Interaction Psychology* (Hillsdale, N.J.: Erlbaum, 1977), pp. 317–31.

26. Wachtel, "Vicious Circles."

27. See, for example, Wachtel, *Psychoanalysis and Behavior Therapy*, and *idem*, "What Can Dynamic Therapies Contribute to Behavior Therapy?" *Behavior Therapy*, 13(1982): 594–609.

28. Wachtel, *Psychoanalysis and Behavior Therapy*.

29. *Ibid.*

30. *Ibid.*, p. 44.

31. Rieff, *Freud*, p. 329–30.

32. Lionel Trilling, *Sincerity and Authenticity* (Cambridge: Harvard University Press, 1971), p. 61.

33. Sennett, *Fall of Public Man*.

34. R. D. Rosen, *Psychobabble* (New York: Avon, 1979), p. 16.

35. Erik H. Erikson, *Childhood and Society* (New York: Norton, 1950), p. 222.

36. Edwin Schur, *The Awareness Trap: Self Absorption Instead of Social Change* (New York: McGraw-HIll, 1976).

37. Lasch, *Culture of Narcissism*.

Chapter Ten: Misunderstanding Narcissism

1. Peter Marin, "The New Narcissism," *Harper's* October 1975.

2. Christopher Lasch, *The Culture of Narcissism* (New York: Norton, 1979).

3. *Ibid.*, pp. 4–5.

4. *Ibid.*, p. 13.

5. *Ibid.*, p. 26.

6. *Ibid.*, p. 7.

7. *Ibid.*, p. 41.

8. *Ibid.*, p. 231.

9. *Ibid.*, p. 232.

10. *Ibid.*, p. 33

11. R. E. Ulrich, T. J. Stachnick, and N. R. Stainton, "Student Acceptance of Generalized Personality Interpretations," *Psychological Reports*, 13(1963): 831–34.

12. Yi-fu Tuan, *Landscapes of Fear* (Minneapolis: University of Minnesota Press, 1971).

13. *Ibid.*

14. Edward Shorter, *The Making of the Modern Family* (New York: Basic Books, 1975), p. 56.

15. Sigmund Freud, "Psychoanalytic Notes on an Autobiographical Account of a Case of Paranoia (Dementia Paranoides)" (1911), *Standard Edition*, Vol. 12, (London: Hogarth, 1958), pp. 3–82.

16. A number of considerations make this source of sampling bias more difficult to evaluate. First, many of the adults in family therapy are there (at least initially) because of a difficulty with a child and might previously have sent the child to a child therapist or analyst but not have been themselves part of the adult patient pool. Thus "removing" them from the pool doesn't change the sample of adults the analyst can see. Second, many people who enter family therapy do not initially view their problem in family terms. They seek simply a "therapist" for the individual in the family identified as the sick one and must be persuaded to include themselves in the treatment process. Those who do go through with it were, of course, persuadable and thus at least somewhat willing to see themselves as part of a system of relationships, but it is unclear to what degree they differ

as a group from those who end up in individual treatment. Finally, family therapists will attest that by no means are all their patients paragons of relatedness. That they are part of a family at all, and involved enough at least to participate in the sessions, suggests that as a whole the sample of people in family therapy is different from the sample who now see analysts, but this particular source of skewing does seem more ambiguous.

17. Lasch, *Culture of Narcissism*, p. 43.
18. *Ibid.*, p. 43.
19. J. Van der Tak, "Our Population Predicament: A New Look," *Population Bulletin*, Vol. 34, no. 5, December 1979.
20. Lasch, *Culture of Narcissism*, Chap. IX.
21. *Nutrition Action*, July–August, 1982.
22. Lasch, *Culture of Narcissism*, p. 4.

Chapter Eleven: Jobs and Work

1. We may tend to exaggerate the change in this latter regard (see, for example, T. Massey "The American Class System and How to End It." *Washington Monthly*, February 1978, pp. 6 ff.). But it is still real and substantial as compared with the preindustrial world.
2. Regarding attribution theory see, for example, D. J. Bem, "Self-perception theory," in L. Berkowitz, ed., *Advances in Experimental Social Psychology*, Vol. 6 (New York: Academic Press; 1972); J. Harvey and W. Smith, *Social Psychology: An Attributional Approach* (St. Louis: C. V. Mosby, 1977); and E. E. Jones, D. E. Kanouse, H. H. Kelley, R. E. Nisbett, S. Valius, and B. Weiner, *Attribution: Perceiving the Causes of Behavior* (Morristown, N.J.: General Learning Press, 1972).
3. Statistical Abstracts of the United States, 1981.
4. John Kenneth Galbraith, *The Affluent Society* (Boston: Houghton Mifflin, 1958).
5. See, for example, F. J. Cook, "Somebody Doesn't Like Hy-fuel," *The Nation*, October 4, 1980, pp. 305–11.
6. See, for example, C. Gersuny and W. Rosengren, *The Service Society* (Cambridge: Schenkman, 1973); and V. Fuchs, *The Service Economy* (New York: National Bureau of Economic Research, 1968).
7. See, for example, Christopher Lasch, *Haven in a Heartless World* (New York: Basic Books, 1976), and various works of Foucault, Illich, or Szasz.

Chapter Twelve: The Myth of the Market

1. See, for example, Milton Friedman and R. Friedman, *Free to Choose* (New York: Harcourt Brace Jovanovich, 1980); George Gilder, *Wealth and Poverty* (New York: Basic Books, 1981); William E. Simon, *A Time for Truth* (New York: Reader's Digest Press, 1978); *idem*, *A Time for Action* (New York: Reader's Digest Press, 1980); and Robert Ringer, *Looking Out for No. 1* (New York: Fawcett, 1978).

2. Sweden, for example, is widely regarded as such a mix, yet its economy is at present 94% privately owned and controlled. See Robert L. Heilbroner, "The Swedish Promise," *New York Review of Books*, December 4, 1980, p. 33, for a discussion of the present and possible future characteristics of the Swedish mix.

3. William F. Buckley, Jr., "Up from Liberalism," quoted in *Yale Alumni Magazine*, April 1978, p. 37.

4. Leonard Silk and David Vogel, *Ethics and Profits* (New York: Touchstone, 1976), p. 75.

5. *Ibid.*, p. 77.

6. *Ibid.*, p. 43.

7. Friedman and Friedman *Free to Choose*, pp. 65-66.

8. That principle, of course, has not always been the basis for elections, but it has increasingly come to be recognized as a requirement for a just order.

9. Friedman and Friedman, *Free to Choose*, p. 13.

10. Adam Smith, *The Wealth of Nations*, quoted in G. Tyler in *Dissent*, Summer 1980, p. 285.

11. John Kenneth Galbraith, *The New Industrial State* (Boston: Houghton Mifflin, 1974).

12. Lester Thurow, *The Zero Sum Society* (New York: Basic Books, 1980), p. 7.

13. George Gilder, *Wealth and Poverty* (New York: Basic Books, 1981), p. 296.

14. Paul Samuelson, *Economics* Tenth Edition (New York: McGraw-Hill, 1976), p. 44.

15. F. X. Sutton, S. E. Harris, C. Kaysen, and J. Tobin, *The American Business Creed*, p. 195, quoted in John Kenneth Galbraith, *The Affluent Society* (Boston: Houghton-Mifflin, 1958), p. 184.

16. Galbraith, *Affluent Society*, p. 184.

17. C. Lindblom, *Politics and Markets* (New York: Basic Books, 1977), pp. 269-72.

18. Samuelson, *Economics*, p. 581.

19. Lindblom, *Politics and Markets*, p. 283.

20. See, for example, J. A. Easterbrook, "The Effect of Emotion on Cue Utilization and the Organization of Behavior," *Psychological Review*, 66(1959): 183–201.

21. Mark Green, "Richer than All Their Tribe," *The New Republic*, January 6 and 13, 1982, p. 24.

22. Samuelson, *Economics*, p. 84.

23. Thurow, *Zero Sum Society*, p. 84.

24. See "America's New Immobile Society," *Business Week*, July 27, 1981, pp. 58–62.

25. Cited in Fred Hirsch, *Social Limits to Growth* (Cambridge, Mass.: Harvard University Press, 1976), p. 128.

26. F. C. Thayer, "Can Competition Hurt?" *The New York Times*, June 18, 1979.

27. *The New York Times*, July 8, 1979.

28. E.g., Galbraith, *Affluent Society*.

29. W. Leiss, *The Limits of Satisfaction* (Toronto: University of Toronto Press, 1976), p. 82.

30. Stuart Ewen, *Captains of Consciousness: Advertising and the Social Roots of the Consumer Culture* (New York: McGraw-Hill, 1976).

31. *Ibid.*, p. 39.

32. See, for example, D. Rosenthal "Changes in Some Moral Values Following Psychotherapy," *Journal of Consulting Psychology*, 19(1955): 431–36; P. Pentoney, "Value Change in Psychotherapy," *Human Relations*, 19(1966): 39–46; and J. Meltzoff and M. Kornreich, *Research in Psychotherapy* (New York: Atherton, 1970).

33. See, for example, Paul L. Wachtel, *Psychoanalysis and Behavior Therapy: Toward an Integration* (New York: Basic Books, 1977); *idem* "Contingent and Noncontingent Therapist Response," *Psychotherapy: Theory, Research and Practice*, 16(1979): 30–35; and *idem*; "The Philosophic and the Therapuetic: On the Value Assumptions of Psychoanalysis." In R. Stern and K. D. Irani, eds. *Science and Psychoanalysis*, Vol. 4 (New York: Haven Press, forthcoming).

34. See, for example, Wachtel, *Psychoanalysis and Behavior Therapy*, Chapters 11 and 12.

35. *Ibid.*

Index